THE
ORPHANED
CAPITAL

THE
ORPHANED
CAPITAL

*Adopting the Right Revenues
for the District of Columbia*

Carol O'Cleireacain

BROOKINGS INSTITUTION PRESS
Washington, D.C.

Copyright © 1997 by
THE BROOKINGS INSTITUTION
1775 Massachusetts Avenue, N.W., Washington, D.C. 20036

Library of Congress Cataloging-in-Publication Data
O'Cleireacain, Carol.
    Orphaned capital: adopting the right revenues for the District of
Columbia / Carol O'Cleireacain.
        p.   cm.
    Includes bibliographical references.
    ISBN 0-8157-6425-1 (alk. paper)
    1. Taxation—Washington (D.C.)   2. Revenue—Washington (D.C.)
3. Revenue sharing—Washington (D.C.)   4. Intergovernmental fiscal
relations—Washington (D.C.)   5. Fiscal policy—Washington (D.C.)
6. Washington (D.C.)—Politics and government—1967–   I. Title.
HJ9216.O27   1997
336.02′753—dc21   97-4634
                                                                              CIP

9 8 7 6 5 4 3 2 1

The paper used in this publication meets the minimum requirements of the
American National Standard for Information Sciences—Permanence of Paper
for Printed Library Materials, ANSI Z39.48-1984

Typeset in Sabon

Composition by Harlowe Typography, Inc.
Cottage City, Maryland

Printed by Kirby Lithographic Co.
Arlington, Virginia

For my parents
Albert H. and Sheila Hanfling Chapman

Foreword

As long-time residents and workers in the District of Columbia, we at Brookings share the concerns of many others about the city's continuing financial problems. In the winter of 1996, while the fiscal situation worsened and the attention of the city government and the oversight agency was focused on curbing budget deficits and providing basic services, Brookings Board of Trustees decided to focus the institution's expertise in the field of public finance on the District's longer-term revenue options. This study was designed to complement and expand the policy debate by bringing a thoughtful analysis to help ameliorate a critical fiscal situation.

In a number of ways Brookings reached out in new directions for this study. We brought in an outsider who would bring a fresh eye as well as experience in local government and public finance to the District's fiscal problems. Carol O'Cleireacain, the former director of the Mayor's Office of Management and Budget and former finance commissioner of the City of New York, began as a visiting fellow in May 1996. We enlisted, with the help of James Gibson of the D.C. Agenda, an advisory group, representing a cross-section of experienced and well-informed District residents, to help the study toward a synthesis that would be rigorous, practical, and credible. Both the author and I thank them for their time, guidance, and reaction and for the special access provided by some to their staffs and institutions for help on particular issues. The author also received the full support of Anthony Williams, the District's chief financial officer, and his staff, without whose cooperation and commitment of time and data this study could not have been completed.

Through the summer and fall of 1996, the author worked with a small group of researchers to mine the District's data. Martha Stark helped focus the study's conclusions and force the work to closure. She and Robert Zahradnik produced the analytical work underlying the city comparisons, the impact of the policy proposals, and the reconciliation of budget neutrality They were also primarily responsibile for the property tax and federal payments analyses and proposals. Research analyst Stephen Mark examined the income, business, and sales taxes and is the primary author of the econometric study. Mark and research assistant Jeremy White produced the initial draft of the chapter on the business climate. White was responsible for keeping track of the published and unpublished resources gathered in the course of this study. The author thanks them for their hard work and takes full responsibility for whatever errors may remain.

The author cannot list all the individuals in the District of Columbia who provided valuable insights and suggestions. She is grateful for the access and help provided by the staff of the District's Department of Finance and Revenue, including Julia Friedman, Philip Appelbaum, Modibo Coulibaly, Mark Grippentrog, Tom Kerwin, and Paul Wright; the federal Office of Management and Budget, including Franklin Raines, Edward deSeve, Carol Thompson-Cole, Joseph Minarik, and Mark Wasserman; the Internal Revenue Service's director, Margaret Richardson, and her staff; and the members of the Financial Authority, Andrew Brimmer, Stephen Harlan, Joyce Ladner, Constance Newman, and Edward Singletary, and their staff, especially John Hill and Dexter Lockamy.

In addition, the author received special help from Charles Betsey at Howard University; Ruth Crone and her staff at the Metropolitan Washington Council of Governments; Philip Dearborn and Carol Meyers at the Greater Washington Research Center; Harley Duncan and Ronald Alt at the Federation of Tax Administrators; Jeffrey Eisenech and Jane Fortson at the Progress and Freedom Foundation; David Fowler and Jeffrey Henig at George Washington University; Stephen Fuller at George Mason University; Joshua Gotbaum at the U.S. Treasury; Larry Herman at KPMG Peat Marwick; Iris Lav at the Center on Budget and Policy Priorities; Robert McIntyre at Citizens for Tax Justice; Robert Shapiro at the Progressive Policy Institute; Margaret Simms at the Joint Center for Political and Economic Studies; and Ray Whitman at the University of the District of Columbia.

The manuscript benefited from the detailed critiques of an early draft provided by William Gale, Jim Gibson, Robert Litan, Robert Reischauer, and Alice Rivlin. The author thanks these readers for the time and effort they gave to improving her work.

Within Brookings the author is grateful for the support of Henry Aaron, E. J. Dionne, William Frenzel, Robert Katzmann, Thomas Mann, Pietro Nivola, Bruce Smith, Kent Weaver, Margaret Weir, Stanley Wellborn, and Joseph White. Linda Gianessi and Evelyn Taylor provided staff support. James Schneider edited the book, and Cynthia Iglesias and Gerard Trimarco checked its factual accuracy.

Funding for this project was provided by the Bauman Family Foundation, Carr America Realty Corporation, the Morris and Gwendolyn Cafritz Foundation, the Ford Foundation, Giant Food, the Philip L. Graham Fund, Robert P. Kogod, Peter Kovler, Marriott International, the Eugene and Agnes E. Meyer Foundation, Frank Pearl, and Francis B. Saul II.

The views expressed here are those of the author and should not be attributed to the individuals and organizations acknowledged above, the members of the Brookings D.C. Revenue Project Business-Civic Advisory Group, or the trustees, officers, or other staff members of the Brookings Institution.

Michael H. Armacost
President

March 1997
Washington, D.C.

Contents

Tables

Figures

CHAPTER 1

The Problem and Proposed Solutions

THE NATION'S CAPITAL is in a fiscal and political crisis. In 1995 Congress imposed a presidentially appointed Control Board when the District of Columbia could not balance its budget, did not have the cash to pay its bills, and was shut out of the capital markets.[1] The expected budget deficit for the current fiscal year is about $74 million. Because spending growth (about 8.5 percent a year) has outpaced revenue growth (1.4 percent a year) since 1990, the District faces a cumulative deficit of almost 10 percent of its total budget without any authority to issue long-term debt to finance it.[2]

The inability of the District's government to provide basic services to its citizens has become legendary. Three agencies are in receivership.[3] The winter of 1996 saw the District's streets impassable with snow and ice long after the streets of Philadelphia and New York, which experienced harsher storms, were clear. Now, on any given day, the tap water is likely to be pronounced unfit to drink, 30 percent of the police vehicles are in the shop for repairs, 25 percent of the school buses are inoperable,

1. *The District of Columbia Financial Responsibility and Management Assistance Act of 1995* (P.L.104-8) became law on April 17, 1995, and established the five-person District Financial Responsibility and Management Assistance Authority, known to everyone as the Control Board.

2. The District has experienced annual operating deficits of $118.2 million in fiscal 1990, $335.4 million in fiscal 1994, $54.4 million in fiscal 1995, and $75.6 million in fiscal 1996. See *District of Columbia Comprehensive Annual Financial Report, September 30, 1995* (1996), p. 77 (hereafter *CAFR, 1995*), for deficits for fiscal 1990–95. Fiscal 1996 number is from *CAFR, 1996*. The accumulated deficit is estimated to be $400 million to $500 million, according to "Moody's Muncipal Credit Report, District of Columbia, January 30, 1997."

3. The Departments of Public and Assisted Housing, Human Services, and Corrections are either fully or partially administered through receiverships ordered by judges of the Federal District Court or Superior Court of the District of Columbia.

and firefighters say they can respond to no more than two two-alarm blazes at once (because of shortages of spare parts).[4]

Middle-class families are leaving the District at a rapid pace. Since 1970 its population has shrunk by nearly one-quarter, moving it from the ninth largest to the nineteenth largest American city by 1992. In the past five years alone the District has lost 53,000 inhabitants, 21,000 more than in the entire decade of the 1980s.[5] From 1984 to 1994 Washington lost one-third of its dual-earner households, which has meant a dramatic decline in real income tax revenues even as personal income rose. Indeed, 55 percent of income tax filers are now single earners.[6]

With 13 percent of the region's people, the District houses 44 percent of the area's poor.[7] Middle-class flight has also resulted in a disproportionately large number of low- and high-income households. As a result, mean household income ($43,866 in 1994)—which has been pulled up by the well-to-do—indicates a rich city by American standards, while median (50th percentile) household income ($30,166) was 7 percent below the national average. The District's population loss is accompanied by intense suburbanization in the region. In 1995 fully 87 percent of the region's people lived outside the District, a figure 11 percentage points higher than it was in 1970. Of comparable metropolitan areas, only the Atlanta area has a greater concentration of people living outside the core city.

The District's economy has been stagnating. The economy is dominated by government, with public employment almost 40 percent of total employment, compared with 33 percent in the region and 17 percent in

4. Residents read about these daily in the *Washington Post*. For useful summaries see David Lamb, "How the Capital Has Crumbled," *Los Angeles Times*, June 26, 1996, p. A1; and the series, "Monument to Decay," *New York Times*, July 25–27, 1996.

5. During the 1970s the annual rate of loss averaged 1.7 percent of the population. During the 1980s the rate slowed to 0.5 percent. In the 1990s it has jumped back to 1.7 percent.

6. See table 4-4.

7. Bureau of the Census, *State and Metropolitan Area Data Book, 1986, 1990*, STF-3 (Department of Commerce, 1995); and unpublished estimates. The growth of urban poverty has been a dominant trend in the past thirty years. Ranked by the number of census tracts of extreme poverty, poverty, distress, and severe distress, and adjusting for population, Washington ranked sixty-second, twenty-first, twenty-eighth, and thirty-third, respectively, among the nation's one hundred largest cities in 1990. In part this is the result of having an economic base that was heavily service oriented long before those of other cities. On the matter of residential segregation, however, the nation's capital ranked tenth among American cities in 1990. See John D. Kasarda, "Cities as Places Where People Live and Work: Urban Change and Neighborhood Distress," pp. 115, 122, in Henry G. Cisneros, ed., *Interwoven Destinies: Cities and the Nation* (Norton, 1993).

Figure 1-1. *District of Columbia Tax Revenue per Capita, Fiscal Years 1983–95*

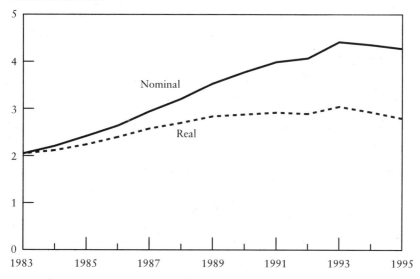

Thousands of dollars

Source: *District of Columbia Comprehensive Annual Financial Reports (CAFR), 1983–95.*

the nation as a whole. For the past fifteen years the District's economy has been growing more slowly than that of the region and is now home to less than one-quarter of the region's private jobs. Although the recession of the early 1990s hit the entire region hard, the District, unlike the suburbs, has not yet recovered. It lost 14,000 jobs—9,700 federal, 2,800 local government, and 1,500 private—from 1995 to 1996.[8] Government downsizing is expected to continue into the next century. The unemployment rate, at an average of 8.5 percent in 1996, is double that in the rest of the region.

With the stalled economy has come significant fiscal pressure. On a per capita basis, real tax revenues are flat in the 1990s (figure 1-1), the population loss has meant total real tax revenues have been falling an average of 2.3 percent a year from 1989 to 1995 (figure 1-2). Property tax delinquencies increased from less than 1 percent in 1989 to about 10 percent in 1995.[9] The District government's response has been multi-

8. Rudolph A. Pyatt Jr., "In D.C., the Tax Base Shrivels and the Fiscal Problem Grows," *Washington Post*, July 11, 1996, p. D10.

9. *CAFR, 1995*, p. 79.

Figure 1-2. *District of Columbia Revenue Changes, Selected Taxes, Fiscal Years 1989–95*

Percent

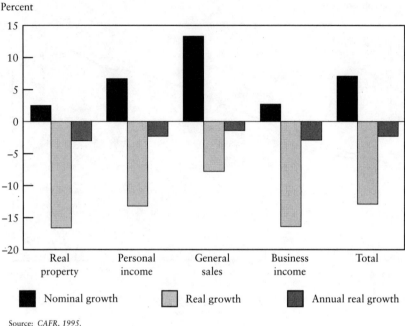

Source: *CAFR, 1995.*

faceted. First, city officials sought increased federal help and received it. There have been significant increases in the annual federal payment, from $454 million in 1989 to $660 million in 1994.[10] The mayor and the city council also resorted to budget gimmickry. To avoid ending fiscal year 1993 with a deficit, for instance, they moved the first of fiscal 1994's semiannual property tax payments into fiscal 1993, a shift of $180 million, which distorted the annual revenue growth from fiscal 1992 through fiscal 1994 and mocked prudent accounting (1994 was, by the way, a mayoral election year).

But attempts at increasing taxes have proved to be marginal, given that the District has the highest per capita tax burden in the region. A

10. The *Financial Responsibility and Management Assistance Act* extends the authorization for the federal payment through fiscal year 1999 and requires that the federal payment be made to the Control Board on behalf of the District. The Treasury may withhold all or part of the federal payment to reimburse itself for amounts due from the District as a result of Treasury advances outstanding. Also, the operations of the Control Board and the inspector general may be funded from the federal payment.

number of services were added to the general sales tax base, and the telecommunications gross receipts tax was raised twice, from 6.7 percent to 10 percent in the 1990s. Several tax increases have been dedicated to special projects.[11] But, other tax increases did not hold. An increase in the general sales tax rate from 6 percent to 7 percent lasted less than three months in 1994; it was replaced by a general rate of 5.75 percent. An attempt to increase property tax rates ended in a return to the status quo during fiscal 1995. The effective business income tax rates (carrying two surcharges) are now 9.975 percent compared with 10.5 percent in 1990–92.

Uniquely, the District of Columbia is isolated in the halls of power. By intention, it is neither a state nor a city within a state. To avoid the inherent conflicts between local and national interest and to ensure the federal government's independence from any state, the drafters of the Constitution established the capital as a "district," and in Article I, section 8, clause 17 retained for Congress the authority "to exercise exclusive legislation in all cases whatsoever, over such district."

This singular status and congressional oversight carry familiar ramifications. Since the District's creation in 1791 and its initiation as the capital in 1800, Congress has defined its physical presence, setting its boundaries and stipulating its appearance, including the height of its buildings. Congress has also defined the political landscape. Through the years, it has changed the District's governance from a three-member board of commissioners, to a mayor and city council appointed by the president, to home rule with an elected mayor and city council, to the present oversight of the Control Board.[12] Citizens residing in the District have been allowed to vote for the president and vice president of the United States only since the 1964 election. But they do not have voting representation in either house of Congress, even though Congress deter-

---

11. The incremental revenues from a 1 percentage point increase in the sales tax rate that applies to restaurant sales of food and beverages and a 2 point increase in the rate that applies to hotel services have been dedicated to a new convention center. The new small business gross receipts tax (called a "fee"), levied on any businesses subject to the District's corporate income tax, unincorporated income tax, or the regulations of the Unemployment Compensation Act, was imposed in 1994 and is dedicated to paying for the new sports arena.

12. For a history of the District as the nation's capital see Howard Gillette Jr., *Between Justice and Beauty: Race, Planning and the Failure of Urban Policy in Washington, D.C.* (Johns Hopkins University Press, 1995). Stanley M. Elkins and Eric McKitrick, *The Age of Federalism* (Oxford University Press, 1993), covers the beginnings of the capital and provides a detailed listing of other historical sources.

mines, ultimately, the District's budget and its taxes. Of all the members of the United Nations that have elected national legislatures, only the United States denies voting representation to the residents of its capital.[13] Truly, this is an orphaned capital.

The Findings

The District's long-term fiscal problems stem largely from its very nature as the nation's capital. On the revenue side of the budget, the implications are overwhelming. As both the nation's capital and a city that is not part of a state, the District has a limited tax base. As an entity unto itself, it has to provide a full range of nonfederal services to its residents, including welfare and medicaid, financed from that limited tax base. In its oversight capacity, Congress has limited the District's taxing powers and revenue sources. The more limited the tax base, the heavier the tax burden on the remaining parts of the District's economy. Increasingly, businesses and residents are fleeing.

This study finds that the District's present revenue structure is not sustainable over the long term and will not ensure ongoing budget balance. There are four threads binding this conclusion.

As a small open economy, the District functions like a city. However, its budget covers a hybrid combination of state and city service responsibilities, financed by an increasingly dysfunctional hybrid tax structure (figure 1-3). Compared with cities, the District levies many more, and higher, taxes on resident households and businesses, who, of course, do not have to remain within its boundaries. For example, the District is one of only a handful of cities to levy a full personal income tax (on unearned as well as earned income). Compared with states, the District lacks both the constitutional standing and the sovereignty to determine whom and what it taxes. For example, its personal income tax looks like a state income tax. But unlike any state, the District is not allowed to tax nonresident earnings.[14] The courts have ruled that this exclusion extends

13. United Nations Population Fund, *Statistical, Administrative and Graphical Information on the Major Urban Areas of the World* (Barcelona: Institut d'Estudis Metropolitans de Barcelona, 1988), pp. 1493–94.

14. See Advisory Commission on Intergovernmental Relations (ACIR), *Significant Features of Fiscal Federalism*, vol. 1: *Budget Processes and Tax Systems* (Washington, 1995), table 21, for a full listing of cities taxing resident and nonresident earnings and other income.

Figure 1-3. *District of Columbia Discretionary Revenues,*
Fiscal Year 1995

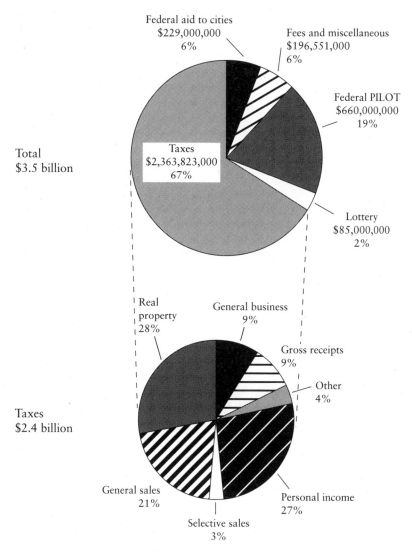

Total
$3.5 billion

Federal aid to cities
$229,000,000
6%

Fees and miscellaneous
$196,551,000
6%

Federal PILOT
$660,000,000
19%

Taxes
$2,363,823,000
67%

Lottery
$85,000,000
2%

Taxes
$2.4 billion

Real property 28%

General business 9%

Gross receipts 9%

Other 4%

General sales 21%

Selective sales 3%

Personal income 27%

Source: *CAFR, 1995*. See appendix table A-1.

Table 1-1. *District of Columbia Revenues Compared with Those of Cities of Similar Size, 1995*

Thousands of dollars unless otherwise specified

Revenue source	District	Baltimore	Boston	Memphis
City-type taxes	993,171	650,248	707,363	399,672
PILOT	660,000	4,955	47,729	29,434
Intergovernmental aid	229,364	960,831	549,221	457,412
Federal aid to cities	229,364	292,342	119,942	92,976
State aid	0	650,054	429,050	355,250
Other	0	18,435	229	9,186
Fees	188,509	112,764	246,443	94,489
City revenues (without PILOT)	1,411,044	1,723,843	1,503,027	951,573
City revenues (with PILOT)	2,071,044	1,728,798	1,550,756	981,007
State-type taxes	1,370,652	1,057,128	993,491	670,062
State fees	85,100	165,981	140,801	120,757
State revenues	1,455,752	1,223,109	1,134,292	790,819
State and city revenues	2,866,796	2,946,952	2,637,319	1,742,392
State and city revenues with PILOT	3,526,796	2,951,907	2,685,048	1,771,826
Per capita comparisons (dollars)				
City-type taxes per capita	1,751	925	1,291	651
State-type taxes per capita	2,417	1,504	1,814	1,091
Total taxes per capita	4,168	2,429	3,105	1,741

Sources: District figures are from *District of Columbia Comprehensive Annual Financial Report, September 30, 1995 (CAFR, 1995)*. The author has allocated revenues as either city-type or state-type. For other cities, all city-type revenues are 1995 actual amounts from their *1995 CAFRs*. All state-type revenues are based on per capita distribution back to each city shown in 1994 Bureau of the Census data.

to nonresidents' income from professional partnerships—the legal, accounting, management, and political consulting firms clustered in the nation's capital.[15]

As a city-state, Washington's per capita taxes are $4,168, compared with combined city and state taxes of $3,105 in Boston and $2,429 in Baltimore, cities of similar size (table 1-1). For households, the tax burden becomes progressively higher as income levels rise and are the highest in the surrounding area at the $100,000 income level.[16] The progressivity of the District's tax burden stems from a low residential property tax, which includes a $30,000 homestead exemption plus heavy reliance on

15. *Bishop v. District of Columbia*, 401 A.2d 955, April 20, 1979. Most state personal income taxes employ graduated rates on income earned and generated within the state, including partnership and consulting (federal schedule C) income. ACIR, *Significant Features*, vol. 1, pp. 49–69.

16. District of Columbia Department of Finance and Revenue (DFR), *A Comparison of Tax Rates and Burdens in the Washington Metropolitan Area* (1995), p. v.

the state-type progressive income tax.[17] For businesses the District tax bill is at least 25 percent greater than elsewhere in the region.[18] The District's high commercial property tax and sales taxes may be a significant factor accounting for the decreasing share of metropolitan area private employment.[19]

Second, the hometown industry is tax exempt. The District's tax base is significantly reduced because it is the nation's capital. Forty-one percent of the property in the District is exempt from property taxes.[20] Sixty-five percent of the exempt property belongs to the federal government. The rest, exempted by the Congress or by executive order, includes property of churches, libraries, hospitals, and universities, plus that of the District government and the foreign governments, multilateral institutions, and national nonprofit organizations that are located in the nation's capital.

Most employment in the District does not generate local income tax revenue; it generates income tax revenue for Maryland and Virginia. Every day, almost half a million workers flow into the District, more than doubling the adult population during working hours. Forty percent of Arlington's residents and one-third of the residents of the nearby cities of Alexandria and Falls Church and Prince George's County hold jobs in Washington. Congress does not allow the District to tax their earnings. There is an estimated $20 billion earnings gap between suburban commuters into the District and residents who work outside, which is worth about $1 billion in revenue annually: $366 million to Virginia and $619 million to Maryland and its counties.[21]

Other economic transactions, by military and diplomatic personnel, as well as by the federal government, go exempt from sales, income, and personal property taxes. The District estimates annual revenue forgone from these sources, at present tax rates, at $120 million.

Third, as a city the District suffers from a lack of state aid. In the rest of America, states redistribute tax revenues to localities in the form of aid. State aid accounts for 28 percent to 38 percent of general revenues

17. Michael P. Ettlinger and others, *Who Pays? A Distributional Analysis of the Tax System in All 50 States* (Washington: Citizens for Tax Justice and the Institute on Taxation and Economic Policy, 1996), app. 1, p. 9, and app. 2, p. 2.

18. See Coopers and Lybrand, "Greater Washington 1996 Comparative Tax Report," prepared for the Greater Washington Board of Trade, July 1996.

19. See appendix B.

20. Reducing the total assessed value from $78.3 billion to $46.3 billion.

21. Author's calculations. See chapter 4.

for Boston, Memphis, and Baltimore (table 1-1). With such aid, the need for local taxes diminishes. The District does receive a unique federal payment of $660 million. But at 19 percent of District revenues, the federal payment represents only half the share of help that Maryland provides Baltimore through state aid. Under the Home Rule Act this payment is justified as a form of compensation for the fact that the federal government and other entities in the District do not pay taxes to provide the public services received.[22] The federal payment is large enough to cover the lost revenue from exempt property, but not large enough to cover the revenue shortages resulting from the lack of state aid and the need to provide state services as well.

Finally, the District's revenue collection system is broken.[23] After nine directors in twenty years and staff reductions exceeding 20 percent since 1990, the city's Department of Finance and Revenue lacks the capacity to enforce and fairly collect the more than 20 different taxes and 115 fees and charges now on the books.[24] External audits point to serious deficiencies in the accuracy of the tax collection numbers and in the accountability for money received. Internal appraisals indicate that many auditors and assessors have not kept up with developments in their professions and have not been trained to use even the outmoded technology available to them. Voluntary tax compliance is languishing, evasion is significant, and business tax revenues derive largely from audits. Many properties are underassessed, some of them perhaps intentionally, while growing backlogs throughout the tax agency offer easy opportunities for outstanding tax bills to remain outstanding. With neither an internal auditor nor a resident inspector general watching over collections or assessments, the serious risk of corruption needs to be recognized and corrected.

Recommendations

The following recommendations are intended to change a dysfunctional revenue structure into one that more closely resembles that of cities of

22. Under the act the mayor must submit to the federal Office of Management and Budget an enumeration of the services and the tax exemptions, but the federal government is under no obligation to link the payment to these measures or, indeed, to take any heed of them.

23. The basis for this conclusion is presented in chapter 6, which provides a list of sources.

24. Appendix A contains a listing of taxes, fees, and charges.

Table 1-2. *District of Columbia General Fund Discretionary Revenues, Current and Proposed, Fiscal Year 1995*

Thousands of dollars unless otherwise specified

Revenues	Current	Proposed	Difference	Current (percent)	Proposed (percent)
City-type taxes	1,653,171	1,179,123	(474,048)	47	38
Property	654,284	477,104	(177,180)	19	15
Personal property	61,305	0	(61,305)	2	0
Gross receipts	210,269	260,269	50,000	6	8
Other	67,313	59,271	(8,042)	2	2
PILOT	660,000	382,479	(277,521)	19	12
Intergovernmental aid	229,364	663,530	434,166	7	21
Federal aid to cities	229,364	229,364	0	7	7
State aid	0	434,166	434,166	0	14
Fees	188,509	188,509	0	5	6
Total city revenues	2,071,044	2,031,162	(39,882)	59	65
State-type taxes	1,370,652	1,015,973	(354,679)	39	32
Personal income	643,676	449,676	(194,000)	18	14
Sales (selective and general)	549,490	549,490	0	16	18
Business income	160,679	0	(160,679)	5	0
Other	16,807	16,807	0	0	1
State fees–lottery	85,100	85,100	0	2	3
Total state revenues	1,455,752	1,101,073	(354,679)	41	35
State and city revenues[a]	3,526,796	3,132,235	(394,561)	100	100

Sources: *CAFR, 1995*; and author's calculations.

a. Also called general fund discretionary revenue.

similar size. Therefore, this study proposes cutting and streamlining District taxes and changing significantly the federal contribution to the District's revenues. The resulting revenue structure would still be a combination of city-type and state-type taxes and aid, and the District's spending responsibilities would remain similarly hybrid (table 1-2). The taxes would, however, be lower, simpler, fairer, easier to collect, more stable and predictable for budgeting, and would result in a tax burden more closely in line with the combined state and local tax burdens in the surrounding area. The aid would be more rationally based, achieve a fair measure of parity with other cities, and be linked to specific shortfalls in revenues stemming from the District's special status.

Specifically, this study proposes to eliminate entirely four taxes on business, including the personal property tax, professional license fee, corporate income (franchise) tax, and unincorporated income (franchise) tax (see chapter 5). In addition, two broadly based taxes should be cut significantly. Real property tax revenues should be cut by 27 percent, with five tax classes simplified into two, the timing of assessments and

Table 1-3. *Proposed Restructured Relationship between the Federal Government and the District of Columbia, Fiscal Year 1995*

Millions of dollars

Category		Amount
PILOT[a]		382.5
Federal government property	280.9	
Traditional local exemptions required by Congresss	69.5	
Foreign property	14.0	
Special act of Congress and executive order exemptions	18.1	
Direct state aid		434.2
Shared costs for state redistributive services (medicaid and welfare)		220.4
Shared costs for other state services[b]		158.2
Total		1,195.3

Sources: Author's calculations based on District of Columbia Department of Finance and Revenue, *Study of Property, Income and Sales Tax Exemptions in the District of Columbia* (April 1995); District of Columbia Department of Finance and Revenue, "Schedule of Organizations in the District of Columbia Exempted from Real Property Taxation, by Acts of Congress, 1996 Assessment"; Philip M. Dearborn and Carol S. Meyers, "The Necessity and Cost of District of Columbia Services," Greater Washington Research Center, August 1996; and *FY 1995 Boston Comprehensive Annual Financial Report.*

a. Not included in the PILOT are other tax exemptions that reduce the District's tax base and the estimated revenue forgone: sales tax on military purchases, $10.9 million; sales tax on diplomatic purchases, $11.2 million; income tax on military personnel, $21.1 million; income tax on diplomatic personnel, $25.6 million; federal and special act of Congress personal property, $52.6 million; and federal sales tax (not available).

b. State services provided by the District include the following: SSI supplements, general relief, need determination, foster care, development disabilities, rehabilitation, child support, health labs, long-term care, mental health, higher education, parole, and vehicle registration.

payments should be simplified to improve cash flow, and the many tax relief programs should be consolidated into one, targeted to those with low (or fixed) incomes. The District's personal income tax should be cut by 30 percent, meaning that all residents with federal adjusted gross income of less than $200,000 would have their taxes cut and that 36 percent of residents would pay no District income tax. The new income tax would be 28 percent of federal liability, with collection and enforcement delegated to the Internal Revenue Service. Discretionary revenue of $50 million would be raised through a low, broadly based business gross receipts tax.

The resulting decrease of about $400 million in the District's discretionary revenue would be offset by a *new fiscal relationship with the federal government*. This relationship would have three elements, each addressing a particular part of the District's revenue shortage that stems from being the nation's capital (table 1-3). The first is a payment in lieu of taxes (PILOT), amounting to $382 million, to compensate the District for the reduction of its tax base by federally owned and otherwise tax-exempt property. This would allow property taxes to be reduced for all property owners. The second is state-type aid of $434 million, an amount

Table 1-4. *District of Columbia Budget Reconciliation, Fiscal Year 1995*
Millions of dollars

Revenue	Current	Proposed	Difference
General fund, discretionary revenue[a]	3,527	3,132	(395)
Other revenues[b]	142	142	0
Federal categorical grants[c]	653	653	0
Federal aid for state-type spending			0
Medicaid and welfare at 75 percent	0	220	220
All other state services at 50 percent	0	158	158
General fund, budgeted revenue	4,322	4,305	(17)
Enterprise funds[d]	848	848	0
Total budget	5,170	5,153	(17)

Sources: *CAFR, 1995*; and Government of the District of Columbia, *A Vision for America's First City: FY 1997 Budget and Multiyear Plan* (May 1996).

a. Includes $3,248 million of appropriated revenues as defined in *CAFR*, plus $85 million in lottery revenue, plus $229 million in federal aid to cities (total federal grants of $882 million less $653 million in categorical human services grants), less the $35 million motor fuel tax, less the $175,000 health care provider fee, and less the $468,000 general fund portion of the arena fee (*CAFR, 1995*, pp. 23, 46).

b. Nonappropriated charges for services and miscellaneous revenues (*CAFR, 1995*, p. 23).

c. Federal grants for human support services, primarily medicaid and welfare (*CAFR, 1995*, p. 46).

d. Total expenditures for the enterprise funds as reported in the budget (*1997 Budget*, p. 35).

comparable to that received by cities of similar size from their state governments. The PILOT and state aid are city-type discretionary revenues to the District. They total $817 million, compared with the present federal payment of $660 million, also categorized as a city-type discretionary revenue (table 1-2).

The third element is a 50-50 sharing of state-type spending on medicaid and welfare ($220 million) and on general programs ($158 million), which together amount to an additional $378 million. This third element partially compensates the District for the fact that it has no state to provide a range of state services. Such payments would not be discretionary revenue to the District. They could be spent only to provide specific (state-type) services and subject to whatever federal sanctions or Control Board oversight Congress might choose to exercise to ensure efficient service provision. As such they are categorized in this study as (state-type) categorical aid (table 1-4). The compensation would not be necessary, of course, if the federal government chose to provide these services directly to District residents. Federal resources in this proposal total $1.2 billion: $817 million in city-type discretionary revenue and $378 million in state-type categorical grants.

At the bottom line, the District's total budget and revenues would be of the same size as presently approved by Congress (table 1-4). This study has not determined whether that amount is correct for the District's budget or whether a local government efficiently providing its services would require a smaller or a larger budget. Further, the reader is cautioned that the numbers displayed here should be treated as orders of magnitude rather than budgetable amounts, since they are estimates based on the less-than-perfect data available to this study.

City-Type Taxes

This study proposes to reduce city-type taxes by almost half a billion dollars. It would cut and simplify the real property tax, consolidate property tax relief programs, and streamline the assessment and collection calendar. Two city-type business taxes (the personal property tax and professional license fee) would be eliminated, and one city-type business tax (a broadly based gross receipts tax) would be increased.

REAL PROPERTY TAX. The real property tax is the main revenue of local governments. The District's present five-class system has resulted in a $2.15 (per $100 of market value) effective commercial rate on occupied property and $5.00 on vacant property. These rates result in commercial tax liabilities that are, on average, 40 percent higher than those in the suburbs. The study's econometric analysis indicates that these differences may be linked to the District's decreasing share of the region's jobs (see appendix B).

We propose a two-class system, a residential rate of $0.90 and a commercial rate of $1.35, with a maximum 150 percent ratio between the two rates, set by statute, to prevent a creeping increase in the commercial rate. A single, income-determined, residential property tax relief program would be better targeted and fairer than the present system for those for whom property tax payments represent a real burden. The District also needs to change the assessment and payment calendar as well as the budgeting of the property tax, including a reserve for delinquencies. These changes will improve cash flow and budget stability. The lower property tax rates, holding other things constant, should result in increased property values and lower rents, for both households and businesses.

Simplicity argues for a single-class system, but the District's present rate structure makes it very difficult to get from here to there. The lowest (residential) rate is now $0.96, and its highest is $5.00; suburban rates range from $0.90 to $1.45 (the most common being $1.07). Imposing a single-class system at the current residential rate would reduce commercial rates in the downtown office building core to a level far below that of the surrounding area. Alternatively, imposing a single-class system at the suburban rates would require a tax increase on all homeowners, which this study has ruled out, given the present low quality of District services, looming assessment changes, and the proposal for an income-targeted relief program. Thus the proposal for a two-class system.

Currently, 53 percent of the market value of the District's property is residential and 47 percent is commercial. Residential property pays 38.6 percent of the levy and commercial property 61.4 percent. Under this proposal, residential property would bear 43 percent of the levy and commercial property 57 percent. Thus, moving to a two-class system and reducing the rates would narrow by about one-third the spread between the shares of market value and the shares of taxes borne by residential and commercial property.

PERSONAL PROPERTY TAXES. The study has determined that the District would be able to meet a further goal of eliminating unenforceable taxes by setting the commercial real property rate to allow the elimination of the business personal property tax ($61 million). The resulting effective tax rate of $1.35 on commercial real property would be a significant reduction from current burdens and would be on a par with the rate in Prince William County. Because surrounding jurisdictions impose a personal property tax, eliminating the District's tax may provide some competitive advantage.

PROFESSIONAL LICENSE FEE. The professional license fee ($8 million) applies largely to professionals doing business in the District and is the remnant of attempts to tax the thousands of legal, accounting, political, and management consulting partnerships in Washington. It is not well enforced, which makes it unfair and discourages potential payers from acknowledging self-employment in the District. It should be eliminated.

GROSS RECEIPTS TAX. In its 1990 report to the mayor on budgetary reform, the Rivlin Commission recommended a broadly based gross business receipts tax, in large measure because it is easy to audit and enforce and, at low rates, issues of fairness are minor. It also does not violate the prohibition on the taxation of nonresident income. The District has implemented a small version of such a tax and dedicated the $10 million in revenue to financing the downtown sports arena now under construction. From data provided by the District's Department of Finance and Revenue, with the present payment structure, collecting five times that amount for general revenue, while continuing the portion designated for the arena, would still keep the tax burden comparable to that in the surrounding area.

Federal Payment in Lieu of Taxes

The federal government should make a full tax-equivalency payment in lieu of taxes (PILOT) on the value of the 41 percent of the property base of the nation's capital that is tax exempt and receives local services. Unlike the present federal payment, the amount of the PILOT should not be negotiable. Its value should be determined by assessments and the commercial property tax rate. It should be a permanent part of the federal budget, incorporated into the grants section with other PILOTs.

Based on existing assessments and the proposed commercial property tax rate of $1.35, the federal payment would be $382 million. Like a state, the federal government has determined which local properties are exempt from taxation. This study proposes, then, to include all tax-exempt properties, except those belonging to the government of the District of Columbia, as part of a federal PILOT. The bulk of the payment would compensate for federal government property, with the remainder covering property owned by traditional tax-exempt organizations and diplomatic, national nonprofit, and multilateral institutions. Many consider these institutions part of the fabric of the nation's capital. If some people question whether the federal government should pick up the costs of the one-quarter to one-third of the exempt property that is not federally owned, the option always exists for the federal government to require national nonprofits, universities, and hospitals to contribute a portion of the PILOT themselves or even to eliminate some or all of these exemptions.

The values for tax-exempt property should be treated with particular caution. Because the assessments of exempt property have never been used for a material purpose, neither the District nor the owners have had an incentive to make certain of their accuracy. Under this proposal, there might be an advantage for both the federal and District governments to form a partnership with the International Association of Assessing Officers to ensure state-of-the-art valuation for some of the unique properties of the nation's capital. There are valuation techniques available to assessors, such as those used by New York City to value Central Park and to arrive at the PILOTs that the state pays for the World Trade Center and Battery Park City.

State-Type Taxes

The District should significantly reduce its dependence on state-type taxes, which will cost it considerable revenue. This study proposes converting the personal income tax into a flat percentage of the federal income tax liability. The new tax would be administered by the Internal Revenue Service. The unenforceable and arbitrary business income taxes should be eliminated. These actions would improve markedly the fairness of the tax structure and the enforcement and collection process.

PERSONAL INCOME TAX. Most cities do not levy a personal income tax on unearned and earned income; states do. Even by state standards, the District income tax is high, higher than Virginia's and similar to those found in the Maryland suburbs. The income base requires a great many adjustments from the federal form 1040, and although the tax is progressive, it is less progressive than the federal tax, causing some residents who receive the federal earned income tax credit to pay District income tax.

The District should follow the lead of two small East Coast states, Rhode Island and Vermont, and piggyback on the federal income tax. The rate should be set to reduce the District's reliance on the income tax as it becomes more progressive. The Internal Revenue Service should administer the tax for the District.

Under this proposal the District would raise about $200 million less than it does now from the personal income tax. District residents would pay a flat 28 percent of federal liability. Virtually no taxpayers would be made worse off; the effective tax rate would decrease for all income classes. The average effective tax rate would fall from 5.15 percent to 4.33 percent, with the largest drop (from 5.42 percent to 3.34 percent) occurring for those with federal adjusted gross incomes of $30,000–$50,000. Those with incomes of $100,000–$200,000 would see a reduction of their effective rate from 6.73 percent to 5.29 percent. Those with incomes greater than $200,000 would receive only small reductions in their District tax liability.

The strongest reason for this simplification is to have the IRS, acknowledged as the best tax agency in the world, administer this tax on behalf of the District. Although the agency would require significant control over the layout of the tax forms and perhaps as long as two years to put the programming and administration in place, this proposal offers significant administrative and enforcement relief to the District.

BUSINESS INCOME TAXES.   The two income-based general business taxes, each seriously flawed, should be eliminated, costing at most $160 million in revenue forgone. To the extent that S-corporation owners and partners of unincorporated businesses are residents of the District, some revenue would flow back through the personal income tax.

The District's corporate franchise tax, structured like typical state corporate income taxes, has an effective rate of 9.975 percent (including two surcharges). Rates in Maryland and Virginia are 7 percent and 6 percent, respectively. The yield from this tax, accounting for only 5 percent of the District's tax revenue, is largely audit driven, making it erratic and unpredictable. Increasingly, the District is being subjected to blackmail by corporations that seek special treatment for remaining in Washington. For this complicated and poorly administered tax, the District's tax collectors have incomplete data and do not know who the biggest taxpayers are, what industries bear the heaviest burdens, or how tax liabilities vary by size or type of corporation. The randomness of the voluntary compliance and the audits indicate that at present this is a very unfair tax.

The unincorporated franchise tax has little justification.[25] Levied at the same rate as the corporate tax, it was intended to create parallel tax treatment regardless of the form of the business and to reach, particularly, the lucrative 4.5 percent of private employment represented by legal services. But because of a 1979 court ruling, the District exempts professional partnerships from this tax, which has effectively been reduced to a levy on small proprietors. About 8,000 payers produce $39 million in revenue. Again, some of this revenue would be replaced by the new gross receipts tax.

The impact of these tax changes on residents is important, but difficult to measure. For households, the effect of the changes in the property tax depend on ownership or rental, and on income, age, and the value of property. For low-income households (earning less than $30,000) and renters, the property tax changes would mean a tax cut. For middle- and high-income homeowners these changes would mean an annual property tax increase of $50 to $215, stemming from a tightening of the tax relief programs, particularly the elimination of the $30,000 homestead exemption. At the same time, however, most households would be getting larger tax cuts through the income tax—from $100 to $2,000. For most, but

---

25. The remaining model for it is New York City's unincorporated business tax (UBT).

not all, District residents, the personal income tax cut will swamp the increase in the property tax.[26]

For typical businesses, this proposal would lower the tax costs by about 30 to 40 percent. For a business services headquarters or a national association, the District would become a lower-tax option than Prince George's County and put it in the running on tax costs with Montgomery and Arlington counties.[27]

State Aid

"A city's . . . fiscal health depends on . . . economic and social factors . . . and on its state-determined fiscal institutions, including its access to broad-based taxes, the taxes collected by overlying jurisdictions, its service responsibilities, and the intergovernmental grants it receives from its state."[28] These grants, known as state aid, constitute a crucial component of cities' general revenue. Massachusetts, for example, in 1995 provided $429 million in state aid to Boston, roughly the District's size. State aid to localities comes from state taxes and is distributed in recognition of special spending burdens, to help provide for services that states expect localities to provide, and to spread revenues more evenly among wealthier and poorer areas.

The federal government should take on the role of state to the nation's orphaned capital and provide $434 million, a figure adjusted for the small difference in population between Boston and Washington. Like other localities, the District contributes to federal collections, although the contribution is a small part of the total. In this way, the District would be to the federal "state" no different from any number of small counties are to their states. They pay taxes; they receive state aid.[29]

26. For example, the author calculates that homeowners with an income of $85,000 and a home valued at $200,000 would receive an income tax cut of $1,500 and a property tax increase of $170, resulting in a $1,330 annual increase in disposable income. A renter with a $25,000 income and one dependent would receive a $1,029 (39 percent) combined income tax cut.

27. The author's calculations are based on the method and data contained in Coopers and Lybrand, "Greater Washington 1996 Comparative Tax Report."

28. Helen F. Ladd and John Yinger, *America's Ailing Cities: Fiscal Health and the Design of Urban Policy* (Johns Hopkins University Press, 1989), p. 14.

29. This argument assumes that taxes are borne in the jurisdiction collecting them. Often that is not the case. States and localities seek to export as much of their tax burden as possible, taxing resident industries in ways that pass on the costs to national and even international customers, shareholders, and workers. To varying and unknown degrees they

For a number of analysts, state aid to *cities* exists in large part to treat fairly the residents of all jurisdictions in a metropolitan area.[30] This does not happen in the District of Columbia. If the amount of aid proposed here ($434 million) seems too burdensome to the federal government, the logic of sharing this cost with the entire region in the form of a tax on nonresident earnings becomes inescapable. The federal government could impose for the District a typical city-type commuter tax (2 percent), as derived in chapter 4, which would be deductible from the income tax of the state of residence. This would generate about $361 million, more than 80 percent of the cost of state aid. It would not impose an additional burden to commuters, who are currently paying tax to their states. It would, however, eat into the almost $1 billion in revenue that Maryland and Virginia presently receive through their taxation of their residents' earnings in the District of Columbia.

State-Type Services

The absence of a state means that the District provides state-type services. This study proposes that the federal government act as the state. If the federal government could provide these services directly, the District's spending and taxes would fall. This study has focused on the revenue compensation necessary should direct federal provision of these services not be feasible.

It is useful to distinguish between redistributive services (medicaid and welfare) and all others. In the case of medicaid (for this discussion the term will include welfare), there is no perfect model for the federal-District relationship because this is a national program in which the federal government already provides at least 50 percent of the funding to states. With the exception of New York City, cities do not pay for medicaid; states do. At the moment, the federal government is treating the District of Columbia as if it were a state. The federal government pays half the costs and the District picks up the other half.

If the federal government were to act as the state to the nation's capital city, it would mean providing medicaid directly to District residents. However, these may not be services the federal government wants to provide or believes itself equipped to provide. If it chose instead to com-

---

succeed. So justifying state aid based on a locality's contribution to the state's coffers makes limited sense.

30. Ladd and Yinger, *America's Ailing Cities*, p. 15.

pensate the District for performing these functions, the results would be less than satisfactory. Full federal funding, with the District providing the services, offers no incentive for the District (with none of its own resources at stake) to operate efficiently. So, this study has fallen back on the imperfect model of New York City, proposing that the federal government pick up an additional 25 percent state share, leaving the District to provide the service and pay 25 percent of the cost. In New York City's case the state sets benefits and monitors results, but there are three states that pay less than 25 percent of medicaid and, like the District, set their own benefits and enforcement rules. So far the federal government has found that arrangement acceptable.

The District also provides courts, prisons, mental health and higher education facilities, and other state-type services. As table 7-1, derived from a recent study for the Control Board, illustrates, the estimated annual cost of these services is $316 million. Here, too, there should be a sharing of costs, a 50-50 split, or $158 million for the federal government. Again, the option remains for direct federal provision.

Implementation

The survival and success of the nation's capital is in the national interest and is a matter of national concern. Restructuring the District's revenues is an essential component for ensuring this. It will not, however, be the initial component of long-run reform.

First, services must improve. Present and potential taxpayers must perceive that there is value received for the District's tax dollars. Second, financial accountability and prudent fiscal management must be put in place. This will ensure the integrity of the budget and financial accounting process and will open opportunities to address outstanding financial problems and meet new needs. For example, resources freed through refinancing existing debt, resolving the ownership of the outstanding pension liability, or the sale of assets can help pay for needed repairs to the District's infrastructure after years of deferred maintenance.

But even if the District were providing services efficiently and operating under state-of-the-art systems, the analysis in this study indicates that its revenues would fail to keep pace with spending over the long term. In addition, as tough management decisions are made, District residents, employees, and political leaders need to know that there will, eventually, be a more rational revenue structure on which the District's budget will rest.

The proposals presented here are budget neutral and can be phased in. For example, the income tax proposal requires that the IRS begin planning for the new process. This planning should begin immediately. Changes in the property tax calendar and payment schedule need to precede cutting the property tax rates (and revenues) if the District is to avoid making bondholders nervous over its ability to repay debt. The property tax cuts can proceed hand in hand with the refinancing of existing debt and the bonding-out of the accumulated deficit over the coming years. Or the gross receipts tax revenues ($50 million annually) might be dedicated to paying off the accumulated deficit. The elimination of the business taxes can be linked to changes in spending or the introduction of an independent economic development agency. The PILOT and the state aid can be paid to the Control Board. The federal compensation for medicaid and other state-type spending should be linked to improvements in the District's delivery of these services and greater efficiencies in their operations and treated as categorical aid that must be spent on those services.

Finally, although the addition to annual federal spending proposed here is not great, the federal government's budget is moving toward balance and its budget constraints are as real as the District's. The case presented here for the federal fiscal role with respect to the District rests on a constitutional obligation set out in Article 1. From the point of view of making up the federal budget, this obligation should translate into both the PILOT and state aid to the District properly scored for the federal budget as mandatory spending, not subject to the cap faced by discretionary spending.

The Focus of This Study

This study concentrated on restructuring the District's discretionary revenues in a budget-neutral way, addressing the goal of achieving long-term budget balance. The analysis of the present revenue sources—taxes and the federal payment—and the proposals for change were framed by these criteria: What is fair? What is competitive? What can the District do well? What is easy for taxpayers to understand? What is stable and predictable for ongoing budget balance? Several of these criteria interact comfortably. Others stand more independently. For example, there is a presumption in this study that how the revenue is collected, and indeed, whether it realistically can be collected, is at this time central to the task of restructuring the District's revenues. This is not only an issue of efficiency, it is also an issue of fairness. One type of fairness is that all taxpayers and users bear their fair share of the cost of government services, either based on the benefits received or ability to pay. Another is that the tax system should seek to treat like-situated individuals or businesses in a like manner, the concept of parallel treatment or horizontal equity. Clearly, the actions (or inaction) of the District's tax collectors and property assessors matter for both.

In the interest of timeliness or because of limitations on resources or a lack of data, there were a number of interesting avenues that this study simply could not examine. Five stand out as items for the District's newly established Tax Reform Commission. First, the sales and use tax needs a thorough examination. The data were not available in time for this study to pursue the problem. Second, the District's smaller revenues, including the proliferation of fees and miscellaneous revenues, offer a rich possibility for elimination and consolidation. A third is the potential for regional revenue solutions.[31] The need to replace the Woodrow Wilson Bridge and the District's growing difficulty in funding the metrobus system as suburban jurisdictions privatize their buses may present a new opening with respect to regional funding and revenue sharing for transportation. Another option this study could not address is the creation of independent authorities, funded with dedicated revenues, to provide necessary District services. Dedicated user fees not only provide ongoing funding to insulate a service from budget cuts and backing for bonds to ensure state-of-the-art plant and equipment, they also can be collected from otherwise tax-exempt entities, greatly increasing the equity in funding basic services.[32] Finally, the effects of technological change on the District's traditional tax bases and revenues need to be thoroughly ex-

---

31. The Washington region has a history of cooperation on integrating public transportation and, subregionally, of administering water supplies and distribution and the airports. The Washington Area Metropolitan Transit Authority administers public transportation throughout the region. The water cooperation includes the District and several Virginia entities. The Airport Authority includes Dulles International and National Airport but not Baltimore-Washington International Airport.

32. The model would be the new Water and Sewer Authority, where District water fees will be collected from both the federal and District governments as well as nonprofit entities.

plored. For example, state and local telecommunications taxes came of age in the era of national regulation. Technology is creating whole new industries, and global deregulation is blurring the lines between them very quickly.[33] The District needs to face coldly its options, especially in light of actions that other jurisdictions are taking.[34]

33. To draw attention to the problem these governments face in the wake of the *Telecommunications Reform Act of 1996*, the Federation of Tax Administrators, the Multistate Tax Commission, the National Conference of State Legislatures, and the National Tax Association sponsored a conference in November 1996 on the taxation of telecommunications and electronic commerce; the conference raised more questions than it answered.

34. As this study was being completed, the District, under MCI Corporation's threat to relocate, was pressured to make significant changes in its corporate income tax by redefining loss carry-forwards and replacing the three-factor formula for the allocation of income by a single-factor formula (sales only). The policy options offered in this study would make the MCI proposal moot. However, the broader issue of appropriate tax policy for a small, open economy like the District's when dealing with a fleet-footed global telecommunications company remains and lends resonance to the analysis and proposals presented in this study.

CHAPTER 2

The Business Climate

THE DISTRICT OF COLUMBIA is the central city of a wealthy and growing metropolitan area. Although its recent fiscal crisis has drawn special attention, the performance of its economy has been poor for some time. Certainly, aspects of the District's recent economic experience are similar to those of other large American cities, particularly in the Northeast and Midwest, which have also lost population and employment in the past three decades as their suburbs have grown. Although some aspects may be universal, this study focuses on the District because it is sufficiently exceptional to require an individual analysis.[1]

As the nation's capital, the District has a large federal work force and is a magnet for business and tourism. Although the federal govenment links it to its suburbs, in the past twenty-five years the District's economy has become increasingly different from that of its suburbs—less diversified and more dependent on its core federal business.[2]

Decisions by businesses and households weighing the costs and benefits of doing business or living in one locality compared with another are the economic calculus of metropolitan growth. This study focuses on policy choices and their associated consequences for the District's relationship with its suburbs. There is a sharp contrast in the recent fortunes of the District and its suburbs. Employment, for example, has decreased in the District and increased in Northern Virginia. It is natural to suppose

1. According to regional economist Stephen Fuller, "the District of Columbia is different from other central cities in its relationship with its suburban economy. These economic linkages are strengthened by the nature of the area's economy, its dominance by federal government and national capital functions. This federal government dominance has resulted in a more physically centralizedd and interdependent economy than would be found in private-sector dominated economies shaped by market forces." See "The Economy of the District of Columbia and Its Impact on the Washington Area and Its Suburbs," Center for Regional Analysis, George Mason University, December 1996.
2. Fuller, "Economy of the District," p. 1.

that these developments are linked, that some of the jobs created in one jurisdiction might, under different circumstances, have been created in the other. Insofar as the data are available, this chapter compares relevant District attributes with their metropolitan area counterparts, in part to explain why businesses locate where they do.

This chapter also addresses possible links between the District's relatively poor economic performance and public policy, particularly taxes and local incentives for economic development. After sketching the District's recent economic history, it compares the costs of doing business in the District to the costs in surrounding jurisdictions. Finally, it examines a strategy to improve the climate for private sector job growth in the District. Appendix B reports the results of a quantitative analysis of the effect of taxes on the District's share of the region's jobs.

Recent Economic History

Between 1974 and 1989 private employment in the District of Columbia increased 30.2 percent, from to 371,509 to 483,664, while regional employment grew 89.2 percent, from 1.066 million to 2.017 million.[3] Since 1989 private employment in the District has declined 2.8 percent (a loss of 13,305 jobs), while jobs in the suburbs have increased by an average of 2.8 percent (5.2 percent in the Virginia suburbs). In August of 1989 the unemployment rate was 4.9 percent in the District and 2.6 percent in the metropolitan area as a whole.[4] Both rates climbed through June 1992, when metropolitan unemployment reached 5.6 percent, the decade's high so far, and the District rate reached 9.2 percent. Subsequently the rate declined in the metropolitan area, but not as much in the city. In August 1996 District unemployment was 8.8 percent while the met-

3. Differences between central city and suburban job growth characterized the 1970s and 1980s in several U.S. metropolitan areas. The Bureau of Economic Analysis in the Department of Commerce tracks employment by county rather than by city, so that comparisons with a wide range of cities and suburbs are impossible. Like the District, New York City grew more slowly than its suburbs during the 1970s and 1980s. Total growth in private employment was 8.1 percent in the city and 25.9 percent in the suburbs between 1974 and 1989. Since then, private employment has declined by 6.5 percent in the city and 6.9 percent in the suburbs. In Philadelphia, too, suburban growth coincided with urban decline. Suburban jobs increased by 51.4 percent between 1974 and 1989, while 10.0 percent of city jobs were lost. Between 1989 and 1994 private employment increased 1.7 percent in the Philadelphia suburbs and declined 7.9 percent in the city.

4. District and metropolitan area unemployment figures are supplied by the District of Columbia Department of Employment Services.

Figure 2-1. *District of Columbia Share of Metropolitan Area Employment, 1969–94*

Percent

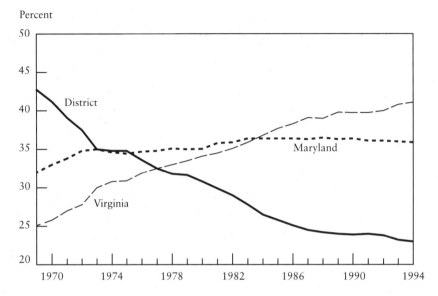

Source: Bureau of Economic Analysis, Regional Economic Information Service, http://www.lib.virginia.edu/socsci/reis/reit2.html.

ropolitan rate was 3.7 percent. The gap between the District and suburban rates has widened significantly in 7 years.[5]

In the past twenty-five years, the District's share of metropolitan area jobs has decreased in direct proportion to the increase in the Virginia suburban share, while Maryland's share has been stable (figure 2-1). The combination of growth in the metropolitan area and cheap undeveloped land in the exurbs gives Washington's suburbs a decided advantage over the District in creating jobs. Realistically, one cannot expect the District to show faster job growth than a newly urbanizing remote suburban county. But the District's continuing loss of jobs, even as the rest of the area recovers, is ominous and has hurt its social well-being through unemployment and its finances through lost business, property, and sales tax revenues. Understanding the causes of the job losses, especially if they are connected to District policy, may provide some guidance in arresting the city's decline and improving its economy and revenue base.

5. The ratio was 1.88 in 1989 and 2.38 in 1996.

The Location Decision

Many factors affect the location decisions of businesses. The hundreds of thousands of private sector jobs remaining in the District and the high rate of growth in the suburban counties both reflect the strong draw the District has for the private sector. The traditional magnets of business location are markets and labor.[6] Profits depend on accessibility to both, and businesses attract both with accessible, central, sometimes prestigious, locations. The District's biggest employer is the federal government, with 210,980 jobs in 1994. Providing goods and services to government agencies and to their employees is a huge opportunity for business. Federal expenditures in the District totaled $21.9 billion in 1995. When firms choose among the many locations spread across the District, Maryland, and Virginia, however, they do take other factors into consideration. To varying degrees they will trade accessibility for reduced rent, or prestige for lower costs. They may also decide a suburban location provides greater accessibility to labor and customers.[7]

Part of the blame for the District's high unemployment belongs to recent federal downsizing in the 1990s. Although federal employment increased steadily between 1988 and 1992, when there were 223,981 federal employees in the District, by 1994 a sharp 5.8 percent drop left the District with 210,980. Federal downsizing in the suburbs has been less dramatic. The eight counties and independent cities around the District had 231,940 federal civilian and military jobs in 1992 and 229,541 in 1994. In general, however, the District's share of metropolitan area federal jobs has been fairly stable, increasing from 51.6 percent in 1970 to 54.7 percent in 1980, but returning to 51.5 percent by 1990 and to 51.0 percent in 1994.

The question remains: Why has the District not benefited from regional growth in private employment? Might District policy affect private sector location decisions and (or) the economic success of District enterprises?

6. F. J. Calzonetti and Robert T. Walker, "Factors Affecting Industrial Location Decisions: A Survey Approach," in Henry W. Herzog Jr. and Alan M. Schlottman, eds., *Industry Location and Public Policy* (University of Tennessee Press, 1991), pp. 221–40.

7. Sixty-eight percent of District workers lived in the suburbs in 1990. Bureau of the Census, *Commuting Data for the Washington and Baltimore Metropolitan Statistical Areas* (Department of Commerce, 1990), table 8.

Creating a Good Business Climate

A good business climate usually consists of a competitive and fair tax structure; factors such as low crime rates, good schools, and efficient transportation that affect the quality of life; and responsive local government. A locality can affect its business climate and its employment and economic growth through an economic development strategy that emphasizes the locality's competitive strengths as well as improving the overall business climate.[8] By the mid-1980s most states and larger localities had implemented economic development strategies or policies to enhance their locational advantage.

Cities can make good use of strategic location, strong market demand, access to regional industries, and other competitive advantages. The central city in a metropolitan area has distinct geographic and demographic advantages over its suburbs in providing businesses proximity to other businesses and centers of economic and political activity. Because businesses are attracted to locations where the business climate is considered favorable, cities can use public policy to create and improve such environments.

But inner cities usually have less vacant land, higher rent costs, more local government regulations, higher taxes, poorer public services, and a less diversified skilled labor force than their suburbs. These factors combine to raise the costs of doing business. Rent, taxes, and poorly skilled workers are direct costs. Government unresponsiveness, regulation, licensing, and other bureaucratic hassles represent indirect costs. To become more competitive, according to Michael Porter, "cities badly need to dismantle these regulatory and bureaucratic mazes to foster economic development. . . . City governments should establish a single entity responsible for all aspects of building, including zoning, permitting, inspections, and other approvals to minimize the costs to business. Turnaround times on permit applications and other approvals should be guaranteed."[9]

In implementing economic development strategies, cities must develop policies that address the needs of their particular economies. Policies to retain and attract business should be comprehensive enough to include

8. Michael E. Porter, "The Competitive Advantage of the Inner City," *Harvard Business Review* (May–June 1995), pp. 55–71.

9. Michael E. Porter, "The Competitive Advantage of the Inner City," Discussion Paper, Harvard Business School, June 22, 1994, p. 3.

diverse businesses, but should also be specific in targeting industries that have a demonstrated need for an urban location. This type of strategic development policy has been lacking in the District. In 1994 the Department of Commerce's Economic Development Administration described the failure of city officials to grasp the importance and scope of economic development.

> Economic development emerged as a crucial political issue, with plenty of debate but often with little understanding. Public and private sector officials came to realize that state and local economic development must be more than local boosterism, business climate ratings, and tax giveaways. Development officials must understand the forces that shape their economies so that they can anticipate problems before they occur and opportunities before they are gone.[10]

Local governments cannot afford to allow regulatory obstacles and a lack of planning to negate the natural competitive advantages of agglomeration that exist within cities. Instead, economic development strategies on the local level should reduce the costs of doing business and enhance the overall business climate to make the market both attractive and profitable.

The Costs of Locating in the District

A recent study conducted for George Washington University's Center for the Advancement of Small Business asked several hundred business managers in the District to rate seven locational attributes as factors providing a reason to stay in the District, or a reason to leave. Taxes of all types controlled by the District topped the list. Three attributes tied for the next strongest reasons to leave: unemployment and workers'compensation costs, the cost of facilities and utilities, and the lack of cooperation and support from the District government.[11]

---

10. James Jennings, "Principles for Planning Place-Based Economic Development in Black Urban Communities in the United States," William Monroe Trotter Institute, University of Massachusetts, Boston, p. 3.

11. Stephen C. Perry, "Factors Which Influence Businesses to Stay in or Leave the District of Columbia," George Washington University, Center for the Advancement of Small Business, 1994.

Taxes

Among the George Washington University study's respondents, District taxes scored highest in determining a decision to leave Washington. Cost of facilities, another category high on the list of pressures pushing firms out of the District, can be connected to taxes. The commercial property tax, for example, must to a great extent be passed along to commercial renters, so lowering it would lower the cost of facilities as well as the tax burden.[12]

A comprehensive list of taxes for all the jurisdictions in the metropolitan area is provided in a report by Coopers & Lybrand for the Greater Washington Board of Trade.[13] Positing four types of private businesses and a "national association," the study calculates major tax costs and total tax liability.[14] In addition to the metropolitan area, the report covers twelve other locations in the United States and Canada. For each hypothetical kind of business the District tax bill is at least 25 percent greater than the total tax liability in other locations in the Washington metro area.[15]

The corporate income tax rates in the District, Maryland, and Virginia are 9.975 percent, 7 percent, and 6 percent, respectively. Although the bases differ, the study shows an expected difference of several thousand dollars in tax liabilities for the four types of private companies. A typical information technology company, for example, would pay $22,078 in income tax in the District, $18,480 in Maryland, and $13,280 in Virginia. The general sales tax rates in the District, Maryland, and Virginia are 5.75 percent, 5 percent, and 4.5 percent (Virginia includes a 1 percent county addition that all of its counties impose). A typical biotechnology

12. See Henry J. Aaron, *Who Pays the Property Tax? A New View* (Brookings, 1975), which contends that the extent of the shifting of the property tax burden onto a building's occupants depends on the availability of untaxed assets (of which there are many) and the presence of lower tax rates on capital (which commercial development in the suburbs provides).

13. Coopers and Lybrand, "Greater Washington 1996 Comparative Tax Report," presented to the Greater Washington Board of Trade, July 1996.

14. The types of companies are information technology, biotechnology manufacturing, nonmanufacturing R&D, and business services.

15. In comparing the District with a number of cities around the country, the study found a more mixed picture, with five cities imposing a greater business tax burden than the District for four of the five hypothetical firms. Chicago, Boston, New York City, Westchester County, and Philadelphia have higher taxes than the District on all but the biotechnology manufacturing company; Chicago and Philadelphia have lower taxes for this business.

manufacturing company (facing the highest sales tax bill of any of the hypothetical firms) would pay $63,250 in the District, $55,000 in Maryland, and $49,500 in Virginia.

Business personal and real property taxes vary by jurisdiction within Maryland and Virginia. The District's 3.40 percent personal property rate exceeds the rate imposed by all the Maryland jurisdictions, including Montgomery County (1.99 percent) and Prince George's County (2.426 percent). Unlike the District, many of the Maryland counties, including these two, exempt manufacturing property. By Virginia standards, the District's personal property tax is reasonable. Arlington, Fairfax, and Prince William counties, and the cities of Alexandria and Falls Church all require a greater personal property tax payment than the District.[16] For the biotechnology manufacturing company, personal property tax liability is nearly as great as real property tax. In the District the bill would come to $126,140 and in Alexandria $130,500. Maryland's rates are much lower; Montgomery County personal property taxes amount to only $8,159 for the same hypothetical firm. Except for Frederick County, which does not impose a personal property tax, Montgomery's tax is lowest among the Maryland counties.

Personal property tax differences matter less for the nonmanufacturing companies. For a business services company, the District personal property tax bill would total $11,220, Fairfax's would be $13,253, and Montgomery's would be $6,567. This distribution is representative of all four of the nonmanufacturing businesses.

The District's commercial real property tax bill is much greater than those found in any of the surrounding jurisdictions.[17] The highest effective rates in Maryland are Prince George's County's $1.38 per $100 valuation and the city of Bowie's $1.55.[18] The next highest suburban effective property tax rate, $1.36, is found in Virginia's Prince William County. The District's effective (and nominal) commercial rate of $2.15 leads to a commercial property tax bill nearly 40 percent greater than that found in the next highest local jurisdiction. An information tech-

16. The biotechnology manufacturing company is an exception. It would pay less in Prince William County than in the District. Prince William County, like Loudoun County and Alexandria, taxes manufacturing equipment at a lower rate than nonmanufacturing equipment.

17. One must look farther afield to find the District's tax rate comparing favorably—to Chicago, Boston, New York City, Westchester County, and Philadelphia among the cities listed.

18. Bowie is in Prince George's County but imposes a surcharge on the assessed real property. Coopers and Lybrand, "Greater Washington Tax Report."

nology company would pay a real property tax of $86,000 (out of a total liability of $127,768) in the District, but just $49,200 in Fairfax County. Its highest area property tax bill outside the city would be Bowie's $62,182. The other firms would face very similar differences. The biotechnology manufacturing company would pay $182,750 in District real property taxes (total liability $383,179), $115,600 ($233,740) in Prince William County, and $93,160 ($164,439) in Montgomery County.

Unemployment Insurance and Workers' Compensation

Unemployment insurance is typically a state-run program intended to support workers who lose their jobs through no fault of their own and are actively looking for work. Most private employers pay into an unemployment insurance fund at rates determined by the job-loss experience of their employees (new businesses pay a special rate). States determine weekly benefit amounts, set by formula to about half a worker's weekly salary, although every state and the District also sets a minimum and a maximum weekly benefit amount.[19] Workers' compensation also charges to employers the loss incurred by workers whose on-the-job injuries prevent them from earning a wage through work. The states set payment formulas for different categories of casualty, and employers often purchase insurance to offset the unpredictability of their obligations. The insurance rates depend on the likelihood of claims and the statutory obligations of the employer.

The District's unemployment insurance costs are significantly higher than Maryland's and dramatically higher than Virginia's. The average cost per employee in 1995 was $406 in the District, $328 in Maryland, and $176 in Virginia.[20] The average payment in the District has been higher than in Virginia since at least 1970 and higher than in Maryland since 1981.

The economic factors causing the District's unemployment insurance costs to be higher are unemployment experience and the wage level. In

19. National Foundation for Unemployment Compensation and Workers' Compensation, "Highlights of the State Unemployment Compensation Laws," Washington, 1996, table 18.

20. The Department of Labor publishes average employer unemployment insurance taxes for each state from 1939 to the present. Combining this with the state's taxable wage base and adding the federal unemployment tax gives an approximation for the average payment per employee. Department of Labor, Unemployment Insurance Service, "Unemployment Insurance Financial Data, 1938–1993 with Annual Supplement," ET Handbook 394.

1994 and 1995 the District led all jurisdictions in the duration of un-employment benefits with an average of 19.9 weeks. In 1995 Maryland averaged 15.8 weeks and Virginia 10.3 weeks. But regulatory differences also affect costs. States impose a maximum on the weekly benefit amount, otherwise determined by a formula. The District's maximum weekly benefit is set at 50 percent of the city's average weekly wage ($359 in 1995), while Maryland's and Virginia's were fixed at $250 and $208, respectively. The District imposes a minimum unemployment compensation tax rate of 1.9 percent on all employers; Maryland's minimum was 0.9 percent in 1995 (0.6 percent was a temporary surcharge), and Virginia's was 0.1 percent.[21] According to the District's Department of Employment Services, 9,804 of 22,813 employers pay the minimum rate, so it has a strong effect on the average.[22] Only five states have minimum rates higher than the District's.[23]

Workers' compensation insurance costs are also higher in the District. Unlike unemployment insurance, these costs should not be affected by economic disparities between the District and the surrounding states. They are determined by the rate of accidents in each job category, and differences result primarily from the jurisdictions' statutes and the claims adjudication process. For nine of the ten largest job categories in the District, the cost of workers' compensation claims is higher than in Maryland or Virginia.[24] Again, these costs are a result of District regulations. Most states fix a schedule of income benefits for specific injuries. Among the forty jurisdictions that establish such a schedule, the District's income benefit is among the four highest for each injury.[25]

21. Department of Labor, "Unemployment Insurance Financial Data," tables 13 and 18.

22. District of Columbia Department of Employment Services, "Distribution of Accounts by Rate, 1995," unpublished data.

23. U.S. Chamber of Commerce, *1996 Analysis of Workers' Compensation Laws* (1996), table 13. The five are Connecticut, Maine, Massachusetts, New York, and Rhode Island.

24. The National Council on Compensation Insurance periodically calculates loss costs for different job categories by state. The rates actually charged will vary by employer and insurer; the loss cost is the portion of the rate attributable to claims.

25. Author's calculations based on data supplied by the National Counncil on Compensation Insurance. For a tenth category—"salesperson, collectors, messengers-outside"—the District rate of 0.36 percent is equal to Maryland's and lower than Virginia's 0.39 percent. For all the categories shown, District rates exceed Maryland's by an (unweighted) average of 28 percent and Virginia's by 37 percent. U.S. Chamber of Commerce, *1996 Analysis of Workers' Compensation Laws.*

Lack of Cooperation and Support

The importance that the George Washington University study's respondents placed on District government cooperation and support echoes a finding by the Washington Committee, a group of area business executives. In focus group conversations, Washington business people complained to interviewers that "government regulatory interaction with business is, in most instances, characterized by an adversarial relationship that results in substantial delays and higher costs to business."[26] An executive in charge of location decisions for a local company whose headquarters recently moved from the District to a suburban county told a similar story. After one meeting with District officials there was little contact, and no firm help. While such anecdotes abound, there is no effective way to incorporate them into empirical work.

The Empirical Studies

Many economic studies, most conducted during the past fifteen years, convincingly demonstrate that local economic conditions are very sensitive to local taxes. Helen F. Ladd has noted that economists were "until recently . . . surprisingly unified in their view that taxes do not matter very much." The principal reasons she cited for the changing opinion are that economic activity has in fact become more mobile and the econometric methods used to study firms' locational decisions and the effects of local taxes have improved.[27]

In a survey of studies on taxes and business location, Timothy Bartik found that 70 percent of respondents listed at least one statistically significant negative effect stemming from taxes.[28] The economic activities affected by taxes ranged from state, local, and metropolitan area employment levels to number of new firms to total value of new building permits. The intra-area studies show stronger reactions to tax rates than comparisons between states and regions. There is reason to believe, therefore, that some of the District's disappointing economic performance in

26. Washington Committee, *Improving the Retention and Attraction of Business in Washington, D.C.* (Washington, May 1992), p. 4.

27. Helen F. Ladd, "Effects of Taxes on Economic Activity," in Helen F. Ladd, ed., *Local Government Tax and Land Use Policy* (Edward Elgar, forthcoming).

28. Timothy J. Bartik, *Who Benefits from State and Local Economic Development Policies?* (Kalamazoo: W. E. Upjohn Institute), table 2.3.

recent years may be connected to its high taxes compared with those of other jurisdictions in the greater Washington area.

To test this we undertook an econometric analysis of the District's employment compared with that of the metropolitan area. The analysis shows that District tax rates, particularly the commercial property tax rate and to a lesser extent the sales tax rate, have had a depressing influence on District employment levels. This suggests that tax policy would be a useful focus for addressing the District's current economic woes (see appendix B).

Studies show a strong inverse relationship between property tax rates and business activity in a community.[29] On average, the proportional increase in economic activity was double the decrease in property taxes that spurred the growth. For example a 5 percent cut in property taxes yielded a 10 percent increase in the proportion of manufacturing firms relocating from Milwaukee to a particular suburb.[30] Increases in the property tax rate significantly reduced the amount of business expansion in the communities that compose the Minneapolis–St. Paul metropolitan area.[31] The results reported in appendix B are very much in line with those found in other work on metropolitan areas.

Targeted Economic Development Policies

Over the years the District has come to face aggressive and increasingly successful efforts by suburban jurisdictions to attract businesses. Both Maryland and Virginia offer a range of targeted tax reduction programs. Several local jurisdictions have set up comprehensive agencies that function as catalysts for economic development beyond the scope of state-initiated programs and financing. The District's economic development efforts fall far short of these, and the lackluster performance may be contributing to the loss of jobs and the District's shrinking share of the region's private sector jobs. Of course, the District, having no state gov-

29. Timothy J. Bartik, "The Effects of Property Taxes and Other Local Public Policies on the Intrametropolitan Pattern of Business Location," in Henry W. Herzog Jr. and Alan M. Schlottman, *Industry Location and Public Policy* (University of Tennessee Press, 1991), pp. 57–82.

30. Michael J. Wasylenko, "Evidence of Fiscal Differentials and Intrametropolitan Firm Relocation," *Land Economics*, vol. 56 (August 1980), pp. 339–49.

31. Therese McGuire, "Are Local Property Taxes Important in the Intrametropolitan Location Decisions of Firms? An Empirical Analysis of the Minneapolis–St. Paul Metropolitan Area," *Journal of Urban Economics*, vol. 18 (September 1985), pp. 226–34.

ernment, bears the full financial burden of all its economic development programs.

The state of Maryland conducts a wide range of economic development activities.[32] Some of these programs include assistance in business location, marketing, financing options (ranging from direct loans to loan guarantees), and employee training programs. The state offers a job creation tax credit, which gives businesses creating sixty new jobs (at a new or expanded facility within a two-year period) a credit of 2.5 percent of annual wages (up to $1,000) per qualified employee.[33] The most comprehensive state program has designated twenty-nine enterprise zones across the state, including four in Baltimore and two in Prince George's County. Companies locating within these enterprise zones are eligible for property and income tax credits as well as loan assistance. There is a ten-year credit against the local property tax for a portion of real property improvements. The credit is 80 percent for the first five years, then decreases steadily to 30 percent in the tenth and final year. Maryland reimburses the locality for one-half of the credit cost. The income tax credit is a one-time $500 credit per new worker up to a total of $3,000 per employee over three years if the employee is from a low-income family.[34]

Virginia also provides incentives and services for businesses seeking to locate within the state.[35] These programs include a job-creation tax credit and other corporate income tax incentives, property tax incentives, and job training programs. Virginia also recognizes twenty-nine enterprise zones statewide, including one in Alexandria. Businesses locating in these zones are eligible for a general tax credit, refundable real property improvements tax credits, investment tax credits for large projects, and job grants. The general tax credit provides 80 percent relief against state tax liability in the first year and 60 percent for the following nine years.

The property improvement tax credit against the corporate income tax provides a credit equal to 30 percent of zone improvement for rehabilitation projects of at least $50,000 and new construction projects of

32. Maryland Department of Business and Economic Development, Division of Marketing, *Business Location Portfolio* (1996).

33. This tax credit went into effect in July 1996 and will remain so until January 1, 2002, according to the Maryland Job Creation Tax Credit legislation.

34. Maryland Department of Business and Economic Development, *Business Location Portfolio*.

35. Virginia Department of Economic Development, "Business Incentives 1995," Richmond, Virginia, May 1995.

$250,000. Businesses creating new jobs also receive grants of $500 per job ($1,000 for zone residents) for a period of three years. These tax credits in addition to several financing options help to attract businesses to suburban Virginia jurisdictions such as Alexandria and Fairfax County.

The Cost of Economic Development Incentives

Measuring the costs of incentives is complicated by the inability to clearly link the incentives with the actual jobs created or retained. Incentives are intended to attract businesses and jobs that would not otherwise locate in a jurisdiction. If a business is willing to move into an area without being offered incentives, then incentives become mere giveaways. In calculating an accurate figure for the cost per job, only the jobs that can be attributed directly to the incentives should be included. These distinctions are impossible to measure since they are based on the intentions of the business, which are not observable. Despite the complications, the cost-per-job calculation is a standard measure of the value of incentive programs.[36] Table 2-1 shows simple costs per job added for tax incentives in various parts of Maryland. The average cost is $18,587.[37]

Policymakers need to consider fairness as well as costs. Offering incentives to one company almost inevitably leads others to seek equal or better deals, a situation that may exhaust resources. An important issue is whether tax concessions should be provided "as of right"—to any business that meets certain criteria, such as relocation or employment of residents—or whether concessions are negotiated case by case. Geographic targeting is usually as of right, with negotiations often focusing on what it takes to keep existing businesses or to lure a particularly

36. On the expensive end, Alabama was recently successful in luring Mercedes Benz to build a plant in the state by offering numerous state and local tax breaks and infrastructure improvements. The final price tag for the plant was an overwhelming $200,000 per job. See Allen R. Myerson, "O Governor, Won't You Buy Me a Mercedes Plant?" *New York Times*, September 1, 1996, p. C1.

37. Anne Arundel County appears to have been the most successful with the Northrop-Westinghouse facility, which resulted in 9,000 new or retained jobs for an investment of $12 million and a cost per job of around $1,000. At the same time, local and state officials invested nearly $13 million in Frederick County, creating only 125 new jobs at a cost per job of $102,400. These amounts are arrived at by dividing the total state and local loans and grants offered to new or existing firms by the number of new or retained jobs. Peter Behr, "Selling an Income Tax Cut in Maryland," *Washington Post*, September 23, 1996, p. F5.

Table 2-1. *Maryland Economic Development Projects since July 1995*

Company	Sector	Location	Number of jobs New	Number of jobs Retained	State and local loans and grants (millions)	Cost per job (dollars)
Avesta Sheffield East	Manufacturing	Baltimore County	150	200	1.8	5,214
Art Litho	Manufacturing	Baltimore County	30	130	1.5	9,500
Bally's Health & Tennis	Services	Baltimore County	100	300	1.6	4,075
CanAm Steel	Manufacturing	Frederick County	110	309	1.6	3,878
Dome-CIDR	Biotechnology	Baltimore City	55	0	0.3	5,454
Filtronic Comtex	Manufacturing	Wicomico	219	181	1.0	4,747
Gene Logic	Biotechnology	Howard	25	0	0.5	20,800
London Fog	Manufacturing	Baltimore City	230	0	0.5	2,173
McCormick & Co.	Distribution	Harford	100	150	5.0	20,000
Marada Industries	Manufacturing	Carroll	120	0	1.9	16,250
Medimmune Inc.	Biotechnology	Frederick County	125	0	12.8	102,400
Northrop-Westinghouse	Manufacturing	Anne Arundel	1,000	8,000	12.0	1,333
Nabisco Foods Co.	Manufacturing	Dorchester	150	0	1.7	11,333
Rohr Industries	Manufacturing	Washington	235	115	3.5	10,000
Staples	Distribution	Washington	700	0	5.9	8,518
Sweetheart Cup	Manufacturing	Baltimore County	100	0	1.2	12,000
Saks Fifth Avenue	Distribution	Harford	70	0	7.0	100,000
Tessco	Distribution	Baltimore County	100	163	3.1	11,787
William T. Burnett/STX	Manufacturing	Baltimore City	15	255	1.0	3,703
Total			3,643	9,803	64.1	18,587[a]

Source: Peter Behr, "Selling an Income Tax Cut in Maryland," *Washington Post*, September 23, 1996, p. F15.
a. Average cost per job.

appealing new company. A recent report by the National Council for Urban Economic Development and the Economic Development Administration recommended using cost-benefit analysis to determine whether certain companies need the incentives they request as well as to ascertain the overall value to the community of a company's presence.[38] When other jurisdictions have predatory policies, however, this may be more easily recommended than followed.

Enterprise Zones

The most common form of geographic targeting for job creation is enterprise zones. Although enterprise zones vary greatly in their characteristics, they are generally distressed geographic areas that are targeted as sites for job creation by programs that lower the costs of doing business there through offering tax cuts, investment incentives, public infrastructure improvements, regulatory relief, and sometimes wage and employment subsidies. Typically, new businesses receive special treatment simply for locating at the site, while existing businesses are granted tax breaks for hiring new workers or hiring people who live in the area. These benefits are as of right.

In 1995 thirty-five states and the District of Columbia had enterprise zone programs, which differed in the number of zones, their size, the incentives offered, and the eligibility criteria. The number of zones varied from 1 in Michigan to 1,422 in Louisiana. The zones can range in size from several city blocks to the entire state of Arkansas. The eligibility criteria usually include measures of unemployment, poverty, median income, and population trends.[39]

Enterprise zones were first introduced in Great Britain in 1981, when eleven unoccupied industrial areas were designated. Studies of the British experience generally concur that the program failed to generate new industrial activity. In fact, most studies found that between 50 and 70 percent of the zone firms had relocated from another part of the country. The program was also expensive, $13,400 to $15,000 for each net new

38. National Council for Urban Economic Development, *Incentives: A Guide to an Effective and Equitable Policy* (Department of Commerce, Economic Development Administration, April 1996), p. 84.

39. Office of Community Planning and Development, *State Enterprise Zone Update* (Department of Housing and Urban Development, 1995).

job.[40] Because relocations have been the source of most economic activity in the zones, the British government has begun to phase out the program; the last two zones are designated to expire in 1999.[41] A critical assessment of the British experience concluded, "The economic incentives provided by the enterprise zones had only marginal effects on firms' investment and location decisions. Perhaps the greatest value of the enterprise zones has been in terms of the publicity benefits to the local communities."[42]

Although early studies of enterprise zones in the United States did not find encouraging results, they suffered from insufficient longitudinal data and methodological problems.[43] More recent studies have linked the zones to new economic growth. Rodney Erickson conducted a study of 357 enterprise zones located in 186 communities in 17 states and found that in a third of them job growth rates were higher than the national rate, with only 9.1 percent of the new investment represented by firms that had relocated.[44] Richard Elling and Ann Workman Sheldon studied enterprise zones in Illinois, Indiana, Kentucky, and Ohio and found only modest success, with an average of 11 companies investing in a zone per year.[45] Leslie Papke analyzed the Indiana enterprise zone program and found an 8 percent increase in the value of inventories attributable to the program and a drop in unemployment claims of 19 percent following zone designation.[46] Barry Rubin and Margaret Wilder studied the Evansville, Indiana, enterprise zone using firm-level data obtained from surveys and income tax returns and found the creation of 1,400 new jobs over three years attributable to the comparative advantage of the enter-

40. Barry M. Rubin and Craig M. Richards, "A Transatlantic Comparison of Enterprise Zone Impacts: The British and American Experience," *Economic Development Quarterly*, vol. 6 (November 1992), pp. 431–43.

41. Leslie E. Papke, "What Do We Know about Enterprise Zones?" NBER Working Paper 4251 (Cambridge, Mass.: National Bureau of Economic Research, January 1993), pp. 47–48.

42. William D. Gunther and Charles G. Leathers, "British Enterprise Zones: A Critical Assessment," *Review of Regional Studies*, vol. 17 (Winter 1987), p. 8.

43. Rubin and Richards, "Transatlantic Comparison," p. 438.

44. Rodney A. Erickson, "Enterprise Zones: Lessons from the State Government Experience," in Edwin S. Mills and John F. McDonald, eds., *Sources of Metropolitan Growth* (New Brunswick, N.J.: Center for Urban Policy Research, 1992), pp. 174–76.

45. Richard C. Elling and Ann Workman Sheldon, "Determinants of Enterprise Zone Success: A Four State Perspective," in Roy E. Green, ed., *Enterprise Zones: New Directions in Economic Development* (Newbury Park, Calif.: Sage Publications, 1991), p. 143.

46. Leslie E. Papke, "Tax Policy and Urban Development: Evidence from the Indiana Enterprise Zone Program," *Journal of Public Economics*, vol. 54 (May 1994), pp. 37–49.

prise zone area. Two-thirds of the job creation was from the expansion of existing companies.[47]

However, there have also been some unfavorable findings. A study conducted by the General Accounting Office on the effect of three enterprise zones in Maryland found that the program did not influence employment growth. The study also surveyed zone businesses to assess the factors that influence business location decisions. Businesses rated market access and community characteristics higher in importance than the elements of the zone policy, such as tax incentives and regulatory relief.[48]

Research on enterprise zones supports theoretical conclusions and practical experience:

> First, zone programs should include those elements best suited to the circumstances of the particular types of firms they wish to attract. . . . Second, what matters most for new and expanding firms is clearly the quantity and quality of administrative resources that support the program. . . . Finally, because property tax relief is so generally available in enterprise zones, and abatements are frequently available from local governments for most firms anyway, it makes sense to expand other opportunities for direct savings for firms. Low-cost financing, access to venture capital, expanding shopsteading programs, and providing fee waivers are some productive approaches.[49]

Thus success seems to require an economic development policy using enterprise zones in coordination with a comprehensive job development strategy. The economic development plan needs to target particular industries for development. Resources need to be allocated to managing the plan and coordinating the enterprise zone program with all the available economic development resources.

The Clinton administration's urban policy uses geographic targeting as its model for economic development. On December 25, 1994, the president designated selected areas of poverty and distress throughout

---

47. Barry M. Rubin and Margaret G. Wilder, "Urban Enterprise Zones: Employment Impacts and Fiscal Incentives," *American Planning Association Journal*, vol. 55 (Autumn 1989), pp. 418–31.

48. General Accounting Office, *Enterprise Zones: Lessons from the Maryland Experience*, PEMD-89-2 (1988), chap. 3.

49. Elling and Sheldon, "Determinants of Enterprise Zone Success," p. 152.

the country as empowerment zones and communities.[50] The policy provides a tiered system of financial incentives for private development combined with new federal grants. In addition, there is the requirement to focus state and local grants and public investments on these communities as part of a larger strategic plan. Selected neighborhoods in these zones are eligible to provide businesses with the benefits of wage tax credits for employing zone residents, accelerated depreciation, and new tax-exempt bond financing. Social service grants provide funds for job training, child care, and transportation to work for zone residents. At the top of the benefit tier are six cities designated as urban empowerment zones (EZs): Atlanta, Baltimore, Chicago, Detroit, New York, and Philadelphia-Camden. At the bottom are sixty-five cities chosen as empowerment communities (ECs), including the District. Between are two supplemental empowerment zones (SEZs) and four enhanced enterprise communities (EECs). In addition, there are no more than thirty rural communities targeted for economic development. All receive varying levels of aid.

Economic Development Programs in the Maryland and Virginia Suburbs

The District of Columbia is ringed by suburbs that have organized and increasingly aggressive strategies to lure businesses to locate there. The goal seems as much to create jobs located near residential development as to increase the tax base, since significant efforts have been made to attract tax-exempt organizations. The states of Maryland and Virginia provide the overarching job development strategy and a structure of tax expenditures and capital investments. Within this strategy and structure, Washington's suburban counties and localities focus on attracting individual companies.

Alexandria, Virginia

Founded in 1981, the Alexandria Economic Development Program (AEDP), a nonprofit partnership between the city and its businesses, has focused on turning Alexandria into a major center for national associations, a long-time staple of the District's economy. Alexandria markets

---

50. Department of Housing and Urban Development, "Urban Empowerment Zones and Enterprise Communities," July 1995.

its proximity to the District, offering its businesses convenient access to Capitol Hill (ten minutes), other major points of interest in the District, and National Airport. The program offers technical assistance for new business owners, an extensive marketing program, and the use of a state enterprise zone (the Mt. Vernon Avenue–Route 1 corridor) to attract and retain business. Businesses within the zone apply for state tax credits and grants. More than 300 jobs have been created in the zone since 1994.[51]

Alexandria's economy has improved recently, particularly attracting national associations. From 1984 to 1992 the number of trade associations in Alexandria increased from 63 to 263.[52] Employment in membership associations grew from 2,318 in 1984 to 4,830 in 1993.[53] Occupied office space has expanded from 4.5 million square feet to more than 15 million square feet in the past decade.[54] Although the District is still home to more trade associations than any other U.S. city, their number has grown only sporadically since AEDP's founding.

Montgomery County, Maryland

Economic development in Montgomery County is conducted by the county Office of Economic Development, which focuses its efforts on attracting and maintaining businesses in such areas as Rockville, Bethesda, the I-270 technology corridor, and along route 29.[55] Following the state's economic development focus, the county has become a center for biotechnology and other life sciences companies, among them the American Red Cross, Medimmune Inc., the Howard Hughes Medical Institute, and Social & Scientific Systems, Inc.[56] From 1984 to 1993 the number of medical laboratory jobs in the county rose from 259 to 1,095 without any county incentives being offered. Medical laboratories and similar research and development firms have been drawn to the county

---

51. Rudolph A. Pyatt Jr., "Jarvis Knows How the District Depends on Gilt by Association," *Washington Post*, October 14, 1993, p. D13.

52. Martha M. Hamilton, "Associations Packing Up, Moving Out," *Washington Post*, September 13, 1993, p. F1.

53. Bureau of the Census, *County Business Patterns* (Department of Commerce, 1993), table 2.

54. Alexandria Economic Development Partnership literature.

55. Montgomery County Office of Economic Development, "Montgomery County Maryland: The Best Location Today for Companies Working for Tomorrow."

56. Montgomery County Office of Economic Development, "Profile of Biological and Medical Science Related Industries in Montgomery County," January 1995.

in large part because of federal government spending and the presence of the National Institutes of Health, the National Institute of Standards and Technology, and the Food and Drug Administration. The county, following the federal and state governments' focus, has invested $30 million in the Shady Grove Life Sciences Center, a 300-acre industrial park geared to the development of life science technology firms and also home to a Johns Hopkins University satellite campus.[57]

Recently, the county has been luring businesses from the District. In September 1996 Watson Wyatt Worldwide, a consulting firm, announced plans to move its headquarters along with 200 employees to Bethesda.[58] The company cited the availability of office space as well as an incentive package worth $800,000 as the main reasons for its relocation. The state of Maryland and the county together contributed $600,000 in loans and a $200,000 job creation tax credit to attract the firm.

Baltimore, Maryland

Like Alexandria, Baltimore has focused economic development efforts on nonprofit institutions. In 1991 the city contracted its development efforts to the Baltimore Development Corporation (BDC), a move that merged three separate economic development organizations.[59] The BDC is funded by the city and has the authority to enter into negotiations and offer incentives to businesses to remain in or relocate to Baltimore. It recently lured the NAACP, the Catholic Relief Association, and the International Youth Foundation to Baltimore. The BDC has been instrumental in developing more than sixty projects, including the renovation of the convention center, the revitalization of Howard Street, and the creation of Inner Harbor East and the South Harbor business incubator.[60]

Baltimore also benefits from its recent designation as a federal empowerment zone. The zone will bring the city $225 million in tax credits and $100 million in grants over ten years to three of the city's most impoverished areas: East Baltimore, West Baltimore, and Fairfield.[61] Since its inception in 1994, nearly 1,600 jobs have been created by forty new or

57. Montgomery County Office of Economic Development staff.
58. David Segal, "Consulting Firm to Move Offices from D.C. to Md.: Watson Wyatt Accepts $800,000 in Incentives," *Washington Post*, September 12, 1996.
59. Baltimore Development Corporation staff.
60. "City of Baltimore Development Corporation Annual Report 1994–95," p. 5.
61. Judith Evans, "Baltimore's Dawn of an Urban Renaissance," *Washington Post*, November 2, 1996, p. E1.

expanding businesses within the zone, at an estimated cost per job of $9,375, about half the state average (see table 2-1). In addition to its federal empowerment zone, Baltimore has benefited from a state enterprise zone, which has provided as-of-right tax benefits and business services.

Economic Development in the District of Columbia

In comparison with the surrounding area, the District has no effective economic development strategy. What it has are several separate policies. First, it has designated three economic development zones, similar to enterprise zones: the Alabama Avenue and Anacostia zones in southeast Washington and the D.C. Village zone in southwest. Businesses locating within these development zones are eligible for tax credits on wages to certified workers during the first twenty-four months of employment and a franchise tax credit of up to 50 percent of worker's compensation premiums.[62] They also receive a five-year reduction in property tax payments, beginning at 80 percent of liability in year one, falling to 16 percent of liability by the fifth year, and may receive a deferral or forgiveness of past due property taxes, special assessments, fees, or water and sewer charges.[63]

Second, the District is developing business improvement districts, most notably in the Georgetown and Franklin Square areas. Businesses located within these districts will pay a BID "charge" to receive additional services such as sidewalk improvements, increased security, and special building improvements.[64] Finally, the District offers industrial revenue bond financing, loan guarantees, and several direct loan programs to firms located throughout the city, regardless of the number of jobs they create.

Organizational Problems

If the District has done hard thinking about where its comparative advantage lies and how it can streamline its interaction with business, it

62. *Economic Development Zones Incentives Amendment Act of 1988: Operating a Business in the District of Columbia*, D.C. Law 7-177.

63. It is not clear whether the ability to defer or forgive water and sewer charges will continue now that there is an independent Water and Sewer Authority.

64. *Business Improvement District Act of 1996.*

is not obvious.[65] The District government has been relying on policy rather than strategy. Unfortunately, compared with its neighbors, its policy tool kit is small, usually pulled out too late, and placed in the hands of inexpert mechanics. Frequently, policy has relied on last-minute negotiations between the mayor and businesses. For example, when the Bureau of National Affairs announced that it would leave the District, Mayor Barry used emergency legislation to structure an agreement that the company, and 1,100 jobs, would remain in exchange for a ten-year property tax deferment. BNA promised to lease 98,000 square feet during this period and ultimately to repay the deferred taxes without penalty or interest. BNA has estimated its tax savings from this deal at $2 million, which works out to $1,818 per job.[66]

While many cities and counties have consolidated economic development agencies, the District government's efforts are so decentralized, dispersed as they are throughout at least eleven main offices and programs, that they might as well be a labyrinth.[67]

In an attempt to improve economic development and business services, the District is now merging several offices into the Business Services and Economic Development Department, a one-stop business center that will be structured to create and implement economic development strategies. But simply merging agencies will not provide the District with an effective and streamlined strategy. The regulations that businesses face to operate in the District are opaque, cumbersome, time consuming, and administered in an unfriendly manner. There is little coordination between regulatory inspections and the economic development effort. The District does not match in any way the welcoming approach of the surrounding jurisdictions.

One encouraging development is legislation pending in the city council to create a Business Promotion Corporation. The BPC would serve as a private marketing and economic development agency to promote the District and provide services to businesses looking to locate there.[68] It would be funded by the District but directed by a professional board of directors, much like Baltimore's Business Development Corporation.

65. There has been considerable discussion regarding a focus on health services as well as tourism and entertainment, although no grand strategy has emerged.

66. Peter Behr, "BNA Gets Tax Deferral to Stay in the District," *Washington Post,* September 5, 1996, p. D10.

67. Government of the District of Columbia, *A Vision for America's First City: FY 1997 Budget and Multiyear Plan* (May 1996).

68. Committee on Economic Development, Council of the District of Columbia, September 1996, personal correspondence.

Administrative Problems

The implementation of economic development programs, according to sources at the city council, has been impeded by administrative delays within the District government. The progression from legislative approval to implementation has taken years to complete. For example, the enterprise zone program was passed by the city council in 1988 but not implemented until 1994. There was no development in the zones until Safeway Stores, Inc., decided to build the Good Hope Marketplace—which meant the construction of a new 56,000-square-foot grocery store and an additional 44,000 square feet of retail space—at 2845 Alabama Avenue, S.E.. The five-year property tax abatement cost could easily reach $750,000.[69]

The District's economic development agencies, like other departments of the District government, lack the capacity to do the job. They cannot develop, sustain, or monitor good economic development programs. They are understaffed and have neither the technology nor the skilled staff to conduct basic research or perform cost-benefit analyses.

Equally troubling, the District lacks the ability to provide basic business services. In various conversations, local business owners agreed that the District's permitting and licensing procedures are a disincentive to business activity. In fact, very few people within the government are aware of the full array of permits and licenses required to do business in the District. There is little reason to believe the policies underlying the permitting process have ever been comprehensively analyzed or justified.

Local government responsiveness is crucial to attracting and retaining businesses. According to the federal Economic Development Administration and the National Council for Urban Economic Development, "the key to success in these [marketing] campaigns often lies in the follow-up activities to the inquiries generated by the advertisements. Inquiries must receive prompt responses and telephone calls."[70] The failure of the District government to respond quickly to businesses has been cited as one

69. It is not clear how many jobs or how much spillover economic activity will take place. In a March 21, 1996, letter to David A. Clarke, chair of the council, the mayor predicted that the project would provide "500 temporary construction jobs and up to 150 permanent jobs." This study has been unable to verify these numbers.

70. National Council for Urban Economic Development, *Bench Marking Practices to Achieve Customer Driven Economic Development* (Department of Commerce, April 1996), p. 13.

of the major reasons they abandon the District.[71] Businesses that once called Washington their home relate a common story of District government lethargy, inability to name a liason to work with them on their problems and needs, and a general lack of interest in their locational requirements.

Proposals

The total burden of taxes in the District is at least 25 percent greater than in the next highest jurisdiction in the region. The commercial property tax stands out particularly, with an effective rate 40 percent higher than any other rate in the region. Economic studies consistently find that taxes do affect business location, especially at the local, intrametropolian area level. These findings are corroborated by our econometric analysis (see appendix B). We therefore recommend dramatically simplifying and reducing the commercial property tax and eliminating several inefficient and inequitable taxes on business (see chapters 1, 3, and 5).

Second, the District must focus on its business climate and must strive for improved business retention as the core of an economic development strategy. Whether the District needs to create an independent economic development organization to devise and implement a strategy for attracting and retaining businesses (such as that proposed in the Business Promotion Corporation legislation) is beyond the reach of this study. But the District government does need to develop a strategic plan for Washington's economy, a plan that would directly address the types of businesses and industries to target, the economic development tools to use, and the employment growth targets that could reasonably be expected. It might help to start with a comprehensive plan for the three existing enterprise zones.

Third, because job growth in the District depends on improving city services, the District government needs to evaluate and streamline its zoning, permitting, licensing, and inspecting policies. Ultimately, the business climate will become favorable when the District can provide

71. Perry, "Factors Which Influence Businesses," p. 20.

safe, clean, and passable streets, drinkable water, quality schools, and a responsive and efficient government. In offering solutions on the revenue side of the District's ledger, this study presupposes that the Control Board and the District's government will bring spending under control and deliver District services efficiently.

CHAPTER 3

The Real Property Tax

T HE REAL PROPERTY TAX is levied on commercial and residential struc-tures and vacant land. It is the District's largest single tax, bringing in revenues of $654 million in fiscal year 1995. The value of the property base is at least $74 billion; but 41 percent of the property is exempt, leaving a taxable base of $42 billion.[1] This situation, the result of being the nation's capital, is perhaps the most distinctive element of the Dis-trict's property base.[2] For most local governments the real property tax is the mainstay tax, representing a far larger share of tax revenue than it does for the District of Columbia. It is a tax uniquely in the control of the local government, which is responsible for determining both the value of the tax base and setting the rate at which that base is taxed. Thus the classification of property, assessment process, rules and calendar, exemp-tions and tax relief, as well as the actual tax rates all form tax policy. This chapter examines all these aspects of the District of Columbia's real property tax policy.

Property taxes historically dominated local government finance, ac-counting for 60 to 70 percent of total local government revenues between 1902 and 1932. With the Great Depression came the federal govern-ment's expanded use of the income tax and state governments' use of the sales tax and the income tax to finance aid to local government. This resulted in a steady decline in reliance on the property tax to 30 percent of local revenues in 1978. However, as federal aid dwindled between

1. This is probably an underestimate of the true value. Although all District properties have been assessed at full market value since 1975, assessors admit that they focus on the taxable properties rather than on those excluded. Thus the value of exempt properties, as well as the entire base, may be considerably understated.

2. The District claims, in Government of the District of Columbia, *FY 1997 Budget and Multiyear Plan* (May 1996), app. 2, p. 570, that this exclusion of properties is the largest proportion of any city in America, but there are a number of cities that have as much as 40 percent of their base exempt.

1978 and 1992 from 9.0 percent to 3.1 percent, and with state aid relatively constant, by 1992 property taxes accounted for 26.5 percent of total local revenues, a twelve-year high.[3] The property tax has been the only local tax to show any revenue growth since the mid-1980s. In fact, from 1986 to 1992 the property tax grew from 24.7 percent to 26.5 percent of local government tax revenues.[4]

That the property tax still constitutes a quarter of local revenues and its share of them has been growing suggests its importance in local government finance. Governments rely on it because it is a stable source of revenue. For one thing, the property tax base is much slower than the sales or income tax bases to respond to changes in the economy. Second, the property tax base is known before the start of the fiscal year, allowing local jurisdictions to adjust the rates incrementally to stabilize revenues. Because the base is so large, small changes in the rate produce large amounts of revenue.[5]

Assessments

The base of the property tax is the value of taxable real property—land and structures—within the taxing jurisdiction. The District of Columbia assesses the value of real property annually. The value it assigns, known as the assessed value, is an estimate of the property's market value. Some jurisdictions assess the value of property at less than full market value, but the District assesses it at 100 percent, or full market value.

The District uses three methods for estimating the full market value of real property: sales comparison, income, and cost. The sales comparison method compares a given property with similar properties that have

3. Between 1932 and 1978, state aid to local governments increased from 12.9 percent to 30.1 percent of local revenues and federal aid increased from 0.2 percent to 9.0 percent. Some of the decline in federal aid is the result of the ending of such temporary programs as the Comprehensive Employment and Training Act (CETA); some is the result of the Reagan administration's "new federalism." Patrick Fleenor, ed., *Facts and Figures on Government Finance*, 30th ed. (Washington: Tax Foundation, 1995), p. 233.

4. During the same period, the sales tax was stable at 5.2 percent, the income tax at 2.0 percent, other taxes at 1.4 percent, and miscellaneous revenues at about 20.1 percent. Fleenor, *Facts and Figures*, p. 233.

5. Hal Hovey, *The Property Tax in the 21st Century* (Washington: Finance Project, 1996), pp. 8–9.; and Dick Netzer, *Economics of the Property Tax* (Brookings, 1966), p. 170.

been sold recently. The value is adjusted to reflect differences in location, physical characteristics, current use, and so forth between the subject property and the comparison properties. This method is typically used in assessing residential properties.[6]

The income method is used to place a value on income-producing commercial properties. Owners of commercial property are required to submit income and expense statements to the Department of Finance and Revenue that provide the data for estimating the market value. To capture the full market value of the property, a capitalization rate is applied to the net operating income, which converts the income stream of the property into a lump-sum value. The capitalization rates, an expression of complex market factors and relationships, are usually derived from market transactions for similar properties, risk, land-to-building ratios, remaining economic lives, and operating expense-to-income ratios.[7]

The cost method of appraisal determines the market value of the property by adding the estimated value of the land on which a property sits to the current cost of constructing a reproduction of the property and subtracting the depreciation. The cost method is used in valuing new commercial properties that have not begun generating income. It is also useful in valuing churches, museums, government buildings, and historic properties that do not generate income and are not frequently sold. The valuation of these is obviously of importance in the District.[8]

The Property Tax Classification System

The District's property tax system taxes real properties at five different rates depending on their use. The five classes fall into three categories: residential, commercial, and vacant. Residential properties have been split into two classes, with class 1 reserved for owner-occupied housing and condominiums and class 2 for rental property. Property owned by cooperative housing associations is considered class 1 if at least 50 percent of the units are occupied by the members of the association.[9]

6. District of Columbia Department of Finance and Revenue (DFR), "Real Property Assessment Process Overview and Assessment Appeals," Information Sharing Series Seminar 1, District of Columbia Government, March 1996, p. 12.

7. DFR, "Real Property Assessment," p. 14; and Joseph K. Eckert, ed., *Property Appraisal and Assessment Administration* (Chicago: International Association of Assessing Officers, 1990), p. 23.

8. DFR, "Real Property Assessment," p. 13.

9. D.C. Code 47-813 (a)(1) and (2).

Class 2 residential property has been assigned a higher tax rate ($1.54 versus $0.96) because the District intends to capture additional revenue from the commercial activity of rental housing. But economic analysts generally assume that property owners pass on the entire tax burden to their renters in the form of higher rents.[10] This study did not attempt to measure the degree of shifting of the property tax burden to renters. There is rent control, which imposes a ceiling on rents in the District, but the rent control law does not affect all rental housing. Beginning in 1976, all new apartment buildings, newly renovated apartment buildings, and buildings with four or fewer units were exempted from rent control. In 1980 the law was amended to allow rent increases of up to 10 percent, based on the cost of living index, with allowances for greater increases in cases of hardship, after capital improvements have been made, and when vacancies occur.[11]

The District's classification of residential property violates the two principles of equity. Horizontal equity holds that equally situated individuals should be treated equally, although encouraging home ownership is not an unusual policy. Taxing renters at a higher rate than owners creates unequal treatment based on the decision to rent rather than purchase. Vertical equity holds that because some individuals are better able to pay higher taxes than others, they should do so.[12] In 1993, renters in the District had a median household income of $24,217 while homeowners had a median income of $46,851.[13] Since homeowners have higher incomes than renters, at least they should not enjoy a lower property tax rate.

Commercial property taxes are also split into two classes: class 3 covers hotels and motels and class 4 includes all other commercial prop-

10. KPMG Peat Marwick, "Comparative Analysis of Kentucky's Tax Structure," prepared for the Kentucky Committee on Tax Policy, July 1995, p. 23; and Hovey, *Property Tax in the 21st Century*, p. 23, n. 19. Hovey notes that the household tax burden model maintained by KPMG Peat Marwick, which has recently been used in tax policy studies in Kentucky, North Carolina, and New York, assumes full shifting to the renter.

11. Steven J. Diner, "The Regulation of Housing in the District of Columbia: An Historical Analysis of Policy Issues," in Steven J. Diner and others, *Housing Washington's People: Public Policy in Retrospect* (University of the District of Columbia, 1993), pp. 46–47.

12. Joseph E. Stiglitz, *Economics of the Public Sector*, 2d ed. (Norton, 1988), pp. 399–400.

13. Bureau of the Census and Department of Housing and Urban Development, *American Housing Survey for the Washington Metropolitan Area 1993*, Current Housing Reports, H170/93-18 (April 1995), pp. 52, 87.

erty.[14] Class 3 is currently taxed at a lower rate than class 4 ($1.85 verus $2.15). In addition to violating horizontal equity, this arrangement does not make practical sense. There is a long-held assumption that, to varying degrees, commercial property owners pass their property tax burden on to consumers.[15] To the extent that hotel and motel owners pass the property tax on in their room charges, the class 3 tax is paid by nonresidents. By taxing these properties at a lower rate than class 4, the District is missing an opportunity to collect additional revenues from the thousands of tourists who visit the District each year. The opportunity is, of course, limited because District hotels and motels must compete with those in the suburbs, particularly Virginia, which is only a fifteen- to twenty-minute Metrorail ride from the Mall.

Finally, class 5 was established in 1990 to penalize property owners for failing to develop vacant land and unoccupied buildings. The rate was set at $3.29 per $100 of assessed value and raised to $5.00 in 1994. The high rate imposed on vacant land is based on a theory that, through the interaction of liquidity and incentive effects, taxing land at a higher rate than improvements will encourage development. The liquidity effect results from increasing the holding cost of land, which encourages landowners to improve their properties or to sell to someone who will. The incentive effect results from decreasing the improvement tax rate, which leads to a decrease in the price and an increase in the quantity of structural services provided. Meanwhile, the increased tax on land cannot affect the supply of land because the supply is fixed.[16]

The class 5 property tax rate derives from the land value taxation idea because it taxes vacant land and buildings at a substantially higher rate than it taxes commercial and residential property. Class 5 is using the liquidity effect by increasing the cost of holding vacant land and unoccupied buildings. An incentive effect is present because property owners can achieve significant tax savings by developing vacant property. However, class 5 is a departure from the land value taxation theory because unoccupied buildings are also taxed at the $5.00 rate. Taxing unoccupied buildings at a higher rate than other commercial property has a potentially harmful effect on revenues because property owners, unlike land-

14. D.C. Code 47-813 (a)(3) and (4).

15. Netzer, *Economics of the Property Tax*, p. 259.

16. Steven C. Bourassa, "Land Value Taxation and New Housing Development in Pittsburgh," *Growth and Change*, vol. 18 (Fall 1987), pp. 44–56.

owners, can avoid the tax by reducing the supply of buildings, by legal means as well as illegal ones such as arson. In addition, large amounts of vacant property, most notably parking lots, have been excluded from the class 5 designation and statutorily taxed at the class 4 commercial rate.[17] In the 1994 tax year, 3,315 properties in class 4 were categorized as "garage/unimproved land" with a total value of $582 million, substantially larger than the $281 million of property taxed at the class 5 rate.[18]

It is not possible to assess whether the class 5 tax rate has increased the development of vacant land and unoccupied buildings. From the start, the District's approach fell short of fully applying the theory of land taxation because it exempted parking lots and included vacant buildings as vacant land. One measure of success might be that the value of class 5 property declined from $423 million in 1992 to $223 million in 1996. However, part of this decline is attributable to property owners' successfully gaining exemptions from the class 5 rate. Furthermore, in multiclass systems with significant rate differences, owners will find creative ways to redefine their property out of the higher tax class, and assessors will be under pressure to assign property that generates higher revenue to the class. Conversations with District property owners indicate some tension with assessors over whether a building is vacant or merely up for sale.

Reductions from the Tax Base

The total assessed value of property in the District was $78.3 billion in tax year 1995. To arrive at the net tax base, the Department of Finance and Revenue first reduces this total by the value of tax-exempt property, yielding the gross tax base, then reduces the gross tax base by the value attributable to property tax relief programs. The net tax base is divided into the five property tax classes, and the rates are applied that result in the tax levy, the amount of money that the property tax is anticipated to raise. The tax levy differs from the property tax revenue figure reported in the District's budget and in other financial documents because the property tax revenue is the amount of money actually collected from the property tax in a given year, consisting generally of the tax levy minus

17. D.C. Code 47-813(c-3)(4)(E).
18. District of Columbia Department of Finance and Revenue (DFR), *District of Columbia Tax Facts, Fiscal Years 1993 and 1994* (1995), p. 35.

current delinquencies plus the collection of delinquencies from previous years.

Exempt Property

Subtraction of the value of tax-exempt property in the District from the total assessed value of $78.3 billion leaves a gross tax base of $46.3 billion (table 3-1). In other words, 41 percent of the total assessed value of property in the District is tax-exempt. Sixty-five percent of this is federal government property; the remaining 35 percent comprises churches, universities, and miscellaneous nonprofit organizations that are traditionally exempt by local governments.[19]

In addition to the federal government property, three types of exempt property are directly attributable to the federal presence in the District: foreign government property, property exempt by special acts of Congress, and property exempt by executive order of the president. Embassies and residencies of foreign ambassadors constitute the "foreign government" row in table 3-1 and were originally exempted by Congress.[20] Congress has also specifically exempted certain institutions, such as the American Association of University Women, the National Education Association, and the National Society of Colonial Dames. Finally, the Organization of American States, the International Monetary Fund, the World Bank, and certain other multinational organizations have been exempted by executive order of the president.[21]

Relief Programs

The structure of the District property tax is also characterized by myriad residential property tax relief programs. Two of these, the homestead exemption program and the senior homestead exemption program, have a direct and substantial impact on the property tax base. The remaining programs, which will also be discussed, have little or no impact.

Among the relief programs the homestead exemption program benefits the most people and has the highest cost. The program allows taxpayers

19. The Brookings Institution is among these. In 1995 Brookings' exemption from the real property tax was worth $250,000.

20. 56 Stat. 826, sec. 1.

21. District of Columbia Department of Finance and Revenue, "Schedule of Organizations in the District of Columbia Exempted from Real Property Taxation by Acts of Congress, 1996 Assessments."

Table 3-1. *District of Columbia Property Exempt from Property Tax, by Type, Tax Year 1995*

Millions of dollars

Type	Value
Total assessed value of all property	78,269
Federal presence property	
Federal government property	20,811
Exempt by special act of Congress	446
Exempt by executive order of the President	893
Foreign government	1,035
Subtotal	23,185
D.C. government property	
D.C. government	3,293
WMATA	193
DCRLA	157
Subtotal	3,643
Not-for-profit property	
Religious	1,265
Educational	1,750
Charitable	271
Hospitals	717
Libraries	9
Cemeteries	133
Miscellaneous	1,001
Subtotal	5,146
Total exempt property	31,974
Gross tax base	46,295
Property tax relief programs	
Homestead exemption	2,709
Senior citizen credit	1,417
Subtotal	4,126
Net tax base	42,169

Sources: District of Columbia Department of Finance and Revenue (DFR), "Study of Property, Income and Sales Tax Exemptions in the District of Columbia," April 7, 1995, app. to chap. 2; DFR, "Real Property Tax Estimates by Class," February 8, 1996; and DFR, "Schedule of Organizations in the District of Columbia Exempted from Real Property Taxation by Acts of Congress, 1996 Assessment."

with owner-occupied residences to deduct $30,000 from the assessed value of the property before it is taxed at the class 1 rate. The deduction is worth $288 to each recipient.[22] In tax year 1996, some 89,646 taxpayers received the deduction at an estimated cost of $26 million. The program is broadly based because there is neither an income nor an age requirement to receive the deduction. In 1996, the homestead exemption exempted $2.7 billion, or 5.9 percent, of the property tax base.[23]

22. The class 1 property tax rate is $0.96 per $100.00 of assessed value. To calculate the tax savings, the following formula is used: [Value of deduction ($30,000)/$100 × Rate ($0.96) = $288].

23. D.C. Code 47-850; and District of Columbia Department of Finance and Revenue

Although the application for the homestead exemption also serves as the application for taxation under the class 1 rate, technically only class 1 homeowners who are subject to the District's individual income tax during the period they occupy their property are eligible for the deduction. Thus someone who owns and occupies a home in the District and is not subject to the District's individual income tax would be eligible for the class 1 rate but not eligible for the homestead exemption. These homeowners include all elected U.S. government officials and some congressional staff members who claim residency in their home state; neither group is subject to the District income tax.

The homestead exemption is generous compared with the property tax relief policies of state governments. A recent comparison of these policies has noted that only the District and fifteen states provide an exemption to homeowners regardless of their age or income. Neither Maryland nor Virginia provides such broad-based property tax relief.[24]

The impact of the homestead exemption can be seen in the property tax rate faced by homeowners. Although the statutory class 1 rate is $0.96 per $100 of assessed value, District homeowners eligible for the deduction have a much lower effective rate. For example, in tax year 1996 the effective tax rate on a class 1 homeowner with the District average assessed value of $185,732 would be $0.80.[25]

Table 3-2 shows the effective tax rates applicable to homeowners falling within a specified range of home values. The rates decrease as the value of the home decreases because the homestead exemption constitutes a larger percentage of a home's value the lower its assessed value. This declining effective rate makes the District property tax less regressive because people with lower incomes have less expensive homes. However, the homestead exemption is not the most efficient or direct means of achieving progressivity because it is not tied to income and thus does not relate the amount of property tax relief to the taxpayer's ability to pay.

A second program that removes a substantial amount of property from the property tax base is the senior citizen tax credit, which allows class

---

(DFR), "Univariate Statistics for Class 1 Residential Properties by Decile of Annual Assessed Value," August 1996.

24. Scott Mackey and Karen Carter, *State Tax Policy and Senior Citizens*, 2d ed. (Denver: National Conference of State Legislatures, 1994), pp. 39, 44.

25. In the example of a house valued at $185,732, the effective property tax rate is calculated as follows:

Home value ($185,732) − homestead exemption ($30,000) = $155,732
($155,732 / $100) × rate ($0.96) = $1495.03
$1495.03 / $185,732 = $0.0080 = $0.80 per $100 assessed value.

Table 3-2. *Effect of Homestead Exemption on District of Columbia Property Tax Rates, Tax Year 1995*

Decile	Home value (dollars)		Effective tax rate (per $100 of assessed value)	Percent receiving deduction
	Minimum	Maximum		
1	89	66,042	0.53	62.6
2	66,045	83,277	0.59	99.1
3	83,278	94,534	0.64	99.5
4	94,535	106,685	0.68	99.8
5	106,686	120,135	0.71	99.8
6	120,137	142,808	0.74	99.7
7	142,812	187,900	0.79	99.7
8	187,901	260,173	0.83	99.8
9	260,180	357,900	0.87	99.9
10	357,917	53,000,000	0.91	99.9

Sources: Author's calculations; and District of Columbia Department of Finance and Revenue, "Univariate Statistics for Class 1 Residential Properties by Decile of Annual Assessed Value," 1996.

1 property owners age sixty-five or older whose annual household adjusted gross income is less than $100,000 to reduce their property tax liability by 50 percent.[26] The relief in this program takes the form of a property tax credit, or specified reduction in tax liability. In 1996 the credit was used by 24,364 taxpayers at an estimated cost to the District of $13.7 million. The senior program removed $1.4 billion, or 3.1 percent, from the gross property tax base. The homestead exemption and the senior citizen credit combined removed 9.0 percent of the value from the gross property tax base at a total cost of almost $40 million (table 3-1).[27]

The District has the most generous senior citizen property tax credit in the region. Maryland does not provide property tax relief based on age. Virginia has a senior citizen property tax credit that is optional for local jurisdictions, but the income cap is $30,000, compared with the District's $100,000.[28] The senior citizen credit further reduces the effective tax rate faced by senior citizens in the District. Table 3-3 shows the effective tax rates applicable to senior citizen homeowners for the same range of home values used in table 3-2. The numbers in table 3-3 assume that all senior citizens who receive the homestead exemption also receive the senior citizen credit. This is true except for seniors who have more than $100,000 in income and are not eligible for the senior citizen credit.

26. D.C. Code 47-863.
27. DFR, "Univariate Statistics"; and DFR, "Real Property Tax Estimates by Class," February 8, 1996.
28. Mackey and Carter, *State Tax Policy*, pp. 39, 45.

Table 3-3. *Impact of Homestead Exemption and Senior Citizen Credit on District of Columbia Property Tax Rates, Tax Year 1995*

| Decile | Home value (dollars) | | Effective tax rate | Percent receiving deduction |
	Minimum	Maximum		
1	89	66,042	0.18	15.3
2	66,045	83,277	0.28	30.6
3	83,278	94,534	0.31	32.5
4	94,535	106,685	0.33	33.2
5	106,686	120,135	0.35	33.3
6	120,137	142,808	0.37	31.5
7	142,812	187,900	0.39	28.3
8	187,901	260,173	0.41	20.5
9	260,180	357,900	0.43	21.6
10	357,917	53,000,000	0.46	14.0

Sources: Author's calculations; and DFR, "Univariate Statistics."

Senior citizens on average are paying property taxes at one-half the rate applied to nonseniors. In fact, someone older than age sixty-five with an adjusted household income of $95,000 and a house valued at $200,000 would pay taxes at an effective rate of only $0.41 per $100 of assessed value.

The District's third largest property tax relief program is the individual income property tax credit, more commonly referred to as a circuit breaker. The circuit breaker is distinguished from the other programs by two features: benefits are related to both income and property tax payments, and the credit is financed by nonproperty tax revenues and thus does not affect the property tax base.[29] Circuit breakers are designed to benefit specific groups such as low-income taxpayers and the elderly who are vulnerable to being overloaded by the property tax. The fact that the property tax is levied on wealth (the value of assets) while paid out of income can create cash hardships and real payment burdens when homeowners' current income declines (as a result of unemployment, illness, or retirement, for example). The tensions arising from being "house rich and income poor" has made the property tax especially unpopular with taxpayers and a political hot potato for elected officials around the country. A circuit breaker, recognizing this potential burden by effectively setting property tax liability at a maximum percentage of income for those with low incomes, has become a widely used policy response.

29. Steven David Gold, *Property Tax Relief* (Lexington, Mass.: Lexington Books, 1979), p. 56.

The District has two circuit breaker programs applying to homeowners and renters, one applying to the elderly, blind, and disabled, and another applying to all others with incomes below $20,000.[30] In 1994, these circuit breaker credits were received by 20,722 taxpayers at a cost to the District of $7.7 million in forgone personal income tax revenue.[31] Each circuit breaker provides an income tax credit that is a percentage of property taxes paid in excess of a certain percentage of household gross income, with a maximum credit of $750. The circuit breaker restricted to the elderly (age sixty-two or older), blind, or disabled, though, provides a more generous scale of credits. For example, for the elderly, blind, or disabled with incomes between $15,000 and $20,000, the circuit breaker credits 100 percent of the property tax paid in excess of 2.5 percent of income, while for the nonelderly it only credits 75 percent of the property tax payment in excess of 4 percent of income.[32]

In the survey of state property tax relief discussed earlier, only the District and ten states provide both a nonelderly and an elderly circuit breaker. An additional nineteen states provide a circuit breaker only for elderly homeowners, and Oregon and Alaska have circuit breakers limited to elderly renters, which brings the total number of states (including the District) with circuit breaker programs to thirty-two. The District's reasoning for providing both categories of relief is its high concentration of poor people.[33]

The District's maximum household income of $20,000 and maximum benefit of $750 compare favorably with the averages of $23,110 and $653 for states with circuit breakers for the elderly. The maximum income of $20,000 and maximum benefit of $750 for its nonelderly circuit breaker program is on the conservative side compared with the averages of $34,180 and $713, respectively, for states with nonelderly circuit breakers.[34]

In terms of fairness, the District's circuit breaker has several advantages over the homestead exemption and senior citizen credit programs. First, the circuit breaker is targeted to income and thus provides the

---

30. For renters, property taxes are taken to be equivalent to 15 percent of rent.

31. D.C. Code 47-1806.6; and District of Columbia Department of Finance and Revenue, "D.C. Income Master File, 1994," June 1996.

32. D.C. Code 47-1806.6; and DFR, "D.C. Income Master File, 1994," June 1996.

33. In 1993 the District had a poverty rate of 26.4 percent, compared with the U.S. average of 15.1 percent. Bureau of the Census, *Statistical Abstract of the United States* (1996), p. 482.

34. Author's calculation based on Mackey and Carter, *State Tax Policy,* pp. 48–49.

property tax with a mechanism for meeting the principle of ability to pay and improving the vertical equity. Second, the circuit breaker automatically compensates for rising taxes resulting from rising property values. Third, it is the only program that provides direct property tax relief to renters, thus improving the horizontal equity of the property tax.[35] Overall, as Steven D. Gold has commented, "If one wants to reduce regressivity, a circuit breaker is the most appropriate policy."[36]

In addition to the three residential property tax relief programs, the District has three smaller programs targeted to specific groups and a deferral program. First, the Lower-Income Home Ownership Tax Abatement Program provides a five-year tax abatement to first-time home buyers, private investors in shared equity investments, and nonprofit housing organizations. Unlike either a deduction and a credit, a property tax abatement eliminates the recipient's entire property tax liability. The purpose of the program is to expand home ownership opportunities for lower-income families at a low direct cost to the District. To qualify, homeowners must meet the income requirement, which changes annually. For example, in 1996 a family of four with household income of less than $49,920 was eligible for the five-year abatement. This program has a higher income threshold and a greater benefit than the circuit breaker program, although it is restricted to first-time home buyers and the benefit lasts only five years. In 1994 the program benefited 2,429 households at a cost of $4.5 million in taxes forgone.[37]

A second targeted program, the Metropolitan Police Department Housing Assistance Program, provides a sliding-scale property tax credit and a $2,000 income tax credit to metropolitan police officers who are first-time home buyers in the District. The program is designed to encourage police officers to live in the District. As of April 1996, twenty-six officers had been granted the $2,000 income tax credit at a cost to the District of $52,000 in taxes forgone. District officials were unable to provide data on the amount of revenue lost as a result of the property tax credit.

The third narrowly targeted program, the Condominium and Cooperative Trash Collection Tax Credit Act of 1990, provides a property tax credit to owners of real property who do not receive District trash col-

35. Gold, *Property Tax Relief*, pp. 72, 90; and Mackey and Carter, *State Tax Policy*, p. 46.

36. Gold, *Property Tax Relief*, p. 314.

37. D.C. Code 47-3501; District of Columbia Department of Finance and Revenue, "Tax Relief Programs," Information Sharing Series Seminar 2, 1996, p. B-2; and DFR, *Tax Facts: Fiscal Years 1993 and 1994*, p. 36.

lection services if their properties are owned as units in a condominium building with more than three dwelling units, owned by members of a homeowners association, or owned by a cooperative housing association with more than three dwelling units. In 1992, when the program became effective, the credit was set at $60 and was to be adjusted for inflation each year. The District was unable to provide data on the number of program participants or on the revenue forgone.

Finally, the District has a property tax deferral program, which is designed to ensure that increases in tax burdens on individual taxpayers are not excessive. The program allows class 1 property owners who have lived on the property for more than one year to pay at a later date property taxes due that exceed 10 percent of the previous year's tax. Once again, the District was unable to provide data on the number of participants or the property tax revenue forgone from this deferral program.[38]

The District's property tax relief efforts manifest themselves in a complex array of programs that are trying to accomplish a variety of policy goals. Two conclusions emerge from this analysis. First, the District has complicated its property tax system by creating programs with similar goals. This is evidenced by the use of a homestead exemption, a senior citizen credit, a circuit breaker, and a low-income exemption to improve the progressivity of the property tax. It is further evidenced by the District's use of both a circuit breaker program and property tax deferral to reduce the burden of property tax increases. Second, the District has further complicated the system by trying to accomplish policy goals such as police officer residency and trash collection that, however worthy, are not efficiently addressed through the property tax system.

The Property Tax Levy

The estimated property tax levy, or yield, for tax year 1996 is $687.3 million, the lowest amount since 1990.[39] The levy experienced an average

38. D.C. Code 47-845.

39. The levy amounts used in this study were derived from assessment data provided by the District. The property tax rate for each class was applied to the net tax base to determine the levy for each class. The levies for each class were then totaled, resulting in the total tax levy for the District. The levies reported in the unaudited statistical portion of the *District of Columbia Comprehensive Annual Financial Review (CAFR), September 30, 1995*, were different from those derived using the above methodology.

Figure 3-1. *District of Columbia Property Tax Levy, 1986–95*

Millions of dollars

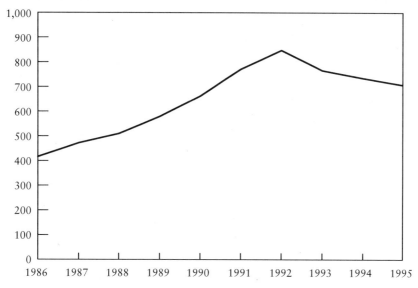

Sources: Author's calculations; and District of Columbia Department of Finance and Revenue (DFR), "Real Property Tax Estimates by Class and Real Property Net Tax Base," February 1996.

growth rate of 10.5 percent in fiscal years 1985–92, reaching a high of $847.5 million in 1992 (figure 3-1). But it then decreased by 9.6 percent in 1993, 4.1 percent in 1994, 3.7 percent in 1995, and 2.8 percent in 1996.

One obvious cause of the decline is the dwindling assessed value of taxable property since 1992 (figure 3-2). During this time the city council has not set the rates to compensate for the declining values. In fact, except for an increase in the class 5 vacant land rate, which accounts for about 1 percent of the tax base, the property tax rates have been frozen since 1990. By freezing the rates, the city council has allowed the assessments to drive the tax levy, which, combined with increased delinquencies, has lead to diminishing revenues.

The performance of the property tax in the District has not paralleled that in the surrounding suburbs since 1991, when property values began to decline as a result of the recession of the early 1990s (table 3-4). From 1986 to 1991 both the tax levies and assessed values grew robustly throughout the region. The District's levy grew slightly faster than the assessed value, whereas in the suburbs the growth of the levy was about

Figure 3-2. *District of Columbia Taxable Assessed Value, 1986–95*

Billions of dollars

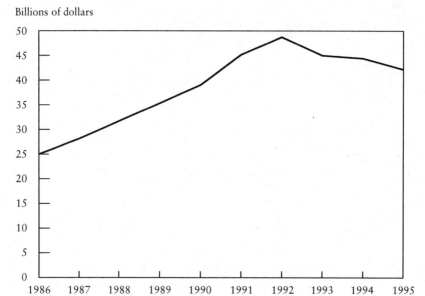

Sources: Author's calculations; and DFR, "Real Property Tax Estimates by Class."

40 percent slower than that of property values. This suggests that while District policymakers were attempting to maximize the revenue from a strong economy, suburban policymakers shared some of the gain with taxpayers.

In 1991–94 the property market was hit by the recession, and property values declined by 6.4 percent in the suburbs and 3.8 percent in the District. The District allowed the property tax levy to decline at a faster rate than the assessed value. Suburban jurisdictions, despite facing a

Table 3-4. *Change in Tax Levy and Assessed Value, District of Columbia and Suburbs, 1986–94*

Percent

Period	District of Columbia		Washington suburbs	
	Tax levy	Assessed value	Tax levy	Assessed value
1986–91	85.1	79.6	71.9	112.0
1991–94	− 4.7	− 3.8	6.5	− 6.1

Sources: *District of Columbia Comprehensive Annual Financial Report*, September 30, 1995, pp. 79–80 (hereafter CAFR, *1995*); Virginia Department of Taxation, *Annual Report, Fiscal years 1986–95*; Prince George's County, *Comprehensive Annual Financial Report* (1995), pp. x-4, x-5; and Montgomery County, *Comprehensive Annual Financial Report* (1996), pp. 160, 162, 164, 165.

Table 3-5. *District of Columbia Property Tax Rates, by Class,
1986–96*[a]

Per $100 assessed value

Year	Class 1 (Homeowner)	Class 2 (Rental property)	Class 3 (Hotels)	Class 4 (Commercial)	Class 5 (Vacant)
1986	1.22	1.54	1.82	2.03	...
1987	1.22	1.54	1.82	2.03	...
1988	1.22	1.54	1.82	2.03	...
1989	1.06	1.54	1.82	2.03	...
1990	0.96	1.54	1.85	2.15	3.29
1991	0.96	1.54	1.82	2.15	2.39
1992	0.96	1.54	1.85	2.15	3.29
1993	0.96	1.54	1.85	2.15	5.00
1994	0.96	1.54	1.85	2.15	5.00
1995	0.96	1.54	1.85	2.15	5.00
1996	0.96	1.54	1.85	2.15	5.00

Sources: District of Columbia Department of Finance and Revenue, *District of Columbia Tax Facts, Fiscal Years
1993 and 1994* (1995), pp. 52–54; and CAFR, 1995, p. 79.

a. Rates are set each year by the City Council pursuant to D.C. Code 47-812.

steeper decline in property values, maintained positive growth in the tax
levy of 6.5 percent to stabilize property tax revenues and to avoid fiscal
problems. The suburban jurisdictions, in short, have adjusted tax rates
to compensate for changes in the tax base and keep property tax revenues
fairly stable in both the upward and downward swings of the market
cycle. District policymakers have not.

Tables 3-5 and 3-6 show the property tax rates for the District and
for selected Maryland and Virginia jurisdictions. The suburban jurisdic-

Table 3-6. *Property Tax Rates in Selected District of Columbia
Suburbs, 1986–95*

Per $100 assessed value

Year	Arlington County	City of Fairfax	City of Falls Church	Montgomery County	Prince George's County
1986	0.95	1.12	0.98	1.16	1.06
1987	0.94	1.08	0.98	1.15	1.06
1988	0.92	0.96	0.92	1.03	1.04
1989	0.89	0.88	0.87	0.91	1.03
1990	0.78	0.84	0.84	0.79	1.01
1991	0.765	0.84	0.93	0.79	0.95
1992	0.765	0.90	0.99	0.88	0.94
1993	0.82	0.93	1.02	0.92	0.96
1994	0.86	0.96	1.03	1.05	0.97
1995	0.897	0.97	1.07	1.07	1.00

Source: Fiscal year 1995 *Comprehensive Annual Financial Report* from each jurisdiction.

Table 3-7. *Property Tax Levy and General Fund Revenue,*
District of Columbia and Suburbs, 1994 or 1995

Jurisdiction	Year	Tax levy	General fund revenue	Levy as percent of revenue
District of Columbia	1995	707,467,800	4,244,420,000	16.7
City of Alexandria	1994	109,338,380	235,820,810	46.4
Arlington County	1994	156,957,136	383,451,255	40.9
City of Fairfax	1994	17,227,693	45,529,782	37.8
Fairfax County	1994	798,258,833	1,417,81,541	56.3
City of Falls Church	1994	10,891,302	24,586,251	44.3
Loudoun County	1994	86,286,574	169,137,599	51.0
Montgomery County	1994	653,006,606	1,239,501,058	52.7
Prince George's County	1995	378,358,042	784,931,538	48.2
Prince William County	1995	159,333,997	295,897,000	53.8

Sources: Virginia Department of Taxation, *Annual Report, Fiscal Year 1995*, pp. 47–51; and Fiscal Year 1995 *Comprehensive Annual Financial Report* from each jurisdiction.

tions do not differentiate property tax rates by use, as the District does with its five tax classes. Taxpayers do, however, face different rates based on where they live in a county and whether they receive any special services financed by property taxes.

Reflecting the city-state nature of the District, Washington's property tax levy accounts for less than 17 percent of general fund revenue, compared with between 37.8 and 56.3 percent for the Maryland and Virginia suburbs (table 3-7). Since the property tax can be an important revenue source because of its stability, the District's lesser reliance on it exposes the city's revenues to the instability of the more economically sensitive income and sales taxes.

Finally, the recent performance of the property tax has also been marked by a significant increase in delinquencies. Collections declined from 97.5 percent of the levy in 1991 to a ten-year low of 89.5 percent in 1994 before rising to 91.7 percent in 1995. A delinquency rate of 10 percent is worth worrying about, not only because of the loss of timely revenue but also because of the administrative work required to restore collections.

The Shares of the Property Tax by Property Class

Because of the District's classification system and generous residential relief programs, in particular the homestead exemption and the senior citizen credit, the relation between a property's value and the amount of

Figure 3-3. *Distributional Impact of District of Columbia Property Tax, by Class*

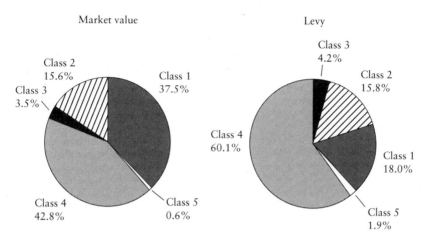

Market value   Levy

Sources: Author's calculations; and DFR, "Real Property Tax Estimates by Class."

property tax it generates is skewed. Figure 3-3 shows the share of market value and tax levy for each property tax class. Class 1 property accounts for 37.5 percent of the market value in the District, yet residential homeowners are only carrying 18.0 percent of the tax levy. Meanwhile, class 4 commercial property accounts for 42.8 percent of the market value, but shoulders 60.1 percent of the tax bill. The distribution of the property tax burden favors class 1 properties at the expense of those in class 4 and, to a lesser extent, classes 3 and 5. This disparity is the result of both the low nominal tax rate paid by class 1 and the expansive residential property tax relief programs, which reduce the statutory rate to an average effective rate of $0.73. Thus commercial property owners are bearing the lion's share of the tax burden and as result face an effective property tax rate of $2.15 that is double that of commercial property owners in the surrounding suburbs.

The Property Tax Calendar

The administration of the property tax in the District is a long and complicated process. At the extreme it can span five years from the time a property is assessed until the time delinquent taxes are reconciled. The normal cycle for taxes that are paid in a timely fashion spans three calendar years from assessment to final payment. The data used in assessing property are often four years removed from the time the taxes are paid.

The administrative process begins with assessing some 160,000 properties in the District. The assessments are made August through December of the calendar year two years before the tax year that will use them. The tax year runs from October 1 to September 30, coinciding with the fiscal year. Thus the assessments for tax year 1997, from October 1, 1996, to September 30, 1997, were made in August–December of 1995. The time lag is even more pronounced because income and expense statements, which provide crucial data for assessing commercial property, are filed in April of the year the properties are assessed and contain data from the previous calendar year. As a result, on April 1, 1995, income and expense statements with 1994 data were filed for tax year 1997 assessments. On March 31, 1997 (the date the first 1997 property tax payment is due), commercial property owners will make a property tax payment for an assessment based on 1994 income and expense data.[40]

By January 1 the preliminary assessments must be completed (figure 3-4). Between January and March taxpayers are notified of their assessments for the tax year beginning October 1. By February 15 the preliminary assessment roll must be compiled; it includes the name of the owner, the address, lot and square, amount, and description and value of the land and improvements of all real property.[41]

If owners believe that their property has been unfairly assessed, they may file an appeal between March 1 and April 30 with the Board of Real Property Assessment and Appeals.[42] A three-member panel reviews a property owner's appeal and determines if the assessment should be changed. The board has the authority to raise or lower the assessment of any real property that it finds to be 5 percent above or below the estimated market value. The board finishes conducting hearings by July 7

40. DFR, *Tax Facts, Fiscal Years 1993 and 1994*, p. 34; D.C. Code 47-802(7); D.C. Code 47-811(b); D.C. Code 47-821(d)(1); and DFR, "Real Property Assessment Process," p. 8.

41. D.C. Code 47-820(a); D.C. Code 47-824; and D.C. Code 47-823(a)(1).

42. The BRPAA consists of eighteen members, all of whom must be residents of the District of Columbia, appointed by the mayor with the approval of the city council to five-year terms. Board members must be knowledgeable about valuation of property, real estate transactions, building costs, accounting, finance, or statistics.

Figure 3-4. *District of Columbia Real Property Tax Calendar*

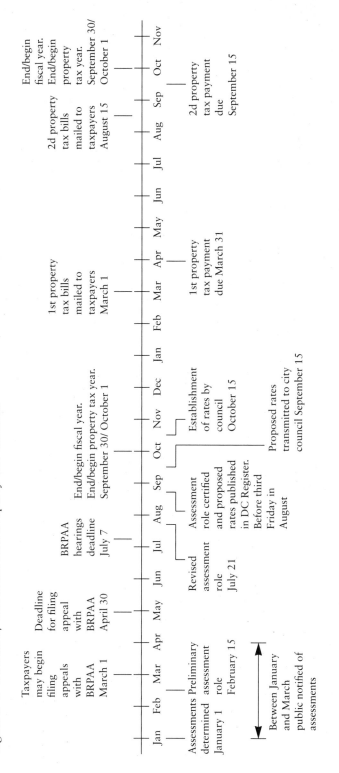

and by July 21 submits the revised assessment role, which is the preliminary assessment role adjusted for the changes in value approved by the board, to the mayor.[43]

If a taxpayer is dissatisfied with BRPAA's ruling, the next level of appeal is the superior court of the District of Columbia. However, taxpayers may only file an appeal with the Superior Court after having appealed to BRPAA. Appeals with the Superior Court must be made by September 30, three months after BRPAA finishes holding its hearings, and the taxpayer must pay the full amount of the taxes that are in dispute. Most cases appealed to the court are referred to a mediation process that was established to settle them before they to go trial. The mediation process typically resolves between 65 and 75 percent of the cases.[44]

On receipt of the revised assessment role from BRPAA, the mayor is authorized to make administrative or clerical corrections to any assessment or to correct any real property classification for the property tax year beginning October 1. Before the third Friday in August, the property tax role must be certified by the mayor. The certified role is an update of the revised assessment role, including any changes made by the mayor, and it serves as the official property tax base, which is used to determine the property tax levy once the rates are set. Also by the third Friday in August, the proposed property tax rates must be published in the District of Columbia Register along with the total assessed value of real property reported by class. By September 15 the mayor must submit the proposed rates to the council for approval. Finally, by October 15 the council must adopt the property tax rates for the property tax year, which began on October 1.[45]

The law allows the council to establish the property tax rates after the start of the property tax year because the first payment is not due until March 31 and is typically billed on March 1. As a result, the council can establish the property tax rates fifteen days after the start of the property tax year and still be four and one-half months ahead of the first property tax billing. The second property tax payment is due September 15, fifteen days before the end of both the property tax year and the fiscal year. If property owners fail to pay property taxes on the prescribed due dates, they are charged a penalty of 10 percent of the unpaid amount plus

43. D.C. Code 47-825.1.

44. D.C. Code 47-825.1(k)(1); D.C. Code 47-3303; and Arthur Andersen, "District of Columbia, Real Property Tax Administration, 30-Day Operational Status Report," Department of Finance and Revenue, 1996, p. 67.

45. D.C. Code 47-825.1(h); D.C. Code 47-815(a); and D.C. Code 47-812(a).

interest at the rate of 1 percent a month until the real property tax liability is paid.

The final element of the property tax calendar is the procedure for the collection of delinquent taxes. On July 1 and October 1 of each year, the assessor of the District of Columbia prepares a list of all real property with delinquent taxes. The council is charged with setting the date of a tax sale at some point after July 1. Both the delinquent tax list and the date of the tax sale must be advertised in the newspaper. If the taxes due, along with penalties and interest, are not paid before the date of the tax sale, the property is sold at public auction at the Office of the Collector of Taxes. The tax sale is held at least three weeks after the publication of the first notice of the sale and continued each day, except Sundays and holidays, until all delinquent property is sold. The purchase price for the delinquent property must be at least the amount of taxes, penalties, and interest owed, and it is paid by the purchaser to the District. The original owner of the property has two years to redeem the property by paying the delinquent taxes, interest, and penalties plus an additional interest charge of 1 percent a month accruing since the sale of the property. If the original owner does not make such a payment within two years of the tax sale, the title of the property is transferred to the tax sale purchaser.[46]

In July 1996 approximately 6,700 properties were offered for sale and only 176, or 2.6 percent, were sold. A possible cause for this low rate is that the District has been cited as an example of a city with a tax sale process that is "cumbersome, confused and lengthy." The District's process is hampered by the fact that the city requires a deposit before the sale begins and takes a long time to settle deposit refunds and redemptions. In contrast, Montgomery County, Maryland, does not have these administrative hurdles and is more attractive to tax lien purchasers.[47]

Implications of the Changed Property Tax Year

In June 1993 the District council passed legislation changing the property tax year. Before the change the tax year ran from July 1 to June 30, not

---

46. D.C. Code 47-1301.

47. Arthur Andersen, "Real Property Tax Administration," p. 22.; and Larry DeBoer, "Property Tax Delinquency and Tax Sales: A Review of the Literature," *Public Budgeting and Finance Management*, vol. 2, no. 2 (1990), p. 336.

coinciding with the fiscal and budget year. The legislation changed the property tax year so that it now runs from October 1 to September 30, coinciding with the fiscal year. This change was enacted to capture additional revenue in fiscal year 1993, but it has had three additional implications: unanticipated property taxes owed, which are realized at time of sale of the property; cash flow issues for the District government; and a significant time lag between property assessments and property tax payments. The time lag has already been discussed; this section will discuss unanticipated taxes owed and cash flow problems.

Before the change (that is, under the July 1 to June 30 property tax year) the first property tax payment was due on September 15 and covered the period from July 1 to December 30, which included three months of one fiscal year and three months of the next. As a result, the September 15 payment was split, with half allocated to the fiscal year ending on September 30 and the other half allocated to the fiscal year beginning October 1. The second payment was due March 31 (see figure 3-5).

In 1993 the District government was faced with a major budget shortfall. The council sought extra revenue by shifting the start of the property tax year from July 1 to October 1 and switching the order of the two tax payments. Under the new property tax year, the first payment is now due March 31 and the second payment is due on September 15. This shift created a one-time revenue increase of $180 million in fiscal 1993 because the District applied the entire amount of the September 15, 1993, payment to fiscal 1993 instead of splitting the payment between fiscal 1993 and fiscal 1994.[48]

On October 1, 1993, the 1994 property tax year and the 1994 fiscal year began. The District received the first property tax payment for both the 1994 property tax year and the 1994 fiscal year on March 31, 1994, and the second payment on September 15, 1994. The September 15 payment is no longer split between two fiscal years, but is entirely allotted to the fiscal year in which it is collected.

Contrary to officials' promises at the time, the change in the property tax year did affect taxpayers. Under the old calendar, the payments were made in the middle of the period associated with each payment, and the city owed three months of services after each payment was made. Since the change, the payments are due at the end of the service period. During

---

48. Margaret K. Webb, "Change in D.C. Real Estate Tax Year Creates Extra Payment," *Washington Post*, October 9, 1993, p. E1.

Figure 3-5. *District of Columbia 1993 Property Tax Year Change*

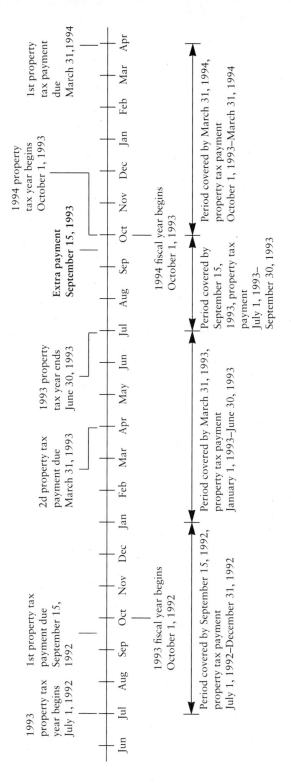

the service period, property owners owe from one to six months of property tax. This debt effectively reduces the value of the property.

The payment made on September 15, 1993, in effect covered only the three-month period from July 1 to September 30. Thus while the taxpayer was making the same payment, the service period covered by the payment was cut in half. The taxpayer's next payment on March 31, 1994, covered the six-month period from October 1, 1993 to March 31, 1994, and each subsequent payment covered the next six-month lagged period.

The implications of this change apparently were discovered when properties began to change hands. At the time of the sale of a property, part of the transaction involves determining the amount of property tax accrued on the property. Consider a hypothetical example. Taxpayer X buys a property on July 1, 1993. As of this date there are no taxes owed on the property because, under the old calendar, the March 31, 1993, payment covered the period from January 1, 1993, to June 30, 1993. On September 15, 1993, taxpayer X makes a half-year property tax payment, which covers only the three-month period from July 1, 1993, to September 30, 1993. On March 31, 1994, taxpayer X makes a half-year property tax payment covering the six-month period from September 30, 1993, to March 31, 1994. Thus as of March 31, 1994, taxpayer X has paid a year's worth of taxes, has occupied the property for nine months, and is only up to date on the property tax.

On July 1, 1994, taxpayer X sells the property to Y. As of July 1, 1994, the property has accrued three months of property tax owed because taxpayer X's last payment covered the period ending March 31, 1994. Y could rightfully ask for a three-month property tax payment from taxpayer X because when the next payment is due on September 15, 1994, Y will be the taxpayer of record and face a six-month payment but will have occupied the property for only three months. Taxpayer X could protest such a payment because he has occupied the property for exactly one year and has made two half-year property tax payments. The additional three months become a point of contention between the buyer and the seller because neither party received services for the tax liability.

This example demonstrates the frustration and complexity engendered by the apparently simple shift in the property tax year. There are direct costs associated with this frustration because additional time and money must be spent to reach an agreement on whether the buyer or the seller is responsible for payment of the additional three months of taxes.

This issue becomes more complex with commercial property. Landlords pass part of their property tax along to tenants in the form of increased rents. If taxpayer X were a landlord and had anticipated the three months of taxes that would need to be reconciled with Y at the time of sale, an additional amount could have been passed on to the tenants in 1993 to cover the three-month amount. Some landlords did impose such a surcharge.[49] Until the property is sold, they are holding and collecting interest on these tenant advances.

The change in tax year has created another problem: a cash flow gap, because the first property tax payment is received six months after the fiscal year begins. Under the old schedule, the District would collect a quarter of the property tax revenue fifteen days before the start of the fiscal year. Now it can no longer earn interest on the revenue. Instead, it may actually incur additional interest expenses through increased short-term borrowing to deal with immediate cash flow needs during the first half the fiscal year. It is hard to see how this change in the tax year improved anything, although it did get the tax year and fiscal year aligned. Now that they are, this study recommends changes to rationalize the ad hoc nature of the present system.

Supplemental Assessments

In addition to the annual property assessment, the District conducts a supplemental assessment that begins January 1, immediately after the annual assessments are completed. The supplemental assessment is designed to capture any additions or subtractions to the property tax base that occur while the property tax roll for the forthcoming year is being finalized. The additions and subtractions to the base may include the construction of new buildings, an addition to an existing building, or a conversion that raises the value.

The first supplemental assessment is conducted between January 1 and June 30 (see figure 3-6). Property owners may file appeals for the first-half supplemental with BRPAA between September 1 and September 30. BRPAA completes the first-half supplemental hearings on October 15. The second-half supplementals are conducted between July 1 and December 30. Property owners may file for appeal of these between March 1 and March 31. BRPAA completes the second-half supplemental hearings on April 15. The first-half supplementals are billed with the regular first

49. J. Fernando Barrueta, "A Rock, a Hard Place, and a Real Estate Tax," *Barrueta Exclusive Quarterly Report*, vol. 2 (August 1994), p. 2.

Figure 3-6. *District of Columbia Supplemental Assessments Calendar*

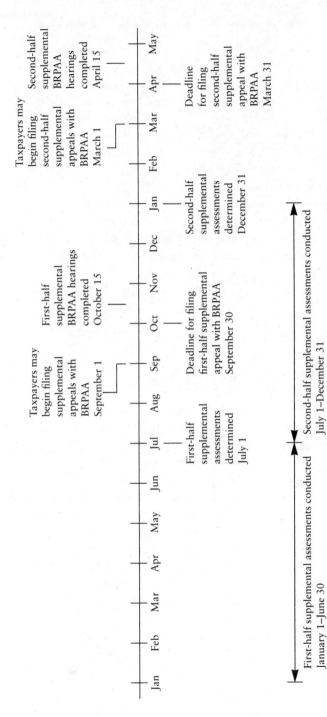

billing and are due March 31, and the second-half supplementals are billed with the regular second billing and are due September 15. Approximately 300 to 500 properties may fall into this category each billing period.[50]

Recent Administrative Problems

During the summer of 1996 the *Washington Post* reported a long list of problems in the District's Real Property Tax Administration (RPTA). The problems came to light when it was reported that two assessors were using square footage to determine the assessment of residential property and ignoring design, location, interior condition, and other factors. Their methodology led to overassessments of inexpensive houses and underassessments of expensive ones. After this discovery, the mayor extended the deadline for filing appeals with BRPAA from April 30 to September 30. In addition, 9,700 properties that had been assessed using the faulty methodology were reassessed. Anthony Williams, chief financial officer of the District, then fired the acting associate director of the RPTA and the director of property assessments. These events exposed fundamental weaknesses in the District's ability to assess effectively and fairly the $42 billion of taxable real estate in the city.[51]

The *Washington Post* reported other examples of the problems that plague the property tax administration. First, District data showed that a quarter of all residential properties in the District were overassessed in fiscal 1996 by more than 10.5 percent and that about the same share were underassessed by more than 15.5 percent, based on actual sales. Second, more than 19,000 assessment appeals have been filed during the past five years, and that number will increase dramatically with the 1996 extension of the filing deadline. Third, the Department of Revenue and Budget's outdated mainframe computer has virtually no space to indicate which of the many relief programs applies to which taxpayers. Finally, if a taxpayer moves from the District and rents his home, there is no

50. D.C. Code 47-829; D.C. Code 47-830; and DFR, "Tax Relief Programs," p. H-2.

51. Vernon Loeb, "Faulty Formula Botches 9,700 D.C. Assessments," *Washington Post*, June 13, 1996, p. B1; Loeb, "Residents Challenge 2d D.C. Assessor," *Washington Post*, June 22, 1996, p. B1; and Loeb, "D.C. Financial Chief Fires 2 Top Assessment Officials in Shake-up," *Washington Post*, July 11, 1996, p. B1.

standard process for removing the homestead exemption, which applies only to owner-occupied property owners.[52]

To assess the depth of the problems in the Real Property Tax Administration, outside consultants were brought in to evaluate the operations and management of the administration and make recommendations. Arthur Andersen's "30-Day Operational Status Report" details personnel, technology, and data problems in the RPTA. The report raises serious questions as to the integrity of the assessment data and the ability of the personnel to use the data in concert with the available technology to produce accurate and fair assessments. The report noted the time lag problem concerning the submission of income and expense data, stating that "by the time the assessment cycle begins, almost nine months of the current year are over and annualized figures are then based on stale data." The report also observed that the District has too many tax relief programs that cannot be effectively administered and, in some cases, produce very little tax relief.[53]

To address the administrative problems, the Anderson report recommended and the chief financial officer proposed a one-year moratorium on property tax assessments. The moratorium froze 1997 assessments so that they would not change in 1998. The stated purpose was "to provide a simple expedient procedure for correcting errors, installing systems, and designing and implementing processes to improve the quality and accuracy of assessments, whether they benefit the taxpayer or the government."[54]

Proposals

For the District of Columbia, as for other local governments, the property tax represents the ultimate backing for its bonds. Creditors look to this tax as the revenue of last resort to meet obligations. This study's examination of the present property tax structure and administration in the

52. Vernon Loeb, "Verdict on D.C. Tax System: 'Garbage In, Garbage Out,'" *Washington Post*, July 10, 1996, p. A1.; and Loeb, "Agency's Problems Tax D.C. Property Owners," *Washington Post*, July 15, 1996, p. B1.

53. Vernon Loeb, "D.C. Considers Moratorium on Tax Assessments," *Washington Post*, August 4, 1996, p. B1; and Arthur Andersen, "Real Property Tax Administration," p. 52.

54. Office of the Chief Financial Officer, "Real Property Tax Administration Stabilization Plan—Interim Update—Proposed Moratorium, FY 1998 Assessments, Briefing Package," August 12, 1996, p. 7.

District of Columbia has generated the following proposals to make this tax simpler, lower the burden, distribute it more fairly, and ensure that the tax is better able to help stabilize the budget.

Create a two-class system with lower rates and a statutory limit on the ratio between the two. The present classification system is complicated, difficult to administer, and unfair. The different residential rates, based on ownership, violate strictures of horizontal equity. Combined with the large homestead exemption for owner occupiers, the classification system affords a strong incentive for fraud. The creation of new commercial classes has led to commercial rates and tax burdens that are significantly higher than those of surrounding jurisdictions and may be linked to the District's shrinking share of the region's private jobs.

This study proposes a residential rate of $0.90 per $100 and a commercial rate of $1.35, which represents a substantial tax cut for all property owners in the District. The ratio of the commercial to the residential rate (150 percent) should be set in law as the maximum ratio between the classes to avoid creeping increases in the commercial rate.

The case for the cut in the commercial rate is persuasive and has been made throughout this study, especially in chapter 2 and appendix B. Although the District's present residential tax rate is not out of line with that of the surrounding areas, the quality of many District services is. Over the years, residential property owners (who are also voters) have managed to secure a number of broadly based exemptions and deductions that have significantly lowered their effective tax burdens and shifted them to commercial properties. These programs are neither fair nor efficient public policy and should be eliminated. But their existence and assumed continuation are reflected in present residential property values. As these tax expenditures are eliminated and, at the same time, assessment changes take place, it would be prudent to lower the nominal residential tax rate.

The new two-class system and lower rates would generate a lower tax levy than the present system. Based on 1995 assessments, at $0.90 and $1.35 the property tax levy would be $477 million (with even lower revenues, considering delinquencies). However, the lower property tax levy is appropriate within a reformed District revenue structure that includes a PILOT and adequate state-type aid from the federal government.

Make all property tax relief income based, ending poorly targeted relief programs and substituting one improved circuit breaker program. The District has a very broad and generous relief program compared with other places.[55] We propose targeting property tax relief on those for whom the payment creates a significant burden—because they may be either unemployed or living on a fixed income. This is fairer. It will result in easier administration, less fraud and abuse, and, for wealthier home-owners, higher property tax payments. It will also save the District tax revenue. Table 3-8 summarizes the proposed consolidation of existing, poorly targeted, relief programs.

There are various ways to improve the circuit breaker program. For example, the formula could be adjusted incrementally, raising the maximum credit and lifting the income eligibility to cover more people.[56] Table 3-9 illustrates one such possible combination of changes, providing a general credit at 85 percent of the property tax in excess of the designated percentage of income, compared with the present 75 percent; increasing the maximum credit from $750 to $1,000; and increasing the income eligibility level from the present maximum of $20,000 to $30,000 of household gross income.[57] Thus households with incomes between $20,000 and $30,000 would be credited with 75 percent of the property taxes paid in excess of 3.5 percent of household gross income.[58] This new structure adds about $21 million to the cost of the circuit breaker, resulting in a total cost of about $29 million and a savings over the present broad system of $23 million.

The effect on District residents of lower rates and more targeted relief would differ between renters and owners. Seventy-seven percent of low-income residents are renters. With taxes on rental property declining sharply if this proposal were implemented, there should be downward

55. Among the twenty-eight states with circuit breakers, the District's average benefit ranks seventh and the cost per capita sixth. See Mackey and Carter, *State Tax Policy*, p. 50.

56. Changes in the property tax rates and the elimination of the homestead exemption and the senior citizen credit will increase the cost of the circuit breaker by $321,000 before any policy changes are made. The cost estimates are based on the author's calculations using DFR, "DC Income Master File, 1994"; District of Columbia Department of Finance and Revenue, "1995 District of Columbia Individual Income Tax Booklet," p. 25; and Bureau of the Census, *American Housing Survey for the Washington Metropolitan Area 1993*, pp. 52, 67, 87, 94.

57. For people with household incomes less than $2,999, the formula would be changed from 95 percent to 100 percent of property tax in excess of 1.5 percent of income.

58. Under the circuit breaker for those aged 62 or older, blind, or disabled, households with incomes between $20,000 and $30,000 would be credited 100 percent of the property taxes paid in excess of 3 percent of income. Expanding the circuit breaker to the $30,000 threshold would increase the cost by $10.5 million. Applying the two policy changes discussed above to households with incomes between $20,000 and $30,000 would add an additional $1.7 million to the cost.

Table 3-8. *The Proposal to Restructure District of Columbia Property Tax Relief*

Current relief programs	Coverage	Current cost (millions of dollars)	Proposal	Cost (millions of dollars)
Homestead exemption	$30,000 reduction in value for homeowners occupying own home	26.0	Replace with enhanced circuit breaker (see table 3-9)	
Senior citizen property tax relief	One-half reduction in property tax liability for homeowners occupying own home who are over 65 with AGI less than $100,000	13.6		28.7
Circuit breaker	See table 3-9	7.6		
Lower-income homeownership tax abatement	Five-year tax abatement for low-income first-time homeowners occupying own home	4.5	Eliminate	0
Metropolitan police housing assistance program	Five-year sliding-scale credit for police officers who are first-time homeowners occupying own home	n.a.	Eliminate	0
Trash collection credit	Credit for owners of condo or coop property who do not receive D.C. trash collection services	n.a.	Eliminate	0
Property tax deferral	Deferral of payment on amount over 10 percent for Class 1 property owners with property taxes 10 percent higher than the previous year	n.a.	Eliminate	0
Total		51.7		28.7

Sources: See text.
n.a. Not available.

Table 3-9. *The Proposal for an Enhanced Circuit Breaker for District of Columbia Taxpayers*

Current circuit breaker		Proposed circuit breaker	
Household gross income (dollars)	Credit formula	Household gross income (dollars)	Credit formula
Claimants less than age 62 who are not blind or disabled			
Less than 2,999	95 percent of tax in excess of 1.5 percent of income	Less than 2,999	100 percent of tax in excess of 1.5 percent of income
3,000–4,999	75 percent of tax in excess of 2.0 percent of income	3,000–4,999	85 percent of tax in excess of 2.0 percent of income
5,000–6,999	75 percent of tax in excess of 2.5 percent of income	5,000–6,999	85 percent of tax in excess of 2.5 percent of income
7,000–9,999	75 percent of tax in excess of 3.0 percent of income	7,000–9,999	85 percent of tax in excess of 3.0 percent of income
10,000–14,999	75 percent of tax in excess of 3.5 percent of income	10,000–30,000	85 percent of tax in excess of 3.5 percent of income
15,000–20,000	75 percent of tax in excess of 4.0 percent of income	. . .	. . .
Claimants age 62 or older who are blind or disabled			
Less than 4,999	100 percent of tax in excess of 1.0 percent of income	Less than 4,999	100 percent of tax in excess of 1.0 percent of income
5,000–9,999	100 percent of tax in excess of 1.5 percent of income	5,000–9,999	100 percent of tax in excess of 1.5 percent of income
10,000–14,999	100 percent of tax in excess of 2.0 percent of income	10,000–30,000	100 percent of tax in excess of 2.0 percent of income
15,000–20,000	100 percent of tax in excess of 2.5 percent of income	. . .	. . .
Maximum credit (dollars)	750	Maximum credit (dollars)	1,000
Total cost (millions of dollars)	7.7	Total cost (millions of dollars)	28.7

Sources: See text.

Table 3-10. *Current and Proposed District of Columbia Property Tax Policies*

Current dollars

Category of homeowner	Tax burden under current policy[a]	Tax burden under proposed policy[b]
Income of $12,500 and home value of $120,492[c]		
Nonelderly	545.31	534.54
Elderly	250.00	250.00
Income of $25,000 and home value of $133,495[c]		
Nonelderly	993.21	923.92
Elderly	496.60	500.00
Income $50,000 and home value of $146,574[c]		
Nonelderly	1,119.11	1,319.17
Elderly	559.56	1,319.17
Income of $75,000 and home value of $164,064[c]		
Nonelderly	1,287.01	1,476.58
Elderly	643.51	1,476.58

Sources: Author's calculations; and Bureau of the Census, *American Housing Survey for the Washington Metropolitan Area 1993*, Current Housing Reports, H170/9318 (Department of Commerce, 1995), p. 67.

a. $0.96 rate, homestead exemption, senior citizen credit, circuit breaker.

b. $0.90 rate, enhanced circuit breaker.

c. Median home values for the stated income levels in the Washington metropolitan area.

pressure on rents. And, with rent regulation, the District can require that the savings be shared with renters. For homeowners, the impact would depend on the value of the home and the owner's income. Those with incomes of less than $25,000 generally would not be worse off (table 3-10).

Treat the property tax differently than it has been treated in the budget process. Because the property tax base is known in advance of the budget year, policymakers can budget exactly how much revenue is needed from the tax and then set the rates to achieve the target. For budget predictability and stability, the target should represent only an incremental increase over the previous year, enough to cover inflation. Most jurisdictions, including the surrounding suburbs, recognize this characteristic of the property tax and take advantage of it, adjusting their rates to ensure a stable revenue stream.[59] Budget policy in the District has instead frozen the tax rates and allowed the assessments to drive the levy, which has

59. Within reason. Obviously, during severe economic downturns or crashes in the property market, maintaining revenue stability may not be feasible and over several years may prove to be impossible.

generated budget problems as well as putting pressure on assessors to be revenue raisers rather than recorders of market value.

In addition, the District should include in the levy a reserve for delinquencies and court refunds. Without a reserve, these adjustments directly lower current-year revenues because they are not anticipated when the levy is set. To improve budget stability, the District should set the desired levy, increase it by the amount of anticipated net delinquencies and court refunds, and then set the rates to generate the amount of the levy plus the reserve.

The District should reorganize the property tax calendar—payment dates, assessment dates, appeals—to streamline administration and receive cash at the beginning of the fiscal year, thus improving cash management and reducing the need for short-term borrowing. Moving the first payment to the beginning of the fiscal year would force a shortening of the property tax assessment calendar. Several administrative dates, including when the council sets the rates, would have to come earlier to ensure that the bills were sent on time. The District should also institute a single date when the property roll is official, eliminating the supplemental assessments. These assessments are cumbersome make-work and not the best use of assessors, whose skills need to be upgraded and used more efficiently. The elimination of the supplementals forgoes, at most, six months' worth of cash on a small number of properties, while freeing assessor time and eliminating unnecessary paperwork.

There is a one-time cost associated with reordering the payments and capturing the cash early in the fiscal year. It is equal to half the annual property tax revenue. Based on fiscal 1995 revenues, that one-time cost is $327 million, significantly more than the $173 million the District gained in fiscal 1993 by changing the ordering of the payments. In essence the District borrowed the $173 million then, rather than acknowledging the deficit, and now it will cost twice the amount to return to a payment sequence that minimizes cash flow problems and the expense of short-term borrowing.

Improve the administration of the property tax. The disclosures of assessment failures as well as the findings of the Arthur Andersen report to the chief financial officer clearly demonstrate fundamental problems: from backlogs in the registration of properties, through classification and assessments, to collections, delinquencies, and the sale of tax liens. Nothing is working well, including the computer-assisted mass-appraisal (CAMA) database. The chief financial officer and his new management team at the Department of Finance and Revenue understand this. Addressing these problems and improving the data in the CAMA system must be of the highest priority. Fundamentally, the fairness of the property tax depends on accurate assessments, which reflect market value. Priority must be given to improving the assessment process in a timely fashion and permanently enhancing the quality and efficiency of the service provided to property owners.

CHAPTER 4

Income Taxes on Residents and Nonresidents

T HE PERSONAL INCOME TAX on residents accounts for more than one-quarter of the tax revenue of the District of Columbia. In the first half of the 1990s this revenue decreased sharply in real terms, largely because of the District's losses of middle-class taxpayers. This chapter examines the structure of the District's personal income tax and the distribution of its burdens on residents. It proposes cutting the resident income tax by 30 percent and simplifying it. The new personal income tax would be an easy calculation of 28 percent of federal income tax liability, with revenues collected by the Internal Revenue Service. In addition, the chapter examines the federal law prohibiting the District from taxing commuters' earnings and its implications for the District's revenues. There is an estimated $1 billion revenue gain to the surrounding area: $366 million to Virginia and $619 million to Maryland and its counties. The chapter offers two alternative nonresident income taxes, which, being deductible from state income tax, would not increase tax payments for commuters. Imposing the equivalent of Virginia's income tax would net the District $737 million. Imposing a flat city-type tax of 2 percent would yield $361 million. This study does not propose a commuter tax but offers these estimates to inform the public debate.

The Resident Personal Income Tax

Forty-three states and the District of Columbia impose personal income taxes on their residents. Eleven states allow city income taxes. The structure of the District's tax and the city's reliance on it make it similar to state income taxes.[1]

---

1. A resident is a person domiciled in the District at any time or one who maintains an abode in the District for 183 days or more during the year.

The rates and the extent of states' reliance on the individual income tax vary widely. The tax contributes 65 percent of Oregon's tax revenue but just 3.6 percent of New Hampshire's and 1.9 percent of Tennessee's, where only dividends and interest are included in taxable income.[2] Thirty-three of the states use a progressive rate structure and nine use a flat rate. Among the progressive structures, the lowest maximum rate is 5 percent in Alabama and Mississippi, imposed on incomes greater than $3,000 and $10,000, respectively. The highest is 11 percent, applied against incomes greater than $214,929 in California and $62,700 in Montana. The flat rates range from Pennsylvania's 2.8 percent to Massachusetts's 5.95 percent (but 12 percent on interest, dividends, and net capital gains).[3]

In recent decades states have increased their reliance on the personal income tax: its share of total tax revenue has expanded from 13.4 percent in 1963 to 31.9 percent in 1993, by far the greatest increase of any category of tax.[4] The personal income tax is largely responsible for the increases in state government tax collections in these decades. As total state tax collections rose by $815 per capita in real terms, the real per capita individual income tax collections increased by $362.[5] Today, states with high revenue needs often turn to the income tax. Of the ten states with the highest effective total tax rates, five have effective income tax rates that are also among the nation's ten highest.[6] Three of the exceptions are Alaska, New Mexico, and North Dakota, which receive a large share of their revenue from severance taxes on the extraction of natural resources.[7]

2. Patrick Fleenor, ed., *Facts and Figures on Government Finance*, 30th ed. (Washington: Tax Foundation, 1995), table E23. Figures are for fiscal 1993.

3. Advisory Commission on Intergovernmental Relations (ACIR), *Significant Features of Fiscal Federalism*, vol. 1: *Budget Processes and Tax Systems* (Washington, 1995), table 15.

4. Of the eleven categories of state taxes shown in Fleenor, *Facts and Figures*, table E18, the relative reliance on two—individual income and general sales, use, or gross receipts—increased between 1963 and 1993.

5. In real 1993 dollars, total tax collections per capita increased from $554 to $1,370, while personal income collections grew from $74 to $436. The calculations are based on data in Fleenor, *Facts and Figures*. The deflator used is from *Economic Report of the President, 1996*, p. 343.

6. The effective rates are equal to per capita revenue from Fleenor, *Facts and Figures*, divided by per capita income from the Bureau of the Census and *Statistical Abstract of the United States, 1995*, table 713.

7. Fleenor, *Facts and Figures*. The shares of total tax represented by severance taxes in Alaska, New Mexico, and North Dakota are 50.5 percent, 11.2 percent, and 14.9 percent. The national average is 1.4 percent.

Eleven states allow cities to impose income taxes on their residents. Except for New York City, these rates are flat and low, ranging from 1 percent of income in Birmingham, Kansas City, and St. Louis to 3.46 percent in Philadelphia.[8] Economists have long argued that progressive taxation at the local level should be avoided because, as long as the possibility of paying less in taxes and experiencing no cuts in services exists in nearby jurisdictions, residents may be induced to move.[9]

The progressive income tax system of the District, with a maximum rate of 9.5 percent imposed on incomes greater than $20,000, is unique among American cities and more typical of states. In 1995 the District raised 26.9 percent of its total tax revenue through the income tax. The average for the states is 31.9 percent.[10] In 1992 cities with populations between 0.5 million and 1 million relied on it for 16.8 percent.[11] The District's reliance on the income tax falls, then, between that of a state and that of a city.

In 1995 per capita income tax payments in the District came to $1,135. The combined per capita state and local taxes for Baltimore residents amounted to $809. Neither Boston nor Memphis, the other two cities of comparable size examined in this study, levy personal income taxes.[12]

Budget requirements have forced a tax rate on District residents that is much higher than average. District residents paid an average 3.8 percent of their income in District income taxes in fiscal 1992. Among the states, only Oregon's 4 percent for combined state and local income tax posed a greater burden. The national average is 2.2 percent.[13] The District, a city with a population of 559,000, administers a mildly progressive, state-type income tax and a relatively complex one.

8. In New York City, the maximum rate is 3.4 percent. ACIR, *Significant Features*, vol. 1.

9. See for example, Wallace E. Oates, *Fiscal Federalism* (Harcourt Brace Jovanovich, 1972).

10. Fleenor, *Facts and Figures*, p. 187; and *District of Columbia Comprehensive Annual Financial Report, September 30, 1995* (1995), p. 78 (hereafter *CAFR, 1995*). State data are based on fiscal year 1993.

11. Fleenor, *Facts and Figures*, table F5. City data are from fiscal year 1992. The personal income tax share of district tax revenue was 26 percent in fiscal 1992.

12. The per capita state income tax attributable to Boston was $937, while Memphis was $19. The District information comes from *CAFR, 1995*. For other cities (and states), see sources for table 1-1.

13. Advisory Commission on Intergovernmental Relations (ACIR), *Significant Features of Fiscal Federalism*, vol. 2: *Revenues and Expenditures* (Washington, 1994), pp. 90, 91.

Table 4-1. *District of Columbia per Capita Income and Income Tax Revenues, Selected Years and Periods, 1984–95*

Thousands of dollars unless otherwise specified

Period	Nominal per capita income (dollars)	Real per capita income[a] (dollars)	Nominal personal income tax revenue	Real personal income tax revenue[a]	Nominal total tax revenue	Real total tax revenue[a]
1984	16,668	24,449	386,635	567,114	1,398,812	2,051,770
1989	22,794	28,015	603,469	741,683	2,204,598	2,709,522
1995	32,036	32,036	643,676	643,676	2,391,041	2,391,041
Change 1984–89 (percent)	36.8	14.4	56.1	30.8	57.6	32.1
Change 1989–94 (percent)	40.6	14.2	6.7	−13.2	8.5	−11.8
Change 1984–95 (percent)	92.2	31.0	66.5	13.5	70.9	16.5

Sources: *District of Columbia Comprehensive Annual Financial Report, September 30, 1995*, pp. 78, 83 (hereafter *CAFR, 1995*); and District of Columbia Department of Finance and Revenue, *District of Columbia Tax Facts, 1984* (1985), and *Tax Facts, 1985* (1986).

a. 1995 dollars.

District Personal Income Tax Revenue

In fiscal year 1995 the District raised almost $644 million in personal income tax revenue. The growth of the tax since 1984 has mirrored the growth of tax revenue in general, increasing by 13.5 percent in real terms (table 4-1). Because taxes overall have grown by 16.5 percent in real terms, the share of tax revenue resulting from the income tax has changed very little, decreasing from 27.6 percent to 26.9 percent.

The revenue growth, however, masks some problems. Although real personal income tax revenue grew 30.8 percent from 1984 to 1989, it declined 13.2 percent between 1989 and 1995. Yet these two periods saw real per capita personal income in the District grow by 17.5 percent and 16.5 percent, respectively. Why did taxes decrease when income was growing? The capital has been losing population (table 4-2). Except for

Table 4-2. *District of Columbia Population, Selected Years, 1970–95*

Year	Population (thousands)	Change (percent)
1970	755.1	. . .
1975	710.3	−5.9
1980	637.6	−10.2
1985	634.6	−0.5
1990	609.9	−4.9
1995	554.0	−9.2

Source: Bureau of the Census, *Survey of Current Business* (various years).

Table 4-3. *District of Columbia Taxable Income, by Filing Classification, 1989, 1994*

Billions of dollars unless otherwise specified

Classification	1989	1994	Change 1989–94 (percent)
Total taxable income, nominal	6.776	7.182	6.0
Total taxable income, real (1995 dollars)	8.328	7.385	−11.3
Married, separate combined taxable income, nominal	1.870	1.890	1.1
Married, separate combined taxable income, real (1995 dollars)	2.298	1.943	−15.4
Single taxable income, nominal	3.030	3.098	2.2
Single taxable income, real (1995 dollars)	3.724	3.186	−14.4

Source: District of Columbia Department of Finance and Revenue, "Statistics on District of Columbia Individual Income Tax," 1991; and "District of Columbia Master Income File."

1984, 1985, and 1986, it has decreased every year since 1969.[14] The 9.2 percent population loss between 1990 and 1995 was exceeded only by the 10.2 percent loss between 1975 and 1980.[15]

The impact of this exodus on real taxable income in the District has been serious, even though the population changes between 1984 and 1994 varied widely among each filing category (table 4-3).[16] Those filing as "married, separate combined," have the highest average taxable incomes and have left in greatest numbers since 1984 (table 4-4).[17] Their

14. The population decline in the 1980s averaged 0.6 percent annually. Since then, the rate of loss has accelerated, returning to the 1.7 percent annual rate experienced during the 1970s.

15. Bureau of Economic Analysis, *Survey of Current Business* (Department of Commerce, various years).

16. District of Columbia Department of Finance and Revenue (DFR), *Statistics on District of Columbia Individual Income Tax* (1991), pp. 32–37. Through June 1991, in which statistics on tax year 1989 were published, the District's Department of Finance and Revenue annually published *Statistics on District of Columbia Individual Income Tax*. Its tables reported distribution of taxable income, standard and itemized deductions, and tax credits, broken down by types of filer. This document has not been published since 1991, but taxpayer distributions for 1990–94 were made available to this project.

17. The category "married, separate combined" allows couples to split their income and deductions between husband and wife in whatever manner minimizes their tax liability.

Table 4-4. *District of Columbia Income Tax Filers, by Filing Classification, Selected Tax Years and Periods, 1984–94*

Year	Single	Head of household	Married, joint	Married, separate	Married, separate combined
1984	160,358	59,455	29,460	8,521	31,264
1989	172,676	62,498	26,789	9,311	56,198
1994	143,858	60,903	25,078	8,655	20,940
Change 1984–89 (percent)	8	5	−9	9	−10
Change 1989–94 (percent)	−17	−3	−6	−7	−25
Change 1984–94 (percent)	−10	2	−15	2	−33
Average taxable income 1994 (dollars)	21,536	13,973	42,100	28,209	90,277

Source: DFR, "Statistics on District of Columbia Individual Income Tax," pp. 32–37.

incomes exceed those of other filers because they represent the incomes of couples, often reflecting two earners. The present 20,940 separate combined filers have a taxable income of $1.9 billion, 26.3 percent of the District's total taxable income. The rapid and accelerating departure of this group accounted for 37.6 percent of the real decline in total taxable income between 1989 and 1994. The district has also lost 15 percent of its married joint filers, the second highest income group. The single filers, whose numbers are much greater, account for another 57.1 percent of the real decrease in total taxable income.

In fiscal year 1994 the District had 269,144 individual taxpayers who contributed an average income tax payment of $2,418. The more typical median payment was $944. As the population of the District has shrunk, the decrease in the number of married filers has outpaced that of single earners by 22 percent to 2 percent, and the distribution of the tax burden has become less progressive. In 1984, for example, a household earning $75,000 paid 7.14 percent of its income to the District in income tax, and a household earning $15,000 paid 2.53 percent. In 1994 a household

With progressive taxation, it is particularly beneficial for couples with large differences between the income of husband and wife, for example when one of them does not work outside the home. Nine states and the District employ this treatment to avoid the so-called marriage penalty characteristic of joint filing in progressive income tax structures (including the federal tax).

earning $100,000 paid 6.67 percent, and one earning $25,000 paid 4.38 percent.[18]

The District's tax rate structure is not especially progressive. The graduated rates are 6 percent for net taxable incomes less than $10,000, 8 percent for those from $10,000 to $20,000, and 9.5 percent for those higher than $20,000. Nineteen states have top brackets beginning at levels higher than $20,000. The District's standard deduction and personal exemption amounts of $2,000 and $1,370 are middle-of-the-pack figures among the states imposing income taxes.[19] As a result of the District's low beginning bracket amounts, the income tax liability represents 3.4 percent of family income for those in the bottom 20 percent of taxpayers (income less than $31,000) and 6.1 percent for those in the top 20 percent (income greater than $111,000).[20] Still, even if the personal income tax is only slightly progressive, it does help the District achieve a tax system less regressive than that in many states.

District income tax rates are higher than Virginia's but similar to those found in the Maryland suburbs. The maximum rate in Virginia is 5.75 percent and the top bracket begins at $17,000. In Maryland, incomes greater than $3,000 and less than $100,000 are taxed at 5 percent. For income in excess of $100,000 the marginal rate is set at 6 percent. Montgomery and Prince George's counties collect an additional 60 percent of the state liability. For incomes greater than $100,000, then, the marginal rate in these counties comes to 9.6 percent, just above the District's top rate.[21]

Definition of Taxable Income in the District

Taxable income in the District differs from federal taxable income, and computing it is done in two steps.[22] Starting with the federal adjusted

18. District of Columbia Department of Finance and Revenue, *A Comparison of Tax Rates and Burdens in the Washington Metropolitan Area* (June 1985), table; and DFR, *Comparison* (June 1995), table 3.

19. ACIR, *Significant Features*, vol. 1.

20. Michael P. Ettlinger and others, *Who Pays? A Distributional Analysis of the Tax Systems in All 50 States* (Washington: Citizens for Tax Justice and the Institute on Taxation and Economic Policy, 1996), app. 1, p. 9.

21. DFR, *Comparison of Tax Rates* (1995), pp. 4, 25.

22. The discussion here on the differences between District and federal income tax laws draws heavily on Emil Sundley, "The Income Tax," pp. 67–106 in *Technical Aspects of the District's Tax System* (Washington: Committee on the District of Columbia, 1978).

gross income (AGI), a taxpayer makes additions and subtractions to produce a District adjusted gross income. Subtracting deductions and exemptions from the District AGI results in District taxable income.

ADDITIONS AND SUBTRACTIONS. The District requires that taxpayers add back to the federal adjusted gross income all federal adjustments to income. These include moving expenses and contributions to individual retirement accounts. By disallowing the deduction of IRA contributions, the District imposes a bookkeeping headache on residents. To further complicate matters, drawdowns from an IRA are taxable at the federal level but are ignored in the District tax code. The District also disallows the federal adjustments that grant self-employed persons the tax protection other workers receive on fringe benefits (the self-employment adjustments are an attempt by the federal tax code to provide equal treatment of employees and the self-employed). The District thus imposes a substantial penalty on the self-employed.

Subtractions from federal taxable income include any income subject to District business franchise income taxes. Franchise income is instead subject to the District's tax on unincorporated business income and income earned by a District-based S corporation, which is taxed by the federal government as personal income of the shareholders but is taxed as corporate income by the District.[23] Should the owners of such franchises reside outside the District and in a state that imposes an income tax, they will be taxed a second time on this income. If they are District residents, they can subtract the business income already taxed from their federal base and must add back in any federal deductions claimed in connection with the franchise.

The District's tax policy distorts decisions on whether to locate or remain there. Businesses that would be subject to these unusual taxes, and the consequent double taxation of some of their owners, could very well decide not to locate in the capital. But the owners of such businesses that have already located in the District have an incentive to remain. Should a significant portion of their personal income be derived from a District-taxed franchise, residence would entitle them to subtract

---

23. Under federal tax law, owners of S corporations, limited to a maximum of thirty-five stockholders and one class of stock, are taxed on their share of the S corporation income, but the corporation itself is not taxed, thus allowing investors to avoid the double taxation of corporate income while retaining limited liability and other privileges of incorporation.

franchise-derived income from their taxable income, which could be a significant adjustment.

The differing tax treatment of S corporations by the District and the federal government places an extra burden on residents subject to District personal income tax who are shareholders and who dispose of the corporations' stock. The cost bases used in calculating capital gains on the S corporation stock will be adjusted by the shareholder's personal income tax payment at the federal level but not at the District level. Thus a District-based S corporation shareholder who also resides in the District must keep two sets of records, one for each level of taxation.

FEDERAL ITEMIZED DEDUCTIONS AND DISTRICT ADJUSTMENTS. All federal itemized deductions (other than state and local income taxes and those expenses incurred while a taxpayer is not a resident of the District) are permissible deductions on the District return. Granting a deduction for state income taxes is unusual and would be tantamount to a significant rate reduction.[24] Income tax payments for fiscal 1994, occurring mostly in calendar year 1994, totaled $651 million, just over 9 percent of the total 1994 taxable income of $7.181 billion. A 9 percent reduction in taxable income would produce a reduction in revenue of roughly the same percentage.

Conformity with the Federal Personal Income Tax

A significant feature of any state or city personal income tax is the extent of its conformity to the provisions and rules of the federal tax code. The Advisory Commission on Intergovernmental Relations distinguishes four levels of conformity.[25]

—No conformity. The tax forms in five states—Alabama, Arkansas, Mississippi, New Jersey, and Pennsylvania—are worked out entirely separately from the federal form.

—Adjusted gross income. The federal AGI is a starting point for the calculation of tax liability in twenty-six states and the District. The states

24. Six income taxing states do allow state income taxes to be deducted; thirty-one do not. The rest of the states either do not tax income, tax only interest and dividends, or use the federal taxable income or federal liability. Using the federal taxable income or liability does imply granting a deduction for state income tax. ACIR, *Significant Features*, vol. 1, table 18.

25. ACIR, *Significant Features*, vol. 1, table 16.

are Arizona, California, Connecticut, Delaware, Georgia, Illinois, Indiana, Iowa, Kansas, Kentucky, Louisiana, Maine, Maryland, Massachusetts, Michigan, Missouri, Montana, Nebraska, New Mexico, New York, Ohio, Oklahoma, Oregon, Virginia, West Virginia, and Wisconsin.

—Federal taxable income. Six states—Colorado, Hawaii, Idaho, Minnesota, North Carolina, and Utah—allow the federal deductions and exemptions and calculate their tax based on the federal taxable income.

—Federal tax liability. Three states—North Dakota, Rhode Island, and Vermont—figure their tax as a percentage of the amount of tax paid to the federal government. Like the District, each has a population of less than 1 million.

States basing their taxes on the federal AGI or federal taxable income can make alterations in the starting point before proceeding with the calculation of tax. North Dakota, Rhode Island, and Vermont, the states conforming to federal liability, and South Carolina make no alterations in the federal exclusions and adjustments. South Carolina imposes its own exemption amounts and its own brackets and rates. Colorado and Minnesota, which use the federal taxable income base, have minor differences from the federal form in their treatment of pensions and social security benefits. The benefit for states that conform with federal taxable income and particularly the federal tax liability is that the tax form is less complicated, saving their taxpayers' time and effort and improving compliance.

Simplifying the District's Personal Income Tax Structure

Like Virginia and Maryland and many other states that base their income taxes on the federal AGI, the District uses additions and subtractions to calculate its own separate adjusted gross income, which is unnecessarily burdensome and, for the self-employed, actually unfair. These anomalies could be reduced and conformity with the federal form increased through relatively easy changes in the District tax laws.

GREATER CONFORMITY WITH FEDERAL AGI. Conformity with the federal AGI is the most common type of state income tax conformity and the one to which Americans are most accustomed. Some simplifications in additions, subtractions, and deductions and exemptions might improve compliance, ease administration, and lift some of the financial burden from District taxpayers.

In terms of additions, because federal adjustments amount to 1 percent of adjusted gross income for the country as a whole, eliminating the need for District residents to add back federal adjustments to achieve District AGI would thus cut about 1 percent from the District's income tax revenue.[26] The benefits would include equal treatment for the self-employed and greater competitiveness with Maryland and Virginia, both of which let the federal adjustments stand. This would mean that the District, like the federal government, would not tax IRA and Keogh contributions but would tax withdrawals from the plans. District taxpayers would no longer need to keep separate federal and District records for all such plans.

One addition all but the District, Indiana, and Utah make to federal adjusted gross income is the interest earned on other states' municipal bonds. For Maryland this addition amounts to 0.3 percent of the state AGI and tends to be concentrated among taxpayers in the highest brackets.[27] It seems safe to assume, then, that taxing this interest would add about 0.5 percent to the District's personal income tax revenues. This addition would cut in half the loss stemming from the restoration of federal adjustments.

Subtractions to the federal AGI could also be adjusted. The District, like the states generally, does not tax interest on U.S. savings bonds and other federal obligations. Taxing this income would boost revenues by perhaps 0.8 percent.[28] The unlikelihood of the District's becoming an exception to those jurisdictions that are subsidizing federal debt makes this a theoretical rather than a practical option.

For deductions and exemptions to the federal AGI there are more alternatives. The District's standard deduction of $2,000 for a single head of household and for a couple married and filing jointly, $1,000 each for those married and filing separately and for singles, and a $1,370 personal exemption are well within the range established by state income tax allowances. But the bottom fifth of the District's income distribution pays a greater percentage of its income in income tax than the bottom fifth of any other state, and more than twice the national average.[29] The average

26. Internal Revenue Service, *Statistics of Income Bulletin*, vol. 15 (Spring 1996), table 1.

27. The State of Maryland annually provides a complete breakdown of the additions and subtractions. In fiscal year 1993 its taxpayers earned $210,783 on the obligations of other states. Their total AGI was $77 billion. See *Statistics of Income, FY 1993* (1995), pp. 19, 26.

28. Maryland taxpayers earned $584 million from U.S. obligations in 1993.

29. Ettlinger and others, *Who Pays?*

federal AGI in the District in 1994 was $37,877 and the median was $23,100, indicating some very high-income filers. An increase in the exemption or the deduction amounts might be a good policy.

Increasing the allowances to match those at the federal level, which would mean tripling the deduction and doubling the exemption, would cost the District just over 10 percent of its income tax revenue, more than $60 million.[30] Smaller increases would produce smaller losses. Were the personal exemption increased by $1,000 to just under the federal level of $2,500, a loss of $25 million would result, about 4 percent of the District's personal income tax revenue. Were the standard deduction doubled to $2,000 for singles and $4,000 for married filers and heads of households, it would still be well short of the federal amount and would cost $17 million, about 3 percent of revenue. Such changes would constitute a tax reduction for all payers and would increase progressivity. Assuming adoption of the federal allowances, the income tax burden on the bottom fifth of taxpayers would decrease from 3.4 percent to 1.2 percent, just below the national average.

ADVANTAGES OF FEDERAL TAXABLE INCOME CONFORMITY. Greater simplification would result from basing the District's income tax calculation on the federal taxable income instead of the federal AGI. Although consulting a tax table would still be required, the tax form would become much less formidable. As with greater conformity with federal AGI, greater conformity with federal taxable income would make the District's tax more progressive as a result of retaining federal deductions and exemptions. Using the District's own system of rates would allow officials to adjust the degree of progressivity. It would also protect the District from revenue swings resulting from federal rate changes.

Proposal: Conformity with the Federal Liability

North Dakota, Rhode Island, and Vermont, three of the nation's smallest states, with an average population of 738,000 (the District's population, again, is 559,000), use federal income tax liability as the base for their personal income taxes. They impose rates of 14 percent, 27.5 percent, and 25 percent, respectively, on federal liability. Their forms are

---

30. These percentage estimates are based on the 1993 income distribution of income tax payers that was provided by the District's Department of Finance and Revenue. The dollar amounts are updated based on the total revenue in 1995.

Table 4-5. *District of Columbia Income Tax Rates Based on Federal Liability*

Percent unless otherwise specified

Federal adjusted gross income (dollars)	Number of filers	Current effective personal income tax rate	Effective rate at 28 percent federal liability	Change in effective rate
Less than 15,000	92,034	0.44	−0.11	−0.56
15,000–30,000	86,852	4.03	2.12	−1.91
30,000–50,000	52,067	5.42	3.34	−2.08
50,000–75,000	24,609	6.08	4.10	−1.98
75,000–100,000	10,504	6.41	4.64	−1.77
100,000–200,000	10,917	6.73	5.29	−1.44
More than 200,000	4,396	7.30	7.28	−0.02

Source: Internal Revenue Service, *Statistics of Income Bulletin*, vol. 15 (Spring 1996), p. 115.

easier to fill out and easier to check than those using other bases. Compliance is improved, administration eased.

This would alter the District's distribution of tax burdens. The federal structure is highly progressive. In the District in 1995, federal filers with incomes between $15,000 and $30,000 paid 8.2 percent of their income to the federal government and 4.03 percent to the District in income taxes.[31] At this level the federal liability was, then, twice the District's. For filers with incomes of more than $200,000, the federal effective rate of 28.1 percent was 3.85 times the District's effective rate of 7.3 percent. For the District personal income tax to generate the same revenue, the tax rate would have to be set to 39.2 percent of federal liability. The effective burden on filers with incomes greater than $200,000 would grow to 10.42 percent, an increase of more than 3 percentage points, which is not feasible.

Our proposal would both simplify and cut the District's personal income tax. District taxpayers' income tax liability should be set at 28 percent of their federal liability, with current income tax credits retained, which would produce a reduction in District income tax liability for all income levels (table 4-5). On the basis of 1994 earnings, this tax change would cost $194 million: revenues would be reduced by 30 percent, from $651 million to $457 million. Income taxes would be simplified and virtually every District resident would pay less.

31. IRS, *Statistics of Income Bulletin*, vol. 15 (Spring 1996); "District of Columbia Master Income Tax File, 1994"; and author's calculations.

Under the proposal the average effective rate in the District would fall from 5.15 percent to 4.33 percent, with the largest drop occurring for federal AGIs of $30,000–$50,000 (from 5.42 percent to 3.34 percent), and those with AGIs from $100,000 to $200,000 would see their effective rate reduced from 6.73 percent to 5.29 percent. Taxpayers with incomes greater than $200,000 would receive only marginal reductions in their liability. The change would remove from the District's income tax rolls those residents without federal income tax liability, who may represent 45 percent of current taxpayers.[32]

Such a cut in personal income taxes and the accompanying simplification of the form might help slow the capital's population losses and the consequent shrinkage of the tax base. Between 1985 and 1990 the District experienced net out-migrations of 14.8 percent for households with incomes between $40,000 and $49,900 and 13.1 percent for those with incomes between $60,000 and $74,900, losses that continued into the 1990s.[33] These are the income categories that would benefit most from the proposed change to using federal liability as a base.

The strongest reason for basing the District's tax liability on the federal liability is that the Internal Revenue Service could administer it. Between 1972 and 1990 federal law offered, free of charge, the administrative services of the Internal Revenue Service to collect states' income taxes if their tax structures conformed closely enough with the federal tax structure, which essentially meant basing state taxes on federal taxable income or federal liability.[34] During this period no state availed itself of the offer.

Although the law has been rescinded, its erstwhile existence makes it clear that the federal government believes it has the capacity to administer the District's personal income tax. IRS administration and enforcement would be eased considerably by basing the District's personal income tax on federal liability, along with allowing the agency a lead role in designing the forms. Even so, it might require as long as two years to work out the administrative details and computer programming. And one would hope that, as under the former law, the IRS would be directed not to charge for this service.[35] Given the District government's budget crisis,

32. See tables 7-2 and 7-3.

33. George Grier, "Comings and Goings in the Washington Area, Report No. 1: Impact of Migration on the D.C. Population," Greater Washington Research Center, April 1994, figure 9.

34. P.L. 92-512, Title II, Oct. 20, 1972; repealed by P.L. 101-508, Title XI, Nov. 5, 1990.

35. However, the State of New York charges a fee to the City of New York for a similar service.

personnel shortages, and the documented deficiencies at the Department of Finance and Revenue, federal administration would reduce costs and increase the efficiency and fairness of the District's tax system.

Nonresident Income Taxation

All state income taxes apply to nonresident income and credit the income tax paid to other states. Except for Washington, D.C., and Baltimore, every American city that imposes an income tax on its residents imposes a nonresident income tax as well. All are flat rate and based on wages and other compensation earned within the city. Because the tax is withheld from paychecks, it generally does not burden wage earners with additional paperwork. But the District is prohibited from taxing nonresident income by section 602(a)(5) of the District of Columbia Self-Government and Governmental Reorganization Act (the Home Rule Act). Were the District to impose a nonresident income tax at a typical city rate of 2 percent, $361 million would be generated.

City nonresident income taxes are justified on the grounds of fairness. First, nonresident workers in a city spend a significant amount of time there and use city services. Although schools and social services are provided specifically for residents, many other services—police protection, firefighting, street and bridge maintenance, trash collection—are provided in unmeasured amounts to residents, commuters, and visitors alike. Provision of these services deserves some reimbursement.

Second, a viable central city benefits the metropolitan area surrounding it. The urban economy crosses county and often state lines, with economic growth spread throughout. The central city houses the higher-paying jobs in most metropolitan economies. In a recent survey of suburban Americans in the largest metropolitan areas, half of the household had at least one member working in the city; two-thirds depended on the city for major medical care; and four out of ten had members attending or planning to attend a city-based institution of higher education.[36]

Third, central cities usually have to care for a disproportionate share of their metropolitan area's poor. Many city services, including education and protection from crime and fire, are more expensive to provide to a

36. Joseph Persky, Elliott Sklar, and Wim Wiewel, *Does America Need Cities?* (Washington, Economic Policy Institute, 1991).

poor population.[37] Nonresident income taxes work to equalize across a metropolitan area the burden of paying for these services.

All these arguments apply to the District of Columbia. According to the 1990 census 67.6 percent of Washington's workers live outside the District. But the costs of services flowing to these 490,000 commuters are real and are borne solely by Washington's residents and businesses. In addition, Washington's suburbs benefit financially from the city's proximity. A recent study has shown that for every dollar of increased economic performance in the District's private sector, the suburbs will gain from $1.44 to $1.57.[38] Meanwhile the District's poverty rate is 16.9 percent, but in the metropolitan area the rate is 6.4 percent.

Of course, the District might distribute part of its tax burden to nonresidents indirectly through business taxes. This has been attempted, but the burden is distributed unfairly. In addition, any tax increases must be carefully limited because businesses can choose to leave. Besides, the business tax base is restricted to the private, taxable sector, which constitutes only half of the economy.[39] And, of course, the District's business income taxation cannot by law include the lucrative professional partnerships. Finally, although commercial property has been taxed at a higher rate than residential property since 1979, reflecting another attempt to tax the broader business community, the resulting higher costs for locating in Washington might very well discourage businesses from moving there and could, again, contribute to the flight of resident businesses to the suburbs.[40]

Under certain conditions, taxing the earnings of nonresidents does not affect location or work decisions. If a person earns income in one state, pays an income tax to that state, and his or her state of residence credits the payment made to the state where the income is earned, the individual's total tax payment will not be altered. Because the employee bears

37. Helen F. Ladd and John Yinger, *America's Ailing Cities: Fiscal Health and the Design of Urban Policy* (Johns Hopkins University Press, 1989).

38. Stephen S. Fuller, "The Economy of the District of Columbia and Its Impact on the Washington Area and Its Suburbs," Center for Regional Analysis, George Mason University, December 1996.

39. Author's calculations based on employment shares. Government is 37 percent. In addition, as much as 19 percent of the private employment may be nonprofit (aggregating the health services, universities, membership organizations, and social services, which amount to 45.5 percent of the service sector's 41.8 share of District employment). See Fuller, "Economy of the District of Columbia," pp. 7, 8, for employment shares.

40. Henry W. Herzog and Alan M. Schlottman, eds., *Industry Location and Public Policy* (University of Tennessee Press, 1991).

no extra financial burden, none can be passed along to the employer. There should be no distortion of business activity; the economic transfer takes place between the states. All states credit the income tax paid to other states. Without such crediting, commuter taxes could have distortionary consequences.[41] Should a nonresident income tax be enacted in the District, payments must be creditable against commuters' resident income tax.

A Nonresident Income Tax for the District?

This study has emphasized that the District of Columbia functions like a city; but as a city without a state, it levies a state-type income tax on its residents. In considering whether it should levy a tax on nonresident income and, if so, how to structure such a tax, it is useful to examine issues peculiar to the taxation of nonresident income by both states and cities.

All states that have income taxes tax nonresident income. Like the city nonresident income tax, the state taxes are based on earned compensation. Fifteen states and the District of Columbia have reciprocity agreements that allow residents to pay income tax only to their state of residence.[42] This eases tax administration and does not represent a loss in a state's income if its residents' income earned in other states approximates and offsets nonresidents' local earnings. The District has such a reciprocity arrangement with Maryland and Virginia. In Washington's case, however, the income earned by nonresidents exceeds residents' earnings outside the city by $19.9 billion.[43] Taxing metropolitan area residents where they live instead of where they work creates a revenue boon for Maryland and Virginia and a revenue disaster for the District.

---

41. Taxes borne by commuters can be passed along to employers through a demand for higher compensation, and losses of jobs in the city doing the taxing could be expected. See for example Robert P. Inman and others, "Philadelphia's Fiscal Management of Economic Transition," pp. 98–115 in Thomas F. Luce and Anita A. Summers, eds., *Local Fiscal Issues in the Philadelphia Metropolitan Area* (University of Pennsylvania Press, 1987).

42. Commerce Clearing House, *State Tax Guide* (1996), pp. 3532, 3533.

43. The Bureau of Economic Analysis reports that $33.558 billion was earned in the District in 1994. It reconciles this figure with a reported earnings by place of residence of $11.509 billion by deducting $2.149 billion in personal contributions for social insurance and $19.900 billion in adjustment for residence—the amount by which nonresidents' earnings in the District exceed residents' earnings outside it.

Although states do credit the income tax paid to a state of employment when no reciprocity agreement is in place, no state offers refunds to its residents when their nonresident income tax payment exceeds the income tax they would normally pay in their state of residence. Were the District's nonresident income tax rates set higher than Maryland's or Virginia's, commuters into the District would take home less pay than their counterparts earning the same salary who live and work in the suburbs. The distortions of business location and workers' choice of employment location would result.

Although all states imposing income taxes credit residents for income tax paid to other states, they vary in their treatment of nonresident taxes paid to cities. New York and New Jersey credit payments to Philadelphia and other local jurisdictions that impose nonresident income taxes, but Delaware does not. Neither are Pennsylvania residents outside Philadelphia compensated for payments to the city. It would be essential that Maryland and Virginia expressly credit a local income tax payment to the District, which they presently do not.

As opposed to the typical state nonresident income tax, a city nonresident tax tends not to require filing and to have a liability that is a straight percentage of earned income. Again, to avoid adverse consequences, Maryland and Virginia would have to credit income tax payments to the District against the state income tax liability they impose.

Estimating Revenue from a District Commuter Tax

To estimate the revenue associated with a possible District tax on commuters, it is necessary to know how many commuters there are and what their incomes are. Washington was home to 304,428 workers in 1990 (table 4-6). Of these, 236,734 worked in the city and 67,694 outside. The total number of people working in the District was 730,448.

The distribution of commuters' incomes in the District must be derived. As table 4-6 shows, the ratio by which the number of workers in the District exceeds the number of residents is smaller in the lower-earnings categories.[44] Table 4-7 shows the number of commuters in each income class. The classes have been aggregated to conform with Internal Revenue Service data on the distribution of District residents' income.

---

44. Any assumption of an even spread of commuters over the income categories would produce an underestimate of potential revenue to the District, to the extent that a progressive income tax is being considered.

Table 4-6. *Distribution of Income of District of Columbia Residents and Workers, 1990*

Earnings (thousands)	District workers who live in District	All District workers	Ratio of all workers to resident workers
No earnings[a]	11,684	16,475	6.54
Less than 5	28,026	37,875	1.35
5–10	26,286	40,804	1.55
10–15	32,644	53,087	1.63
15–20	42,121	77,613	1.84
20–25	39,134	87,919	2.25
25–30	29,654	78,784	2.66
30–35	21,787	67,882	3.12
35–50	37,441	134,123	3.58
50–75	21,644	90,839	4.20
More than 75	14,007	45,047	3.22
Total	304,428	730,448	2.40

Source: Bureau of the Census, *1990 Census Transportation Planning Package.*
a. Because this category is based on census rather than tax return data, people who identified themselves as workers but received no pay are included. This group includes volunteers and trainees.

The aggregated figures are shown in the first and third columns. In each income group the number of commuters into the District is equal to the total number of District workers adjusted for the number of reverse commuters. Assuming the commuters from the District have the same income distribution as District residents in general, the 67,694 commuters from the District (column 4) are allocated by income categories. The ratio of commuters to resident workers is shown in column 6. Table 4-8 presents the wages of District residents by federal AGI classes corresponding to the earnings classes in table 4-7 and computes commuters'

Table 4-7. *District of Columbia Residents and Workers, Reverse and Conventional Commuters, by Income, 1990*

Earnings (thousands)	Resident workers	Percent by class	District workers	Reverse commuters[a]	Conventional commuters[b]	Ratios of commuters to residents[c]
Less than 15	98,640	32.4	148,241	21,934	71,535	0.725
15–30	110,909	36.4	244,316	24,662	158,069	1.425
30–50	59,228	19.5	202,005	13,170	155,947	2.633
50–75	21,644	7.1	90,839	4,813	74,008	3.419
More than 75	14,007	4.6	45,047	3,115	34,155	2.438
Totals	304,428	100.0	730,448	67,694	493,714	...

Sources: Author's calculations; and Bureau of the Census, *1990 Census Transportation Planning Package.*
a. Percent in column 2 times 67,694.
b. Number in column 3 minus number in column 1 plus number in column 4.
c. Column 5 divided by column 1.

Table 4-8. *District of Columbia Resident Wages and Computed Commuter Wages, 1994*

Federal adjusted gross income (thousands)	Resident wages (thousands)	Ratio of commuters to residents	Commuter wages
Less than 15	564,698	0.725	409,527
15–30	1,587,452	1.425	2,262,458
30–50	1,657,135	2.633	4,363,233
50–75	1,175,074	3.419	4,017,966
More than 75	2,571,830	2.438	6,271,211
Totals	7,556,189	. . .	17,324,395

Source: IRS, *Statistics of Income Bulletin* (Spring 1996), p. 115.

total wages by federal AGI class by showing their comparative numbers at each level of income.[45]

Table 4-9 presents the hypothetical revenues generated by imposing a nonresident income tax, at the Virginia, Maryland, and District effective rates, on commuters.[46] Although the revenues have been estimated at all three sets of rates, as discussed previously, the Virginia rates represent

Table 4-9. *Estimated Revenue from Three Hypothetical District of Columbia Nonresident Income Tax Rates*

Thousands of dollars unless otherwise specified

Federal adjusted gross income class	Commuter wages	Rate 1		Rate 2		Rate 3	
		Virginia tax rates	Portion due District	Maryland tax rates	Portion due District	District tax rate	Portion due District
Less than 15	409,527	2.83	11,581	4.27	17,500	1.27	5,221
15–30	2,262,461	4.12	93,286	5.26	119,051	4.51	102,025
30–50	4,363,233	4.64	202,400	5.85	255,253	5.90	257,645
50–75	4,017,959	4.92	197,684	5.95	239,024	6.54	262,735
More than 75	6,271,149	5.38	337,413	6.08	381,179	7.41	464,404
Total	17,324,329	. . .	842,364	. . .	1,012,008	. . .	1,92,029

Source: Author's calculations.

45. The Internal Revenue Service *Statistics of Income Bulletin* provides distribution of income by state and for the District. In addition to gross income, the data include total wage income and other categories of income.

46. The Virginia Department of Taxation publishes in its annual report an effective income tax rate equal to liability divided by Virginia adjusted gross income. These rates are shown in column 2 of table 4-9. The Treasury of the State of Maryland (*Statistics of Income Supplement*) and the District's Department of Finance and Revenue (unpublished computer run) also collect income tax distribution data. Tax payments as a percentage of state AGI were computed for the District and Maryland from these reports and are also shown in table 4-9.

Table 4-10. *Washington Metropolitan Area Wages and Salaries and Proprietary Income, 1994*

Billions of dollars

Item	Wages and salaries	Proprietary income
Earned in metropolitan area	8.307	. . .
Earned by residents of metropolitan area	. . .	8.144
Earned in District	2.853	. . .
Earned by residents of District	. . .	1.999

Source: Bureau of Economic Analysis, Regional Economic Information System, http://www.lib.virginia.edu/socsci/reis/reit2.html.

the maximum rates the District could impose on nonresidents without risking the loss of businesses and workers to the suburbs.

The commuter earnings in table 4-9 have been associated with an AGI class in order to apply the appropriate income tax rate for that class against the District earnings. Family income will in some cases increase the AGI class and thus the effective tax rate (or bracket). Without a reciprocity agreement, states maintain the right to tax the income of nonresidents who earn income within their borders.[47] When states impose an income tax on nonresidents, they typically ask the filer to report all income, calculate adjustments, and compute a liability based on this total.[48] Then a ratio equal to income earned in the taxing state divided by total AGI is multiplied by the liability to produce the amount due. Because these data are not available, earned income is used as a conservative proxy for AGI and the associated effective rate. This calculation produces an estimated $842 million in nonresident income tax revenue based on wages earned in the District, applying Virginia's rates.

To this estimate one needs to add the distribution of nonwage income, which is harder to estimate precisely. Table 4-10 reports $8.144 billion in "proprietary income" earned in the District and the counties surrounding it in 1994.[49] Levying a state-type income tax, the District would tax such income were it earned within the city. Because proprietary income

47. Emil M. Sundley and Gail R. Wilensky, "Personal Income Tax," pp. 67–106 in *Technical Aspects of the District's Tax System: Studies and Papers Prepared for the District of Columbia Tax Revision Commission*, House of Representatives, 95 Cong. 2 sess (GPO, 1978).

48. We studied state nonresident tax forms from Delaware, New York, and South Carolina. All used this method. The District, Maryland, and Virginia also use such a system for individuals who reside in a state not participating in reciprocity.

49. This represents earnings from partnerships and self-employment and is reported by residence of the earner.

is derived from commercial activity, it is reasonable to suppose the location of its earning is divided in the same proportions as wages. With 34.4 percent of the area's wages paid in the District, a reasonable estimate of proprietary income derived from the District is 34.4 percent of $8.144 billion, or $2.798 billion. This exceeds by $798 million the amount reported by District residents and would represent an additional 4.6 percent in District-based earnings paid by commuters (over the wage income estimated above to be $17.423 billion), which increases the revenue estimate for the District by 4.6 percent as well.[50]

The estimated fillip from additional earned income comes to $39 million, bringing the total revenue up to $881 million at the Virginia rates.[51]

Revenue Associated with a Flat, City-Type Nonresident Income Tax

Across the country, city nonresident income tax rates range from 0.5 percent to 4.3125 percent, with most falling between 1 percent and 2 percent. In the District, commuters have been estimated to earn $17.234 billion in wages and $797 million in earned income for a total earned compensation of $18.031 billion. Taxed at a flat rate of 1 percent, a city-type nonresident income tax would yield $180 million. At 2 percent it would yield $361 million, and at 3 percent, $540 million.

Revenue Loss from District Residents Who Work Elsewhere

In 1990 about 22.2 percent of District residents worked outside the District. The District personal income tax revenue for fiscal year 1994 was $651 million. On average, District taxable income is about 95 percent of wages, so that almost all revenue will be lost from this segment of the base.[52] About $144 million in revenue can be attributed to these reverse commuters. The District's net gain from taxing workers where they work rather than where they live would be $881 less $144 million,

---

50. This estimate is probably conservative because proprietary income is likely concentrated among workers with higher incomes and higher tax rates.

51. For the Maryland and District rates shown in table 4-9, the estimated additional earned income would be $1.06 billion and $1.14 billion, respectively.

52. "District of Columbia Income Tax Master File, 1994," shows a total District taxable income for 1994 of $7,181,913,093. IRS, *Statistics of Income Bulletin* (Spring 1996), p. 115, shows total wages paid to District residents of $7,556,189,000.

or $737 million, assuming the progressive type of state nonresident income tax at Virginia's tax rates.

We assume that if the federal government were to allow the District to levy a city-type nonresident earnings tax, it would also ensure that Maryland and Virginia did not consider it a violation of reciprocity.[53] Philadelphia taxes New Jersey commuters, for example, but Pennsylvania and New Jersey maintain a reciprocity agreement for the rest of their residents who work in the other state. Lexington and Louisville tax commuters' earned compensation, but Kentucky maintains income tax reciprocity with seven states, including Virginia.

Revenue Gains to Maryland and Virginia under the Present Prohibition

Finally, in estimating the revenues to be gained by the District from a tax on nonresident income, we have also estimated the revenue value to Maryland and Virginia from the present prohibition. As Table 4-9 demonstrates, taxing commuters on District wages at Maryland rates would produce $1.012 billion in tax revenue.[54] Adjusting for nonwage earned income would increase the amount to $1.059 billion.[55] According to census figures, 58.4 percent of commuters into the District are residents of Maryland and subject to the Maryland income tax. Assuming commuters' incomes are divided between Maryland and Virginia in the same proportions as their numbers, Maryland and its counties gained $619 million from taxes on commuters' incomes in 1994. Virginia imposes its income tax on the 41.6 percent of commuters into the District who live in Virginia. The state should therefore derive $366 million in income tax revenue from its residents' Washington-based earnings. The estimation also calculates that the District derives $144 million of its income tax earnings from residents who work outside its borders. Were the District to levy a state-type tax on nonresidents, it would discontinue its participation in the reciprocity agreement.

53. Were the agreement deemed to be violated, the $144 million would have to be subtracted from the revenues projected earlier.

54. State plus local rates.

55. The Bureau of Economic Analysis has an income category called proprietary income, composed of self-employment earnings and partnership income. The BEA allocates these earnings by residence, but they would be subject to income tax in the state of earnings were reciprocity not in effect.

CHAPTER 5

Business and Sales Taxes

THE DISTRICT OF COLUMBIA imposes a variety of taxes on business activity and sales. Three general taxes are levied on businesses and together contributed $222 million to the general fund in fiscal year 1995. The corporate franchise (or income) tax, levied on the net income of all corporations, including banks, doing business in the District contributed $121 million from about 20,000 taxpayers. The unincorporated business tax, levied on the net income tax of proprietorships and nonprofessional partnerships, contributed $39 million from only 8,000 businesses. The personal property tax is levied on all tangible property, except inventories, used for business. A common tax in the region, although levied on slightly different bases and at varying rates, it yielded $61 million from a rate of $3.40 per $100 of assessed value. The District also imposes gross receipts taxes on selected industries—public utilities (gas, electric, and telephone companies), long-distance telephone connections (the toll telecommunications), and insurance. Together these contributed $210 million in fiscal 1995. Finally, the general sales tax, at $486 million, is the District's third largest tax. About one-half the revenue comes from general merchandise and services, one-quarter from restaurants, and one-fifth from hotels.

Business Taxes

The District's two business income taxes have underperformed even a disappointing District economy (table 5-1). The revenues from these taxes are suspect because they lurch up and down annually, out of step with the other taxes and the local economy. The District's Department of Finance and Revenue was unable to provide records of annual collections net of audits, penalties, or payments rightly attributed to other tax

Table 5-1. *District of Columbia Corporate and Unincorporated Business Franchise Tax Revenues, 1989–95*

Thousands of dollars unless otherwise specified

Year	Corporate tax	Change (percent)	Unincorporated business tax	Change (percent)	All taxes[a]	Change (percent)
1989	125,144	...	31,270	...	2,204,598	...
1990	112,273	−10.3	27,468	−12.2	2,279,127	3.4
1991	102,767	−8.5	30,512	11.1	2,371,732	4.1
1992	62,751	−38.9	25,126	−17.7	2,384,300	0.5
1993	105,038	67.4	35,960	43.1	2,557,852	7.3
1994	113,981	8.5	36,227	0.7	2,470,053	−3.4
1995	121,407	6.5	39,272	8.4	2,391,041	−3.2

Source: *District of Columbia Comprehensive Annual Financial Report, September 30, 1995* (hereafter *CAFR, 1995*); District of Columbia Department of Finance and Revenue, *District of Columbia Tax Facts, Fiscal Years 1993 and 1994* (1995); and District of Columbia Department of Finance and Revenue, *A Comparison of Tax Rates and Burdens in the Washington, D.C. Metropolitan Area* (1995).

a. Changes in total tax revenue were affected by several rate changes. Between 1989 and 1990 the homeowner rate on the property tax was decreased and the commercial rate was increased. The general sales tax increased from 6 percent to 7 percent late in fiscal 1994, but was lowered to 5.75 percent in October 1994. Between fiscal 1990 and 1991, the excise tax rate on electricity, gas, and telephone gross receipts increased from 6.7 percent to 9.7 percent. The rates climbed to 10 percent for fiscal 1994. Increases in the corporate and unincorporated business franchise tax rates are listed in the text.

years. Thus revenues reported by the department and represented here do not indicate present business activity and are of limited value to policymakers who need to relate tax collections to local economic activity. A rate increase of 0.25 percentage point (10.25 percent to 10.50 percent) in 1990, and decreases of 0.25 percentage point in 1993 and 0.275 in 1994 (10.5 percent to 10.25 percent to 9.975 percent) do not help explain the dramatic turns these revenues seem to have taken.[1] The poor revenue collection system has led the District's independent auditor to issue a qualified opinion, because of "business tax information system inadequacies," with respect to the revenue figures reported in the District's 1995 financial report and again for 1996.[2]

The Corporate Franchise Tax

State corporate income taxes accounted for 6.9 percent of state tax revenues in fiscal year 1993. This portion has declined somewhat in the past decade and a half, after reaching a postwar high in 1979 and 1980

1. These rates are inclusive of the surtax. District of Columbia Department of Finance and Revenue (DFR), *District of Columbia Tax Facts, Fiscal Years 1993 and 1994* (1995).

2. KPMG Peat Marwick, "Independent Auditors' Report," in *District of Columbia Comprehensive Annual Financial Report, September 30, 1995*, p. 18 (hereafter *CAFR, 1995*); and *CAFR, 1996*.

with 9.7 percent.[3] The District's corporate franchise tax produced 5.1 percent of tax revenues in fiscal 1995. Since 1983 the tax has represented more than 6 percent of District tax revenues only twice, in 1986 when it was 6.6 percent and in 1987 when it was 7 percent. Only four states impose rates higher than the District's 1995 rate of 9.975 percent.[4] Virginia's rate is 6 percent and Maryland's 7 percent.

The District's corporate and unincorporated franchise taxes are levied on business net income, or profits.[5] They are modeled on the federal corporate income tax. The tax base begins with gross receipts or income. Payers deduct from that all the expenses incurred in connection with doing business, including interest on debt, the costs of meals and entertainment, taxes paid to other governments inside and outside the United States, and, of course, the depreciation of capital and outlays for research and development. Capital losses can be deducted only insofar as they offset capital gains. These deductions can be applied in the year the losses are incurred or in preceding or succeeding tax years. Net operating losses can be applied against income as well, and can be carried back and forward. The intention of this flexibility across time is to not penalize those firms with more volatile profits.[6]

As with the personal income tax, the bases for states' corporate income tax vary from the federal base and differ across states. Often preferences are offered to certain kinds of businesses. For example, state policymakers set depreciation schedules for different kinds of capital to benefit certain industries, depending on the economic structure and policy goals

---

3. Patrick Fleenor, ed., *Facts and Figures on Government Finance*, 30th ed. (Washington: Tax Foundation, 1995), p. 184. The personal income tax has enabled less reliance on the corporate income tax because the income tax share of state tax revenues increased from 26.1 percent in 1979 to 31.9 percent in 1993.

4. Two, Iowa and North Dakota, impose a progressive structure with maximum rates of 12.0 percent and 10.5 percent imposed on corporate income greater than $250,000 and $50,000, respectively. Connecticut and Pennsylvania impose flat rates of 11.5 percent and 10.99 percent.

5. Economists do not agree on the incidence of the corporate income tax—whether it is ultimately paid by the owners of capital, passed on to customers, or passed back to workers, and to what extent. See Joseph A. Pechman, *Federal Tax Policy* (Brookings, 1987), pp. 135–40.

6. Pechman, *Federal Tax Policy*, chap. 5. The past fifteen years have seen many changes in the federal corporate income tax. The definition of taxable corporate income has changed with changes in the treatment of (accelerated) depreciation, taxation of foreign earnings, completed contract accounting for defense contractors, and interest and other expenses. There have also been changes in the length of time over which losses can be carried forward. In addition, federal tax reform has eliminated and then reintroduced a federal minimum tax for corporations.

of the state. States also differ in the number of years net operating losses can be carried back and carried forward. The District is relatively generous, matching the federal allowance of three years back and fifteen forward.[7]

Starting from the federal base, the District requires the addition of foreign and local business income taxes and federally exempt foreign interest, and allows the subtraction of interest and dividends on federal securities and state income tax refunds. All states and the District also provide some credits against corporate income liability. The District's credits include 50 percent of wages and workers' compensation insurance payments and below-rent subsidies to child care centers as long as these expenditures are made within certified economic development zones. Maryland also offers an enterprise zone credit. Like many states, Virginia provides a long list of credits against corporate income tax liability, including neighborhood assistance, enterprise zones, and a job tax credit for major business facilities.

After calculating net income, a corporation must determine the portion attributable to the District. Like forty-three states, the District uses an apportionment formula equal to the simple average of three factors: the fractions of property; payroll; and sales situated, paid for, or transacted in the District.[8] The District's tax auditing staff also report that an increasing number of corporations are attempting to carry losses from other activities and locations into the District to offset even the limited income allocated to the District. Indeed, the accounting flexibility involved with booking income (and losses) combined with the tax advantage of being able to carry losses forward to offset future income allows for an unhealthy latitude of negotiation during audits.

The District joins only six states in not recognizing federally defined S corporations as different from other corporations. S corporations, limited to a maximum of thirty-five stockholders and one class of stock, are not subject to federal corporate taxes. Instead, shareholders are taxed on their share of the S corporation income.[9] Such treatment allows investors

---

7. Twenty-two states and the District allow the full range. Twenty-four states and the City of New York allow no carrying backward of net operating losses. Commerce Clearing House, *State Tax Guide*, 10-106 (Chicago), p. 2573 (page updated December 31, 1996).

8. Advisory Commission on Intergovernmental Relations (ACIR), *Significant Features of Fiscal Federalism*, vol. 1: *Budget Processes and Tax Systems* (Washington, 1995), pp. 78–87.

9. Commerce Clearing House, *1996 U.S. Master Tax Guide* (Chicago, 1996), pp. 117–25.

to avoid the double taxation of corporate income, while retaining limited liability and other privileges of incorporation.[10] The District taxes S corporations as other corporations are taxed. So as not to double tax this income, it allows resident individuals to subtract S corporation distributed income from their federal base in calculating District taxable income for the personal income tax. But they must add back any deductions the federal income tax allows the S corporation to pass along to shareholders.

The differing tax treatment of S corporations by the District and the federal government poses a problem upon disposal of the stock. The cost bases used in calculating the capital gain will be adjusted by the shareholder's tax payment at the federal level but not at the District level because the shareholder does not pay an income tax to the District. Thus a shareholder in a District-based S corporation who also resides in the District must keep two sets of records, one for each level of taxation. Treating S corporations as the federal government treats them would eliminate this record-keeping burden. It would decrease the District's revenue from the corporate franchise tax but, to the extent shareholders are District residents, would increase revenue from the personal income tax. Further, if the District is to retain a corporate income tax, it is hard to imagine that it will be able to continue to ignore the growth of S corporations and the special tax treatment that states around the country are granting to limited liability companies.

The Unincorporated Franchise Tax

The District taxes unincorporated businesses at the same 9.975 percent rate that it taxes corporations, and net income is multiplied by an apportionment factor determined by the same formula applied in the corporate income tax calculation. It is intended to ensure that the business tax structure is neutral with respect to business form—corporate or noncorporate. The unincorporated business tax is peculiar to Washington and New York City (states and the federal government tax net income from unincorporated businesses as part of personal income). For New York City, where many of the partners in the major unincorporated businesses—investment banking, stock brokerage, law, accounting, ar-

---

10. The double taxation of income is created by the coexistence of the corporate and individual income taxes. Corporations may not deduct dividend payments, so that these distributions are an after-tax expense. Shareholders must include them in their taxable income under the individual income tax, so that they are taxed twice.

chitecture, and other professional firms—are not residents, the unincorporated business tax represents the exportation of a progressive tax burden, which partly compensates for the small, flat 0.45 percent non-resident income tax the city imposes.[11]

For the District of Columbia, however, such exportation is thwarted. In *Bishop v. District of Columbia,* handed down April 20, 1979, the District of Columbia Court of Appeals ruled that the unincorporated business tax, which the District Council voted to extend to professionals in 1975, was a tax on the income of nonresidents and therefore in violation of article 602 (a)(5) of the Home Rule Act, which disallows any tax on nonresident income. As a result the District now exempts professionals from taxation as unincorporated businesses.[12] Since the court's decision the District's unincorporated business tax has become in effect an income tax on proprietors and small businesses.[13] For District residents, this income is not taxed a second time, because income subject to the corporate (in the case of S corporations) or unincorporated business tax is subtracted from federal taxable income in calculating the District's personal income tax base. Were the unincorporated business tax eliminated, some part of its base would be added to the base of the District's personal income tax.

The exemption of professionals produced an associated change in incentives for choosing places to live. Between 1975 and 1979, professionals could avoid a second taxation on the same income only by residing in the District, where income subject to the District unincorporated franchise tax could be subtracted from taxable income. If they lived outside the District, a deduction for the franchise tax payment would be possible, but their net gain from business income would still be subject

11. ACIR, *Significant Features*, vol. 1, p. 72. New York City Department of Finance unincorporated income tax data for 1992 indicate that "about half of the tax revenue for which the residence of the taxpayer could be inferred went to suburban residents." See Dick Nitzer, "The NYC Economy: Strategies for Growth," statement prepared for the Panel on Tax Policy Conference held by New York City Comptroller Alan Hevesi, December 1996, p. 7.

12. A company must meet a two-part test for exemption: first, more than 80 percent of its gross income must be derived from personal services actually rendered by the individual or the members of the entity, and second, capital must not be a material income-producing factor. District of Columbia Department of Finance and Revenue, "1995 Unincorporated Business Franchise Tax Booklet," p. 1.

13. No characterization of unincorporated business taxpayers is published or made available in written form. Their characterization as small businesses is based on conversations with Department of Finance and Revenue officials.

to state and federal taxation. For this interval, professionals who commuted suffered taxation of income by two jurisdictions. Nonresident proprietors of businesses still subject to the unincorporated business tax continue to face this unusual burden, as do nonresident shareholders in District S corporations.

Selective Gross Receipts Taxes

The District imposes a flat 10 percent tax on the gross receipts of public utilities (gas, electric, and local telephone companies) and on telecommunications (long-distance carriers). In fiscal year 1995 the tax produced revenue of $131.0 million.[14] Maryland imposes a 2 percent tax on gross receipts of utilities, and Virginia a progressive rate of 1.125 percent on the first $100,000 of gross receipts and 2.3 percent on gross receipts in excess of $100,000. Receipts in the telecommunications industry are taxed at 2 percent in Maryland and 1 percent in Virginia. In fiscal 1995, revenues from the District telecommunications tax were $44.5 million. Insurance premiums generated in the District are subject to a 2.25 percent tax; in 1995 the tax generated $34.7 million.[15] The rate in Maryland is 2 percent. In Virginia the rate varies from 1 percent to 2.75 percent for insurance companies. Together the three selective gross receipts taxes produced $210.2 million for the District.

Although the tax rate on utilities' gross receipts is much higher in the District than in Maryland and Virginia, consumption-based taxes in Virginia counties raise the price of gas and electricity there. Arlington businesses pay a 10 percent sales tax on consumption of these utilities. Virginia's other suburban counties mitigate high utility consumption tax rates with maximum monthly payments. Fairfax County, for instance, imposes sales tax rates of 10 percent, 22.2 percent, and 10 percent on electricity, telephone, and gas usage, but only the first $10,000, $1,600, and $3,000, respectively, of these purchases are subject to tax.

14. *CAFR, 1995* reports all the gross receipts revenue amounts.

15. District of Columbia Department of Finance and Revenue (DFR), *A Comparison of Tax Rates and Burdens in the Washington Metropolitan Area* (1995), p. 46. The base is the gross premiums less dividends paid to policyholders, premiums received for reinsurance assumed, and returned premiums. The insured, individual or group, must reside or be headquartered in the District. DFR, *Comparison of Tax Rates*, p. 30; and conversations with DFR staff.

The Broad-Based Gross Receipts Tax

In 1990 the Commission on Budget and Financial Priorities of the District of Columbia (the Rivlin Commission) recommended a comprehensive gross receipts tax.[16] As a result the District has recently imposed a broad-based gross receipts tax but has dedicated its small revenues to a specific purpose. This tax is levied in addition to the gross receipts taxes on specific industries outlined above.[17] First imposed in 1994 and called the public safety fee, the package of rates produced $10,097,000 in that year and $9,961,000 in 1995. In its second year its payers numbered 25,044, and its revenues were dedicated to the Sports Commission. It is now referred to as the Arena fee.

In addition to providing $10 million annually for the Sports Commission, the broad-based gross receipts tax represents an experiment for the District. In the opinion written by Associate Judge Kelly in *Bishop v. District of Columbia*, the unincorporated business tax cannot be extended to professionals because it is a tax based on net income, but "a tax on gross receipts is not an income tax."[18] A tax on gross receipts is an appealing alternative to the present business taxes, and its two-year history suggests it can provide a steady source of revenue. The Department of Finance and Revenue is also documenting the 25,000 payers, sorting them by industry and amount of gross receipts. There is no comparable tracking for the franchise taxes.

The structure of the Arena fee is shown in table 5-2. Assuming gross receipts of $100,000, a company faces an effective tax rate of 0.025 percent. Assuming gross receipts of $350,000, the effective tax rate is 0.014 percent. If gross receipts total $750,000, the effective tax rate becomes 0.013 percent. Table 5-3 shows the distribution of payers and receipts for eleven sectors of the economy (SIC categories), and table 5-4 provides breakdowns of payers at each level of gross receipts for six of the eleven SICs. Based on these District data, the Arena fee is taxing gross receipts at a weighted average of 0.036 percent.

16. "Financing the Nation's Capital," Report of the Commission on Budget and Financial Priorities of the District of Columbia, November 1990, p. 7-3.

17. The only businesses exempted are those specifically identified as tax exempt in the franchise tax code.

18. *Bishop v. District of Columbia*, 401 A.2d 960.

Table 5-2. *Rate Structure of District of Columbia Arena Fee*

Dollars

Gross receipts	Fee
Less than 200,000	25
200,001 to 500,000	50
500,001 to 1,000,000	100
1,000,000n to 3,000,000	825
3,000,001 to 10,000,000	2,500
10,000,001 to 15,000,000	5,000
More than 15,000,000	8,400

Source: District of Columbia Department of Finance and Revenue, *District of Columbia Tax Facts, Fiscal Years 1993 and 1994*, p. 13.

Alternative Types of Taxes for Business

On what bases should the District impose business taxes? This study has focused on five: fairness, competitiveness with the surrounding area, ease of understanding, ease of administration, and contribution to budget stability. One measure of fairness is the benefit principle. A strong argument can be made that businesses should pay local taxes because, and to the extent that, they benefit from location within a jurisdiction.[19] Because the value of benefits received is impossible to measure and com-

Table 5-3. *District of Columbia Business Income Tax Revenue and Number of Returns, Eleven Industrial Classifications, 1995*

Classification	SIC code	Returns	Amount (dollars)
Agriculture	0–1499	122	7,169.22
Construction	1500–1799	1,715	603,942.81
Manufacturing	2000–3999	633	259,942.81
Transportation, communications	4000–4999	458	242,947.71
Wholesale trade	5000–5199	663	1,298,309.61
Retail trade	5200–5999	4,562	1,298,309.61
Finance, insurance, real estate	6000–6999	4,066	1,205,576.03
Hotel, motel	7000–7099	127	178,511.58
Personal, business services	7200–7399	4,144	1,198,106.55
Other services	7500–8999	5,758	2,221,643.32
Miscellaneous	. . .	2,796	751,740.83
Total	. . .	. . .	8,426,069.07

Source: District of Columbia Department of Finance and Revenue (DFR), "Arena Fee Paid by SIC Code," October 8, 1995. The receipts shown do not add up to the total revenue generated by the Arena fee, so these totals cannot be considered accurate. The intention is to give some sense of the distribution of payers.

19. J. Richard Aronson and John L. Hilley, *Financing State and Local Governments*, 4th ed. (Brookings), p. 103.

Table 5-4. *District of Columbia Arena Fee Revenues, by Industrial Classification, 1995*

Thousands of dollars

Industrial classification	Fee classification (dollars)						
	25	50	100	825	2,500	5,000	8,400
Construction							
Filers	1,045	243	173	146	77	11	20
Amount	35.9	12.2	17.4	121.7	193.2	55.0	148.0
Retail trade							
Filers	2,567	825	520	437	158	29	26
Amount	81.1	41.5	52.4	360.5	397.8	146.6	218.4
Finance, insurance, real estate							
Filers	2,959	415	200	250	188	13	41
Amount	84.8	20.9	20.2	206.0	469.9	65.3	338.5
Personal and business services							
Filers	2,493	589	455	395	164	25	23
Amount	74.0	32.3	46.0	326.6	413.7	120.7	184.8
Other services							
Filers	3,225	1,009	618	515	259	52	80
Amount	106.1	54.2	63.2	427.3	648.2	261.9	660.8
Miscellaneous							
Filers	1,990	324	168	175	95	21	23
Amount	54.0	16.4	16.9	145.4	239.5	103.1	176.5

Source: See table 5-3.

pare, the standard proxy is income. Which measure of income, gross (receipts) or net (profits), is fairer? Gross receipts, reflecting both business activity and size, stand out as more closely tracking the benefits received as well as the costs imposed on the District from a business's location.

But gross receipts are a poor measure of a company's ability to pay, which is the other major measure of fairness in taxation. The argument that businesses should not have to pay taxes if they do not make a profit has gradually won out. In addition, elements of unfairness arise because the relationship between gross receipts and profits varies significantly from industry to industry. Retail stores make the case that with high receipts relative to net income, a gross receipts tax punishes them simply for the nature of their business.[20] Another problem is that start-up businesses, which may take years to make a profit, would have to pay a gross receipts tax from their first customer. However, a low gross receipts tax, like the Arena fee, or an exemption from taxation until the third year of business would seem to cover this problem.

20. Virginia's business privilege operator's license tax addresses this problem by imposing the tax at different rates for different categories of business.

Relying on the fairness of the net income tax because of the ability-to-pay argument is not without its problems. Determining net income has become very complex, generally requiring even small businesses to use professionals for tax preparation.[21] For the District of Columbia, both the corporate and the unincorporated net income taxes require a large amount of auditing, suggesting that compliance is spotty or the laws are unclear or both. When compliance is less than automatic, the burden of the tax is bound to be uneven and fairness is compromised. Data provided by the Department of Finance and Revenue on auditing activity in fiscal year 1995 indicate that all the business taxes produce significantly more revenue per audit hour than the average tax. Although this might seem good news for audit revenues, it indicates a lack of voluntary compliance in filing and meeting the tax code. Fairness is further muddied because of the limitations on the reach of the unincorporated franchise tax. Although it was meant to extend parallel treatment to all businesses regardless of corporate form, in the absence of the ability to tax professional partnerships, it is hard to argue that the District's business tax structure is fair at all.

Levying business taxes also demands that they be competitive. Because the District is a small open economy, its level and structure of taxation will be compared with that of the surrounding area. The corporate income tax rate in the District is 2.975 percent higher than Maryland's and 3.975 percent higher than Virginia's. Although there are differences in the bases, the burden a company faces in the District is consistently higher than it is in the suburbs. A recent study found that the total corporate income tax bill was higher in the District than in Maryland or Virginia for the four kinds of private firms it considered.[22] Maryland does not impose a gross receipts tax; Virginia does. The advantage of the gross receipts tax is that the base (the volume of business activity) is very broad, so the rates can be low and will not usually affect location decisions.

The District's business net income taxes are not easy for taxpayers to understand and tax collectors to manage. For businesses, filing itself, not to mention the costs of dealing with subsequent audits, presents a signif-

---

21. And the complexity of the tax code is certainly no guarantee of fairness, since it may be rife with special treatments won by lobbyists and the advantages go to those who understand it best.

22. The four types of companies are information technology, biotechnology manufacturing, nonmanufacturing research and development, and business services. Coopers and Lybrand, "Greater Washington 1996 Comparative Tax Report," prepared for the Greater Washington Board of Trade, Washington, 1996. See chapter 2 for a fuller discussion.

icant burden. For the tax collector, increased reliance on auditing to produce revenue has overburdened a shrinking work force. As the tax codes have become more complex and business more far-flung, the District's auditors openly admit to finding themselves outflanked by businesses' more experienced accountants and lawyers.

In addition, the District appears to have given up trying to analyze the effects of its business taxes. It cannot produce data to show the distribution of payers by income or category of business. The revenues shown for each fiscal year move up and down haphazardly enough to make the figures suspect, which does not contribute to predictability or budget stability. Although in theory business income taxes should fluctuate with the economy, in reality local apportionment and loss carry-forwards are enough to put tax liability for the District on its own (less predictable) cycle. The present business taxes appear not to be contributing significantly to budget stability.[23]

Sales Taxes

The District of Columbia imposes a general sales tax on retail purchasers of five categories of goods and services. It also imposes selective sales (excise) taxes on the importation or manufacture of alcoholic beverages, importation of motor vehicle fuel, and purchase of cigarettes. A flat per room tax is imposed on hotel occupancy, an ad valorem tax on motor vehicle titles, and a registration fee, set according to weight, on motor vehicles.

The five categories of purchases subject to the general sales tax are retail sales, a broad category of tangible goods and services, taxed at 5.75 percent; liquor sold to be consumed off the premises, taxed at 8 percent; restaurant meals, liquor sold for consumption on premises, and rental cars, taxed at 10 percent; parking in commercial lots, taxed at 12

---

23. This need not necessarily be the case. Econometric forecasting estimates the behavior of profits by industry, and the results can be matched with the industry distribution of tax returns. With efficient data collection the tax collector should know, on a quarterly basis, both estimated payments and accumulated loss carry-forwards, although these are subject to adjustment throughout the year. These approaches can combine to narrow the range of prediction for budget revenues. Of course, audit agreements can change payments and carry-forwards. But revenues from audits of previous years should be tracked and budgeted separately.

Table 5-5. *District of Columbia Sales Tax Revenues and Rates,*
1988–95

Percent unless otherwise specified

Fiscal year	General sales tax revenue[a] (millions of dollars)	Revenue growth	Retail trade (millions of dollars)	Trade growth	General sales tax rate	Tax rate on restaurant meals	Tax rate on hotel accommodations
1988	390.6	. . .	2,763	. . .	6	8	10
1989	428.8	9.8	2,793	1.1	6	9	11
1990	466.6	8.8	3,070	9.9	6	9	11
1991	451.6	−3.2	3,194	4.0	6	9	11
1992	442.5	−2.0	3,225	1.0	6	9	11
1993	410.1	−7.3	3,760	16.6	6	9	11
1994	458.6	11.8	3,763	0.1	6/7[a]	9	11
1995	485.7	5.9	3,643	−3.2	5.75	10	13

Sources: Revenue figures are from *CAFR, 1995*; rate history is from *District of Columbia Tax Facts, Fiscal Years 1993–94*, pp. 58–59; retail trade from Bureau of the Census, *Monthly Retail Trade Survey* (revised April 1995), table ST11DCE.

a. There was a temporary increase in June.

percent; and hotel or motel accommodations, taxed at 13 percent. The rates applying to restaurant meals and hotel and motel accommodations were increased by 1 and 2 percentage points, respectively, for fiscal year 1995, with earmarking for purposes other than the general fund.[24]

In fiscal year 1995 the general sales tax generated about $486 million, making it the District's third largest tax revenue (table 5-5), and the selective sales tax nearly $100 million. The general sales tax revenues have reflected nominal growth but real decline since 1986, while tax revenues overall grew slightly in real terms. Because nominal sales tax revenues increased at a bit slower rate than other taxes, general and selective sales taxes have decreased slightly from 21.4 and 4.3 percent, respectively, of total tax revenues to 20.3 and 4.1 percent.

Based on receipts for fiscal year 1995, which were made available to this study, 49 percent of the District sales tax revenue can be attributed to the general sales tax rate, 24 percent to the restaurant sales tax, and 21 percent to the hotel accommodations tax. Given the total audited revenue of $485.651 million, the revenues generated by the three tax

24. One percentage point of the receipts from the restaurant tax is dedicated to the Washington Convention Center Authority. Two and one-half percentage points of the receipts from the hotel tax are also reserved for that purpose. The remainder of the general sales tax revenue flows into the District general fund.

rates were an estimated $238 million, $118 million, and $102 million, respectively.[25]

On average, states depend on sales and gross receipts taxes for a third of their tax revenues.[26] The District's dependence on these sources grew from 31.3 percent to 33.2 percent from 1986 to 1995, but the growth was due entirely to the gross receipts tax, which more than doubled because of significant rate increases. The District's relative dependence on sales taxes is, then, typical for a state. Cities rely on sales and gross receipts taxes less heavily: the fifty-two largest cities in fiscal 1992 received about 16 percent of tax revenue and 10 percent of all own-source revenue from general sales taxes.[27] The District's reliance on sales taxes is excessive compared with that of other cities.

Forty-five states and more than 6,000 municipalities impose a sales tax. There are strong reasons, largely political, for its popularity.[28] First, the federal government does not impose a sales tax, so a state or local tax does not compound an existing burden. Second, for consumers it represents small, if frequent, payments and no paperwork. Merchants are the statutory payers of the tax, but they merely serve as the conduit: they pass along the tax to customers on every transaction, then they forward the customers' payments to the District government. Filing the sales tax does represent a relatively complex undertaking for merchants, especially because many stores sell products taxed at different rates or not taxed at all, requiring good record keeping. However, merchants are a small proportion of the population, so the complexity of the system may cause more economic than political problems. Related political arguments are that the principal alternative to the sales tax is the income tax, which is disproportionately paid by those with higher incomes who have more political influence than the poor. And the sales tax levied on items of consumption is thought to encourage savings.

Third, the sales tax has been popular because it is relatively easy to administer. Although the costs of administration are minimized by having merchants serve as tax collectors, there are accompanying costs of inves-

25. District of Columbia Department of Finance and Revenue, "Sales and Use Tax—Paid Returns," March 2, 1996. This report shows cash receipts for each month. The total cash receipts for fiscal 1995 were $466 million, much of which came from fiscal 1994 payments at the previous year's tax rates: 7 percent for general sales, 9 percent for restaurant meals, and 11 percent for hotel accommodations.

26. Fleenor, *Facts and Figures*, table E18.

27. Fleenor, *Facts and Figures*, p. 237.

28. This draws heavily on John F. Due and John L. Mikesell, *Sales Taxation, State and Local Structure and Administration*, 2d ed. (Washington: Urban Institute Press, 1994).

tigation and auditing that can be significant when the economy has a large number of cash businesses, such as bars and restaurants, for which the tax rate is high. And in the District, which makes detailed distinctions within the category of food as to what is exempt (groceries) and what is taxed (snacks and takeout food), collecting and filing can be burdensome and generate political problems.

Fourth, lawmakers like the sales tax because they expect it to be a generally stable source of revenue, relatively unresponsive to local business cycles. The argument for revenue stability rests on the proposition that consumption is more stable than income. However, a large portion of sales tax revenues depends on consumer durable purchases, which are cyclical and subject to swings in consumer confidence.[29] With few remaining department stores and virtually no new car dealerships, consumer durables may represent a decreasing share of the District's sales tax base. The exemption of groceries, a stable item of household consumption, combined with the taxation of restaurant meals (at a higher tax rate than general goods) may also contribute to instability in the District's sales tax base and revenues.

There are two important economic problems with the sales tax: it is regressive, and consumers can easily avoid it by shopping in another jurisdiction or, increasingly, by catalog. In spite of the widespread exclusion of groceries from the sales tax base, low-income families pay a greater share of their income in sales taxes than do families with greater incomes.[30] Families whose income is in the lowest fifth of their state's income distribution pay 4.7 percent of their income in sales taxes in the District, 4.6 percent in Maryland, and 5.2 percent in Virginia. The wealthiest 1 percent of families pay 0.7 percent, 0.7 percent, and 0.8 percent, respectively. The District's sales taxes do not, however, impose as great a burden on low-income families as do those elsewhere. Families in states' lowest-income quintile pay an average 6.7 percent of income in sales taxes. The District's heavy reliance on the slightly progressive personal income tax partially offsets regressive taxes, so that although the general sales tax rate exceeds that in neighboring states, overall the District's

---

29. John Mikesell, "Sensitivity of Taxes," *Public Budgeting and Finance*, vol. 4 (Spring 1984), p. 37.

30. Michael P. Ettlinger and others, *Who Pays? A Distributional Analysis of the Tax Systems in All 50 States* (Washington: Citizens for Tax Justice and Institute on Taxation and Economic Policy, June 1996), finds this to be the case for all fifty states. The report reviews other studies that find different levels of regressivity associated with sales taxes (pp. 9–12).

reliance on sales taxes is far less than the national average. This lessens the burden on the District's lowest-income families.

Cross-border shopping poses a serious problem for a jurisdiction as small as the District. The 1994 McKinsey study for the Federal City Council emphasized the explosion of retail development on the city's borders. These developments have provided safe, attractive shopping with adequate parking and, sometimes, public transportation. Suburban Washington added 19.4 million square feet of retail development during the 1960s, 1970s, and 1980s, while the District added perhaps 700,000 square feet.[31] This trend has undermined the District's sales tax base, compounding the effects of decreasing population and numbers of jobs. Although residents who purchase goods in a state other than their jurisdiction of residence are liable to their home state for the sales tax on the purchase, this use tax is frequently uncollected and is considered unenforceable.[32] Delaware and New Hampshire, two of the five states with no sales tax, are very small geographically and their retailers are thought to benefit greatly from the consequent interstate shopping.

As a small jurisdiction with general sales tax rates higher than those of its neighbors—the rate in Maryland is 5 percent and in Virginia 3.5 percent—the District should have serious concerns about the border tax problem for retail stores. But the surcharges on restaurant meals and hotel accommodations imposed by the nearby counties in both states bring the total rates for these select categories to levels that are sometimes comparable with the District's (table 5-6).

Exportation of Sales Taxes

Hotel and motel accommodations are taxed everywhere in the United States. Their popularity seems to stem from two elements: much of the tax burden will be borne by nonresidents, and the poor bear little of it.[33] These observations also apply, to a somewhat lesser extent, to the tax on

---

31. McKinsey & Company and Urban Institute, "Assessing the District of Columbia's Future: A Report to the Federal City Council," Washington, October 1994, p. 7 and exhibit 15. The list of suburban shopping center development is impressive: in the 1960s, Tyson's Corner, Montgomery Mall, Wheaton Plaza, Beltway Plaza, Prince George's Plaza; in the 1970s, Springfield Mall, Landover Mall, Lakeforest Mall, Mall in Columbia, Manassas Mall, White Flint; in the 1980s, Pentagon City, Potomac Mills, Fair Oaks, Landmark Center, Tyson's II. The District's retail developments were Chevy Chase Pavilion and Georgetown Park.

32. Due and Mikesell, *Sales Taxation*, 2d ed., p. 93.

33. Due and Mikesell, *Sales Taxation*, 2d ed., p. 93.

Table 5-6. *Metropolitan Washington Area Sales Tax Rates on Hotels and Restaurants, by Jurisdiction, 1995*

Percent

Jurisdiction	State rate	County surcharge on restaurant meals	Total sales tax on restaurant meals	County surcharge on hotel accommodations	Total sales tax on hotel accommodations
District of Columbia	...	...	10	...	13
Charles County	5	...	5	5	10
Montgomery County	5	...	5	7	12
Prince George's County	5	...	5	9	14
Alexandria City	3.5	4	7.5	6	9.5
Arlington County	3.5	5	8.5	6.25	9.75
Fairfax City	3.5	4	7.5	3	6.5
Fairfax County	3.5	...	3.5	3	6.5
Falls Church City	3.5	4	7.5	6	9.5
Loudoun County	3.5	...	3.5	2	5.5
Prince William County	3.5	...	3.5	2	5.5

Source: District of Columbia Department of Finance and Revenue, *A Comparison of Tax Rates and Burdens in the Washington, D.C., Metropolitan Area* (1995), p. 51.

restaurant meals. As the nation's capital the District offers unique opportunities for tourism and business transactions. A high tax on hotel accommodations and meals may thus be sensible, and the rates are very high. The hotel tax is not far out of line with the rates imposed elsewhere in the metropolitan area, but the restaurant tax is the highest rate in the area by 1.5 percentage points. A recent analysis of visitor spending in the Washington area indicates that the District's share of the total is 52 percent. It receives 63 percent of the money spent on hotels and 53 percent of the spending on meals, but only 33 percent of the retail spending.[34]

Exportation of the tax base is, of course, not confined to hotels and restaurants. Tourists and commuters who use the District's streets and police protection also shop in its stores, so the sales tax can represent an appropriate spreading of the burden to the true users of District services. Many sales to tourists and suburban visitors, however, are free of tax because federal law does not permit the District to impose sales taxes on transactions taking place in the Smithsonian Institution, National Gallery, Kennedy Center for the Performing Arts, Hirshhorn Museum, National Air and Space Museum, National Armed Forces Museum, Wood-

34. Stephen S. Fuller, "Presentation to the District of Columbia Home Rule Charter Review Seminar on the Fiscal Condition of the District of Columbia," December 1996, figure 2.

row Wilson International Center for Scholars, Museum for African Art, and the Museum of the American Indian.[35]

In fiscal year 1989, real estate services and data processing and information services were included in the general sales tax base and taxed at 6 percent. This expansion, expected to yield $35 million, was also designed to export the sales tax burden. In 1989 also, the sales tax rate on restaurant meals (and drinks served on premises) was increased from 8 percent to 9 percent and the rate on hotel accommodations from 10 percent to 11 percent. These increases were expected to raise an additional $11 million from restaurants and $7 million from hotels (table 5-5).[36] The annual data have, however, been difficult to analyze.

Proposals

The District's business income taxes should be eliminated. Voluntary compliance is patchy at best and these taxes are not and cannot be enforced efficiently or fairly. Eliminating these taxes will reduce the District's reliance on state-type taxes and cost it revenue. In place of the net income taxes on business, the District should move further toward the simpler taxation of business gross receipts.

It would seem that a general fund gross receipts tax has the most potential for satisfying the requirements of fairness, competitiveness, ease of filing and administration, and predictable revenues. To get a sense for the potential magnitude of a general fund gross receipts tax, one needs to compare the rates of the present Arena fee (table 5-2) with those found in the nearby jurisdictions. Although Maryland does not levy a gross receipts tax, Virginia cities and counties do impose it, at different rates for different industries. In the Virginia metropolitan counties, the highest rate professionals face is Alexandria's 0.58 percent and the lowest is Fairfax County's 0.31 percent. For the retail sector the rates vary from 0.17 percent in Fairfax, Loudoun, and Prince William counties to 0.20 percent in Arlington, Alexandria, and the city of Fairfax. The District could quintuple rates in some sectors and multiply them by greater factors in others and still be competitive with the rates in Virginia, leaving the

35. District of Columbia Department of Finance and Revenue, "Study of Property, Income and Sales Tax Exemptions in the District of Columbia," April 7, 1995, p. 24.

36. Sales tax regulatory history and impact estimates are from DFR, *Tax Facts, Fiscal Years 1993 and 1994.*

Arena fee in place and dedicated to the Sports Commission. Such a gross receipts tax would constitute a very small tax burden for District businesses and a broad-based, dependable source of revenue, totaling about $50 million a year, for the District's general fund.

In 1979 the Rivlin Commission commented that although "a gross receipts tax is regressive, it recommends the tax because it is broad based, easy to administer, simple to calculate for the taxpayer, and generates considerable revenue at a very low percentage rate."[37] As has been noted, the regressivity can be assuaged and, with very little reliance on the tax, presents less concern. The District has addressed the regressivity through the progressive structure of the Arena fee and has addressed companies' differing abilities to pay by imposing a very low rate. Substitution of a small, broad-based gross receipts tax for the two net income taxes would not compromise fairness. Although write-offs, allowances for depreciation and losses incurred in past and succeeding tax years, and other deductions, as well as the factor formula itself, are intended to make the business income tax burden more fair, they also reward sophisticated firms whose behavior and accounting are designed, in part, to minimize their tax burden. The intention of the unincorporated business franchise tax has been thwarted since the *Bishop* decision, and many District businesses remain untaxed. A comprehensive gross receipts tax, applied independently of business status—incorporation, limited liability company, partnership, and so forth—would not distort a firm's decision on how to organize itself and would treat businesses of similar size in similar endeavors equally, irrespective of their legal form.

Improvements in assessing or collecting the District's general sales and excise taxes are more difficult to recommend. District records of sales tax receipts have had problems. A history of receipts by rate and industry was requested from the Department of Revenue and Finance for this study. Only after three months, and too late for our analysis, was such a document produced. The department's policymakers do not have immediate access to this information and do not consult it regularly. Therefore they cannot monitor the performance of the complex package of rates the District imposes. Also, the data we received were organized by date of receipt of payment rather than date of transaction. Many months show revenue garnered at rates that no longer exist. Disaggregating receipts by transaction dates would provide retail activity figures that would each be properly associated with a month and year.

37. "Financing the Nation's Capital," p. 7-3.

There are important questions yet to be answered concerning the District's sales taxes. To what extent are sales in the various sectors sensitive to the tax rates? How much of the burden is borne by residents, by commuters, by tourists? Without better record keeping, there will not be reliable answers. The most important change involving administration of the sales tax would be to provide to policymakers a monthly report of sales tax revenues and transactions organized by sector and date.

CHAPTER 6

The Administration and Collection of Taxes

"**N**O MATTER how well particular taxes are meant to apply, they will be only as good as their actual operation."[1] In the District of Columbia, the Department of Finance and Revenue handles the administration and collection of taxes: billing for payment; collecting and posting the correct payments to taxpayer accounts; fining, pursuing, and reaching settlement with delinquent taxpayers; auditing taxpayer returns and business accounts to ensure compliance with tax laws and correct payment; and educating and fielding questions from taxpayers and their representatives about more than twenty taxes.

The Department of Finance and Revenue thus has a huge responsibility to the District government: to collect the revenue quickly, minimizing cash flow problems; do it efficiently, minimizing the costs of overhead and maximizing voluntary compliance; forecast and track collections accurately, maximizing budget, spending, and program stability; and present the best face of government.

The department also has a major responsibility to taxpayers. It has enormous power and access to the most private financial information. It can subpoena accounts, place liens and confiscate property for nonpayment, and if necessary, pursue, prosecute, and punish evaders. Tax agency employees carry the heaviest of public trusts and the burden of not only being honest in handling billions of dollars worth of accounts, but of being seen to be honest. The stakes are high, the temptations are large, the task is crucial, and the rewards are not often obvious.

---

1. Richard A. Musgrave and Peggy B. Musgrave, *Public Finance in Theory and Practice* (McGraw-Hill, 1973), p. 212.

Organization and Staffing

Because the District's chief financial officer is reviewing the DFR's organization and structure along with the entire financial component of the District government, a detailed description of the organization of the department would likely be outdated before this study is published. But it would be safe to say that the hybrid nature of the District's tax structure has been reflected in the department's organization and functioning. Oversight of the city-type property tax is largely a self-contained operation within the department, accounting for one-quarter of its personnel. This operation is vertically integrated from recording the deeds of ownership and transfers of property to assessment of 168,000 properties to billing and collections to disposal of delinquent properties. All components of the real property tax, including individual payments and delinquencies, are public information.[2]

The rest of the DFR resembles a state tax agency, a line operation handling large numbers of taxpayer accounts, posting, tracking, and certifying the accuracy of billings and collections. This part of the department is organized along functional lines—data management, collections, audit, compliance, and so forth—rather than by tax. The day-to-day operations employ another one-quarter of the staff, with the remaining half involved in various follow-up audit, compliance, and delinquency collection activities. On this side of the department there can be no revelation of a particular taxpayer's circumstances to nondepartment personnel.

A small Office of Tax Policy functions as a staff arm for management; it is also responsible for the annual forecasting of budget revenues and, throughout the fiscal year, the monthly tracking and reconciliation of revenues with budget forecasts. In addition, it analyzes the impact of tax legislation.[3] There is at present no effective internal auditing or anti-corruption program in place anywhere in the department.

During the 1990s, authorized staffing at the DFR has declined about 22 percent, an annual average loss of 3 percent. From the equivalent of

2. With the exception of statements of income and expenses filed by owners of commercial property, which, if Proposition 51, passed in November 1996, holds, may become public as well.

3. Significant restrictions on access to confidential information on taxpayers tend to keep tax analysis in-house in state tax departments, especially since useful information-sharing arrangements with the IRS require strict enforcement of limitations on which officials may have access to tax-secret information.

almost 600 full-time staff in 1990, the department is now functioning with about 470. If the decrease were the result of technological improvements, reorganization, or other initiatives that increased productivity, smaller staffs would indicate constant or improved efficiency and services. However, there have been no major improvements in technology or information systems in the department, and neither District officials nor taxpayers claim to have noticed improved efficiency. The loss of personnel is worrisome and has likely resulted in deteriorating services.

Department of Finance and Revenue Deficiencies

All the audits, investigations, and internal studies of the Department of Finance and Revenue portray an agency in need of fixing.[4] They agree that the department does not collect taxes efficiently or fairly, does not post or forecast collections as accurately as it should, and does not present a competent image of government to the public. Administrative failures have turned what were intended to be fair tax laws into unfair and arbitrary ones and have left a generally cumbersome and overly complex system. Specific shortcomings vary tax by tax and have been presented in the chapters on individual taxes. Here, drawing on all the studies available, we highlight areas for concern.

---

4. This section draws from *District of Columbia Comprehensive Annual Financial Report, September 30, 1995* (1995); Office of the District of Columbia Auditor, "Review and Analysis of the District's Accounts Receivable," January 16, 1996; Aurthur Andersen, "District of Columbia Real Property Tax Administration: 30-Day Operational Status Report," August 28, 1996; Arthur Andersen, "Report of Preliminary Recommendations, CFO 2000 Performance Improvement Initiative," July 24, 1996; KPMG Peat Marwick, "Independent Auditors' Report on the Internal Control Structure," Washington, January 1996; KPMG Peat Marwick, "Independent Auditors' Report on Compliance with Laws and Regulations," Washington, January 1996; Internal Revenue Service, "Assessment of Revenue Collection Process for the District of Columbia," April–May 1995; Metropolitan Business Associates, "Solutions to the D.C. Department of Finance and Revenue Malaise," Washington, February 1996; Vernon Loeb, "Faulty Formula Botches 9,700 D.C. Assessments," *Washington Post*, June 13, 1996, p. B1; Loeb, "Residents Challenge 2nd D.C. Assessor," *Washington Post*, June 22, 1996, p. B1; Loeb, "Verdict on D.C. Tax System: 'Garbage In, Garbage Out,'" *Washington Post*, July 10, 1996, p. A1; Loeb, "D.C. Financial Chief Fires 2 Top Assessment Officials in Shake-up," *Washington Post*, July 11, 1996, p. B1; Loeb, "Agency's Problems Tax D.C. Property Owners," *Washington Post*, July 15, 1996, p. B1; and Loeb, "D.C. Considers Moratorium on Tax Assessments," *Washington Post*, August 4, 1996, p. B1.

Accuracy and Accountability

Major innacuracies in tax revenue accounting indicate two problems. One is with the data themselves. The other, perhaps more serious, is with the tax collection process. Given present tax law, improvements at the department could significantly bolster the District's revenues.

The revenue data are undependable, especially when considered over time. For some taxes, there is no accurate collection history, either in the aggregate or from individual taxpayers. Accurate record keeping has become a victim of antiquated technology. For some taxes and some years, the files have been destroyed and collections are not verifiable.

The amounts recorded for the sales and business taxes fluctuate enough from year to year to raise serious questions as to whether monthly or quarterly collections were recorded when they were collected or were moved for the purpose of balancing the fiscal year budget. Sales tax data are missing for a whole year. The business tax records are in such a bad state that the DFR cannot provide a distribution of taxpayers by size of payment or type of business. This study's aggregation of the real property levy, taken from the public assessment data, does not yield the same levy as reported in the financial statement. It is not clear where the discrepancy lies. The outside evaluation of the assessments performed for the chief financial officer by Arthur Andersen states that the "information . . . is inconsistent, incomplete, and at times inaccurate."[5]

More important, it would appear that revenue collections could be improved and probably increased through careful attention to both administration and enforcement. Wide differences in assessed values for similar properties, well-publicized cases of assessor incompetence, and significant adjustments made during appeals provide strong evidence that assessments are not accurately reflecting market values. The relief programs, particularly the $30,000 homestead exemption, have not been audited for a decade, which may have allowed many owners to take advantage of an owner-occupier privilege without being in residence. In addition, the historic inability of the District to pursue full-scale auditing of both residency and unearned income indicates that the number of taxpayers has been underestimated and the base of the personal income tax is likely to be underreported.

The District's elected officials and its taxpayers cannot be sure that taxpayers have paid what they should, that they have been credited

5. Arthur Andersen, "Real Property Tax Administration," p. 3.

properly with either payments or refunds, and that the money was actually received. This is the result of widespread employee access to taxpayer accounts, which is also a security problem because taxpayer information is legally confidential. The disorganization also dampens the efficiency of revenue collection. And, disturbingly, it raises the possibility of corruption.[6]

Operational Efficiency

The department has for a long time suffered from a lack of stable leadership. In the past twenty years, a generation in which tax collection and enforcement have been radically transformed by computerization, the department has had nine directors. In the same two decades the property tax division has witnessed the comings and goings of twelve associate directors, six chief assessors, and nine people in charge of the office responsible for helping property owners.[7] Until very recently managers have not been held responsible for poor performance by individual employees or for the deterioration of the agency's performance. Nor is there evidence that employees have been held responsible for their own performance.

The skills needed to do the job and the training that has been provided have also been inadequate. In property assessment, existing software has been used inefficiently and ineffectively. There has been as well "a lack of knowledge . . . of financial calculators . . . [and] only nominal knowledge of other office [skills], such as adjustments to printers, use of fax machines, and ability to transfer telephone calls. Although instructions are available . . . the people prefer to rely on the one person who is deemed an expert in the use whenever there is a problem."[8]

The deficit in skills and performance is pervasive: from top to bottom and from managerial to technical to professional personnel. And the reasons are not difficult to find. First, most managerial personnel serve in an acting status, which undermines their ability to initiate and sustain change. Supervisory personnel tend also to serve temporarily and "at times unwillingly," since they often suffer a reduction in pay or the same

---

6. The independent auditors as well as the consultants to the chief financial officer all emphasize the lack of security in the revenue posting and tracking system that allows easy access for too many people to what should be confidential and inviolable data. Arthur Andersen, "Real Property Tax Administration."

7. Arthur Andersen, "Report of Preliminary Recommendations," p. DFR-10.

8. Athur Andersen, "Real Property Tax Administration," p. 33.

pay with increased responsibility.[9] Meanwhile, "technicians are not being trained to eventually move into the assessor positions," and assessors are not being "groomed for promotion to supervisor, nor do many . . . aspire to become supervisors."[10]

Training is not provided and poor performance is not corrected. Without compensation for continuing education, many of the department's professionals have simply fallen behind in their fields.[11] Few assessors can "articulate the rationale and the technical points behind assessment . . . practices. . . . Few assessors are involved with IAAO or other professional valuation organizations. None are certified within the District of Columbia."[12] The auditors, who daily confront business taxpayers, do not demonstrate knowledge of auditing standards and tax laws, nor has management established uniform audit procedures.[13]

Finally, the DFR's information technology systems and the software handling the taxes are obsolete. The department has no unified database, which means it functions tax by tax rather than taxpayer by taxpayer. This costs the District money because often the enforcement personnel handling one tax do not know what other payments might be outstanding for a given taxpayer. Like New York City's, the District's database grew tax by tax. Computerization came to each tax at a different time, resulting in a hodgepodge of databases programmed in a variety of computer languages (many now obsolete), most of which cannot easily communicate with each other. Further, although most of the tax databases at the department have become computerized, there are still manual files and operations. And these are handling state-type taxes.

The property tax information system is both self-contained and segmented. Different files contain a host of assessment-related physical information as well as ownership, billing, and payment histories for every parcel of land and every building in Washington. This enormous amount of information is complicated and difficult to integrate, especially because registered owners—those ultimately liable for the tax—often are not the entities billed or those from whom payment is received. Further, the calculation of the assessed value and the tax classification of property may change over the years, and the assessment, ownership, and billing

---

9. Arthur Andersen, "Real Property Tax Administration," p. 42.

10. Arthur Andersen, "Real Property Tax Administration," pp. 33–34.

11. The District no longer pays for course tuition, although time away from work is compensated. Arthur Andersen, "Real Property Tax Administration," p. 33.

12. Arthur Andersen, "Real Property Tax Administration," p. 36.

13. Arthur Andersen, "Report of Preliminary Recommendations," p. DFR-15.

data have not been kept up-to-date. For example, a two-year backlog in verifying name and address changes from deed documents (the Maps and Titles Department) cripples the District's ability to send property tax bills to the right person in the right place, which means reiteration of work for the department, delays in payments, and increased delinquencies.[14]

These obsolete systems, combined with managerial and staffing deficiencies, result in errors, long turn-around times, and growing backlogs that drain the District's current funds and compromise collection of future revenue. When the District launched a collection initiative in 1996 to catch up on money owed, inaccurate taxpayer information resulted in a flood of notices returned as undeliverable. There was no staff to handle the returned mail even when the Postal Service had provided new address information. The bills languished in bins, and after several months were thrown away—another missed opportunity to increase revenues and improve the currency of the department's data.

Fair and Equal Treatment

A poorly managed and ill-functioning agency with inaccurate and outdated information operates haphazardly and careens from crisis to crisis. Under these conditions tax receipts will flow from the biggest, most obvious, most easily identifiable and available sources. Tax evaders will calculate probabilities as to whether an overworked staff will find them and, if it does, whether staff skills and information will allow the department to pursue and collect. The larger, older, and more established a business taxpayer, the greater the likelihood of payment. However, the department's ability to catch up with small, cash-dominated businesses while they have the resources to pay taxes due has deteriorated badly. And when the District does levy a correct bill for unpaid taxes, the process often devolves to a negotiation over the justifiable amount of interest and penalties, given that most taxpayers can convincingly argue that payment notices were not received, different staff members instructed them to use different procedures, or deadlines had been extended. This is certainly not fair to law-abiding taxpayers. Neither is it an efficient way to collect revenue.

14. Arthur Andersen, "Real Property Tax Administration," p. 101.

Toward the Future

The state of the Department of Finance and Revenue requires that reconsiderations of its capabilities, requirements, and limitations be foremost in making decisions about tax reform and revenue collections. The District cannot treat tax revenues as simply a function of tax rates, or treat tax equity as a matter to be addressed only when writing tax legislation. Increasing the flow of revenues and ensuring that all taxpayers pay their fair share requires turning the department into a first-rate, state-of-the-art tax collection agency. In particular, those interested in tax reform in the District of Columbia must address the following problems in the department.

Corruption and Incompetence

The Department of Finance and Revenue risks a serious potential for corruption as well as the perpetuation of incompetence. This study did not seek to investigate corruption, and the line separating corruption from incompetence may be hard to distinguish. But there are warning signs that cannot be ignored. Any organization, public or private, that handles large amounts of money has to have controls to discourage and expose corruption. The probability that corruption takes place increases with weak internal management, inadequate controls, lack of external oversight, lack of a professional ethos, greater tax liabilities, and chaotic organizational structure. The lack of management, controls, and oversight at the DFR has been well documented. In addition, the department has no resident inspector general. Neither managers nor employees have had anyone checking on them. Because employees will sometimes yield to temptation, accepting bribes and committing outright theft, in even the most tightly run agencies, it is reasonable to assume that such behavior is more than a theoretical issue in the District's revenue operation.

There are specific situations to worry about. First, the District has as many large underassessments as overassessments. Undervaluation of property may be the result of incompetence or overwork, or it may be intentional. It should be systematically investigated. Second, because tax payment information can be recorded and changed by so many employees, there is no way to know who canceled an account due or whether the action was proper or improper.[15] Until the accounting systems are

15. Arthur Anderson, "Report of Preliminary Recommendations," p. DFR-10.

upgraded to limit and record access, special oversight and permission for account changes should be instituted. Third, controls over cash are inadequate. "Temporary employees and the lowest-grade employees are walking deposits to treasury unescorted, [and] too many people are handling receipts."[16] This practice should have been remedied already, but other aspects of the operation, including inadequate systems, indicate a sloppiness in handling and accounting for cash. Fourth, growing backlogs of work offer opportunities and temptations to move files to the bottom of the pile, to change numbers, or to see that outstanding bills or taxpayers disappear.

Finally, audit personnel, uneasy in their understanding of the tax laws, unfamiliar with audit procedure, and facing a savvy business community, may be losing the District as much money with one hand as they collect with the other. When audit staff are stretched, the opportunity arises to play favorites, to allow cases to languish or avoid handling them and still meet minimum revenue targets. Without strong oversight there is no way of knowing how important these forces tugging at department employees may be, nor can one distinguish or measure the effects of political favoritism, special pleading, incompetence, or corruption in revenue collection. Ensuring that there is no corruption and rooting out incompetence should be top priorities.

Voluntary Compliance

Voluntary compliance with the District's tax laws is in serious trouble. Tax evasion is impossible to measure, but the District's tax collectors openly admit that evasion is of significant proportions. Historically, the data for property tax residency exemptions have not been electronically matched against the income tax residency claims, and the District has not demonstrated an ability to enforce the relevant laws on who is a resident and should pay taxes. Matches of District and IRS computer databases by residency have resulted in an inability to collect in 76 percent of the cases.[17]

The business tax revenues are audit driven. According to the audit staff, businesses act as if they are not liable for District tax or consciously decide to minimize their liability and await an audit. Certainly, not all

16. Arthur Andersen, "Report of Preliminary Recommendations," p. DFR-12.
17. Office of the District of Columbia Auditor, "Review and Analysis of the District's Accounts Receivable," January 16, 1996, p. 8.

are audited. Those that are generally accept some liability but consistently await the auditor's challenge on specific items. With fewer than forty-five people, however, the audit staff is too small, and it is too poorly trained and lacks adequate information to cover compliance with the business income, personal property, and sales taxes that are most typically and more and more frequently evaded.

Eighty percent of the approximately $35 million in audit revenues received each year stem from two taxes: sales and corporate income.[18] Although the full range of taxes is audited, the only other audits of real significance cover the personal income and personal property taxes. Despite this narrowed focus, the management of the audit staff appears not to have pursued a strategy of maximizing revenue per auditor hour. An examination of the audit hours and revenue yield for fiscal years 1994 and 1995 indicates that audit revenues could be increased by moving auditors from work on taxes where the dollar yield per hour is lower into auditing the sales tax or even the corporate income tax.[19] The department could also focus on high-profile cases to generate voluntary compliance, something it seems not to have tried.

Public Support for DFR Activities

Public support for what is considered a hostile tax agency has been flagging. Although no one really likes the tax collector, people recognize that the job has to be done and want it done professionally and in the most helpful way possible. The modern governmental approach to tax collection has, thankfully, moved past the era of the Sheriff of Nottingham's pay up or else. Tax agencies understand that they can make collecting taxes easier and reduce compliance costs if they provide better information, clearer and simpler tax forms, and well-trained and competent employees. They can also reach out to ordinary taxpayers as well as to tax professionals.

The District government has been indifferent on most of these matters. Most District taxpayers consider the Department of Finance and Revenue a hostile and unapproachable entity. They doubt whether they will be

18. This discussion is based on unpublished data provided by the District of Columbia Department of Finance and Revenue.

19. It is possible, of course, that moving some auditors into corporate tax auditing, which involves complex issues of factor apportionment, is not possible, given their skills. But the sales tax issues are usually simple, and revenue improvements would likely result just from that staff reallocation.

able to reach someone who can answer their questions and whether the answers will be correct—and they have good reason. Openness and customer service have not been the hallmark of the department's staff or leadership, especially in supplying assessments, which are public information.[20] District assessors, for example, do not make public their methodology for classifying mixed-use properties, a major source of irritation for owners of buildings with street-access stores and apartments above. Nor do managers ordinarily allow assessors to disclose the basis for calculating the market value of commercial property. Such secretive behavior, while not unusual in state tax collection agencies, violates at least the spirit of the public nature of the property tax. It also generates a larger number of formal protests and appeals than a more transparent system might.

Technology and Unrealized Expectations

District officials and citizens may have unrealistic expectations about the possible contributions of improved technology to greater productivity at the DFR, given the department's other deficiencies. Technology is not a magic bullet, and it will need to be managed in a way the District so far has not done. Computers aid tax collection largely through their capacity for sorting, organizing, and manipulating mountains of information. But however good the hardware and software, the system will be no better than the quality of the information that goes into it and the ability of the staff using it to understand the system's output, its limits, and its potential. New technology is a necessary but not sufficient means to improve efficiency, revenue collection, and customer service.

The District's experience with computer-assisted mass appraisal (CAMA) demonstrates this. The CAMA system is meant to aid in assessing the 168,000 properties in the District by following the values of similar properties based on the latest sales information. But updated property information is often "not entered in a timely manner, if entered at all . . . information is lost during uploading and downloading of the computer files; [and] updating the property specific information . . . is now performed on a random, ad hoc basis." In addition, often "the sales information applied in the derivation of trending factors [and] multiple regression analyses is incorrect," generating large disparities between

20. Arthur Andersen, "Real Property Tax Administration," p. 50.

market sales prices and assessed values.[21] Finally, once CAMA performed its work, the District's assessors rarely applied a professional human review and oversight to the results.[22] All these problems led the District's chief financial officer to describe CAMA and the District's assessment system as "garbage in . . . garbage out."[23]

Given this experience, it is a wonder that District officials can seriously believe a proposed new computer system at the DFR will by itself produce efficient tax collection. Patterned after New York City's FAIRTAX and scheduled to be set up by the same consultant, this computer database system is meant to "enable officials in all DFR offices—delinquency, real property tax, audits, assessments, etc.—to pull up taxpayer records with a single keystroke."[24] Impressive, but what information will appear on the screen after the keystroke? Will it be accurate? What will be the price in resources and time to get it there? Clearly, the District must move into the computer database age. But given the current situation, the department will have to make a major effort at the basic tasks of information gathering, data cleansing, and training. New York City's FAIRTAX system, handling roughly the same number of taxes, although many more taxpayers, took more than six years to build and still falls short of fully integrating the property tax with all the others.

So, it might make more managerial sense for the District not to plunge into building an information database until it has addressed the fundamental shortcomings. First, to preempt future problems and prevent large amounts of consultant and staff overtime, the District must allocate resources to update the mailing address of every piece of returned mail as it comes in. No matter what direction District officials take on tax policy and structure, up-to-date information on taxpayers will be crucial.

Second, the type of database information system that is needed will depend on the tax structure. FAIRTAX and similar systems exist for state-type tax programs. The District must examine the implications of a dramatic simplification of its tax structure, along the lines recommended by this study, for such a database. The future may lie with a much simpler tax system, one without property classification, with IRS administration of a piggybacked personal income tax, and with a low gross receipts tax rather than the complex corporate and unincorporated

21. Arthur Andersen, "Real Property Tax Administration," pp. 49, 54.
22. Arthur Andersen, "Real Property Tax Administration," pp. 56, 65.
23. Loeb, "Verdict on D.C. Tax System," p. A1.
24. Ruth Levine, "Catching Up on Taxes," *Washington City Paper*, October 4, 1996, pp. 11–12.

business taxes. If so, the type of database needed would change, as would the need to handle a high volume of audit, enforcement, and collection problems.

Conclusion

Deficiencies at the Department of Finance and Revenue are costing the District serious money. Some of the costs are visible in the flagrant attitude of tax evaders; the backlogs of taxpayer information that have not been processed; the piles of returned mail that get thrown away without anyone noting the change of address; and the warning signs of possible corruption. Revenue losses are compounded when the backlogs, poor data, ill-trained staff, and obsolete operating systems lead to tax moratoriums and freezes—on assessments and on pursuing tax delinquencies, for instance—that will cut budgeted revenues in coming years.

The District is unable to enforce and fairly collect the taxes currently on the books. This study recommends that its priority be to focus on paring down the number of things it must do and then doing each thing well. Its next focus should be to build a user-friendly, technologically efficient Department of Finance and Revenue. Simplifying the District's tax system will not, in itself, bring order and efficiency to this department, but it will constitute a huge step in that direction.

CHAPTER 7

The Federal Role

T HE DISTRICT receives an annual payment from the federal government to compensate for the impact of the federal presence on local resources. At $660 million in fiscal 1995, this lump-sum appropriation was the District's single largest source of discretionary revenue. It has been authorized by Congress to remain at this annual amount until the end of the century.[1] The District receives the payment within the first quarter of the fiscal year or quarterly.

The present federal payment is unrelated to the size, importance, or responsibilities of the federal government in the District. There is no formula or expressed logic to the appropriated amount. Instead, the amount is at the annual discretion of Congress. Over the years, the federal payment has represented no consistent pattern or trend to its role in the District's discretionary revenue. In the era of home rule it has served only occasionally as a countercyclical budget stabilizer. As currently structured, it does not fully compensate the District for serving as the nation's capital and for its unique status as a city without a state. As a result, the District must levy taxes on its own residents that are dramatically higher than those in the surrounding jurisdictions, other cities, and most states.

This chapter measures the direct impact of the federal government on the revenues of the nation's capital. It proposes a formula-based logic for the federal payment, and the measurement, for three distinct elements in a new fiscal relationship. This would replace the existing federal payment. Part of the payment would be discretionary revenue, part categorical payments for specific state-type services. A formula-based approach would provide the District with much-needed budgetary stability, because both the city and the federal government would be able to calculate

1. District of Columbia, "Official Statement Relating to the Issuance of $170,580,000 General Obligation Bonds (Series 1996A)," October 1, 1996, pp. 13, 20.

the amount in advance, providing a measure of certainty. It would also provide the District with an incentive to improve its estimates of tax exemptions. Further, as this study demonstrates, if the federal fiscal relationship were to recognize specifically the burden of state-type spending and the need for state aid, the District would be able to reduce state-type taxes on both businesses and individuals, which would bring the tax burden in the District more closely in line with the surrounding area. Finally, with the federal government acting as a state, the nation's capital city would achieve parity with other American cities. It would no longer be an orphan.

An Independent Capital

The problem of governing any capital is difficult because there is always a conflict of interests between the national government and the people who live in the capital city. The government wishes to control and develop the capital in the interests of the nation as a whole, while the people of the city naturally wish to govern themselves to the greatest extent possible. In addition, the government of a federal capital presents a special problem which is inherent in the very nature of federalism: if the national capital of a federal union comes under the government of any one state of the union, that state is in a position to dominate the federation's capital, and the central government does not have control over its own seat of government.[2]

The drafters of the Constitution foresaw those inherent conflicts and chose a federal capital that placed the interests of the national government above those of the people who live in the city.

As a special entity the District of Columbia belongs to the nation. Every taxpaying American supports the nation's capital through federal taxes. These resources pay for the upkeep of federal buildings and monuments that are appropriately federal expenditures. They also cover the federal payment to the District, which, at $660 million, amounts to less than five cents a week, $2.50 a year for each American. All citizens benefit from the existence of the capital. People from the entire country have free access to the seat of government, their elected representatives, the

2. Donald C. Rowat, ed., *The Government of Federal Capitals* (University of Toronto Press, 1973), p. xi.

home of their president, the monuments that record much of their history, and the museums that hold the nation's treasures. On a more intangible level, all citizens benefit from the existence of an independent capital city that is free from the parochial politics of any one state. Such independence requires that Congress, on behalf of the nation's citizens, act as a responsible caretaker and provide the resources to allow the District to furnish the required services without imposing a punitive tax burden on its residents, who, although not represented in Congress, are fellow citizens of the United States.

The Federal Payment from 1790 to Home Rule in 1973

The nation's capital was created by the Constitution.[3] Article I, section 8, clause 17 states: "Congress shall have the power to exercise exclusive legislation in all cases whatsoever, over such district (not exceeding ten miles square) as may, by cession of particular states, and the acceptance of Congress, become the seat of the government of the United States." Created in 1791, the District of Columbia has served as the capital of the United States since 1800.[4] The Constitution did not define the fiscal relationship between the District and the federal government, and until 1870 there was no formalized fiscal relationship. A federal payment was made in only twenty-three of the first forty-five years of the District's existence and represented almost 24 percent of municipal expenditures during the period. From 1836 to 1870, contributions continued to be irregular but represented a little more than 41 percent of the District's expenditures.

During the 1870s, Congress debated the federal payment along with more general governance issues related to the District. In June 1874 the House Committee on the Judiciary released the Poland Report, which concluded that the District should receive a regular and predictable federal payment equal to at least one-half of its total budget. The report was the first to recommend a fixed percentage formula for the federal payment, although it did not include legislation.

---

3. This section draws heavily on Michael E. Bell, "The Federal Payment to the District of Columbia," in *Technical Aspects of the District's Tax System*, House Committee on the District of Columbia, 95 Cong. 2 sess.; and "Financing the Nation's Capital: The Report of the Commission on Budget and Financial Priorities of the District of Columbia," November 1990.

4. District of Columbia, "Official Statement," p. ii.

In December 1874 the Joint Select Committee on the Affairs of the Government of the District of Columbia recommended another formula in the Morill Report. The report suggested that the federal payment provide the necessary revenue to balance the District's budget after the inclusion of locally raised revenues collected through taxes and fees set at rates comparable with those prevailing in other communities. The report thus introduced the concept of a link between the federal government's fiscal responsibilities and the District's tax burden.

In 1878, after consideration of the Poland and Morill reports and further debate, Congress passed the District of Columbia Organic Act, which, in addition to establishing a commission form of government, enacted the 50-50 funding arrangement suggested in the Poland Report. This formula prevailed until 1921, when it was replaced with a 40-60 formula, with the District responsible for the larger share. In 1925 Congress abandoned the percentage formula and began instead to negotiate a lump sum payment to the District.

The Revenue Act of 1939 legally sanctioned Congress's actions since 1925; use of the lump-sum payment became official. But in passing the legislation, Congress ignored two additional congressional reports about the proper formulation of the federal payment. A 1929 report by the Bureau of Efficiency had identified two important criteria in calculating the federal payment: the taxes the federal government would pay if it were a municipal taxpayer and the cost attributed to the federal government's extraordinary presence in the District. In 1937 the Jacobs Report had provided another reason, this time political, for the federal payment: compensation to the District for the lack of home rule. As with the Morill Report of sixty-three years earlier, the calculation of the federal payment was to be based on the federal government's providing the additional revenue needed to balance the District budget after the District set tax rates comparable to the local tax burden in cities of similar size and with similar service responsibilities.

The Federal Payment since Home Rule

The federal payment became a topic of renewed debate during the home rule deliberations of the early 1970s.[5] The 1972 *Report of the Commis-*

5. This section is drawn primarily from District of Columbia Appleseed Center for Law and Justice, "The Case for a More Fair and Predictable Federal Payment for the District," November 2, 1995.

sion of the Government of the District of Columbia (the Nelson Commission) concluded that there was no objective, mathematically precise formula for calculating the federal payment. In 1973 the House of Representatives rejected a bill setting the federal payment at an amount equal to 37.5 percent of the District's own-source revenue for fiscal year 1974, with the percentage rising to 40 percent for subsequent years. Instead it authorized a lump-sum payment.

Although it rejected a formula-based calculation, Congress directly acknowledged the unique position of the District of Columbia in the Home Rule Act. In Title V it requires the mayor to detail costs and benefits to the District of its unusual role as the nation's capital when preparing the District's annual budget. The act also identifies the categories of information that rationalize a federal payment. Most of the criteria are familiar because the act mimics several of Congress's reports. The mayor is required to the extent feasible to provide information describing:

—revenues unobtainable because of the relative lack of taxable commercial and industrial property;

—revenues unobtainable because of the relative lack of taxable business income;

—potential revenues that would be realized if exemptions from District taxes were eliminated;

—net costs, if any, for providing services to tax-exempt nonprofit organizations and corporate offices doing business only with the federal government;

—recurring and nonrecurring costs of unreimbursed services to the federal government;

—other expenditure requirements placed on the District by the federal government that are unique to the District;

—benefits of federal grants in aid relative to aid given to other states and local governments;

—recurring and nonrecurring costs of unreimbursed services rendered to the District by the federal government; and

—the tax burden of District residents compared with that of residents in other jurisdictions in the Washington metropolitan area and in other cities of comparable size.[6] Although Title V mandates that the District estimate the federal government's impact on it, Congress is not required

6. *District of Columbia Self-Government and Governmental Reorganization Act*, 87 Stat. 774.

to use the information to calculate the federal payment. And it appears not to have done so.

In 1991 Congress returned to a percentage-based formula to calculate the federal payment. The District of Columbia Budgetary Efficiency Act of 1991 established a formula for fiscal years 1993 through 1995 in which Congress agreed to give the District a federal payment equal to 24 percent of the District's audited own-source revenues for the fiscal year two years earlier. As a result the District received $636 million in fiscal 1993 and $648 million in fiscal 1994.

In setting the payment the House committee report also identified four extraordinary costs caused by the federal presence that justified the federal payment: Congress's refusal to allow the District to impose an income tax on nonresidents who work in the city; the congressionally imposed limitation on the height of buildings in the District; the presence of large amounts of federal tax-exempt property; and expenses caused by federal events such as parades and demonstrations.

In 1994 Congress abandoned the percentage-based formula again and returned to a lump-sum payment. The Payment Reauthorization Act of 1994 set the 1995 federal payment at $660 million. The law creating the District of Columbia Financial Authority authorizes the federal payment at $660 million through 1999 and requires that the payment be made to the authority on behalf of the District.[7]

Unfair and Unstable

We agree with the Poland Report that the federal appropriation to the District should "be made regularly and upon some well-informed principle." The federal payment—whether a percentage of the District's budget, a percentage of its own-source revenue, a negotiated lump-sum, or a flat amount—has never been based on a calculation of the impact of the federal presence. Because of that, the payment has been hard to justify to the nation as a whole and to Congress.

Congress has recently chosen a stable and predictable federal payment at the expense of fairness. The $660 million a year authorized through 1999 is not based on a careful determination of the District's needs and does not adequately compensate the District for the costs of being the nation's capital. Instead it is a set amount frozen through the end of the

7. District of Columbia, "Official Statement," p. 48.

Figure 7-1 *Change in Federal Payment and District of Columbia Own-Source Revenue, Fiscal Years 1987–95*

Percent

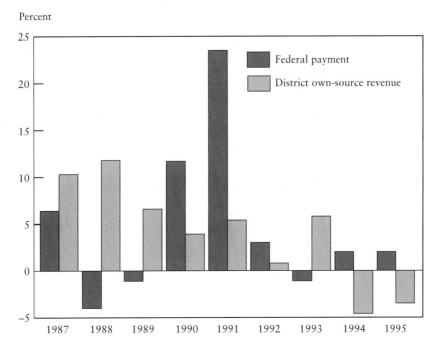

Source: *District of Columbia Comprehensive Annual Financial Report, September 30, 1995,* exhibit S-1 (hereafter CAFR, 1995).

century for the sake of budgetary predictability and simplicity. The lack of empirical grounding for the amount is indicative of the recent history of the federal payment.

Figure 7-1 shows the percentage change in the federal payment and the District's own-source revenues from 1987 to 1995. At times the federal payment served as a countercyclical budget stabilizer, particularly in 1994 and 1995 when it increased as own-source revenue declined. Overall, however, in very recent years the federal payment has performed no consistent stabilizing function for the District's discretionary revenues.

Tracking the federal payment from the start of Home Rule in 1974 makes clear the variation and instability in the amount. Figure 7-2 shows that the federal payment as a percentage of own-source revenues declined dramatically in the 1970s, stabilized at approximately 25 percent in the mid-1980s, declined to a fifteen-year low of 18.1 percent in 1989, and recently has been steadily rising toward the 25 percent level of the 1980s.

Figure 7-2. *Federal Payment as Share of District of Columbia
Own-Source Revenue, Fiscal Years 1974–95*

Percent

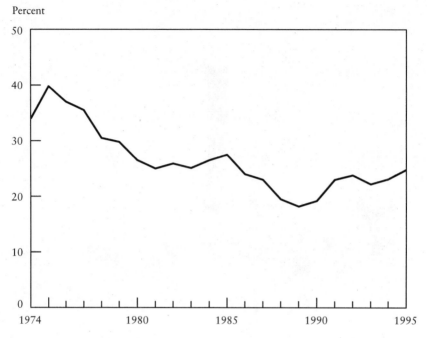

Sources: *District of Columbia CAFR, September 30, 1983*, exhibit S-4; *CAFR, 1985*, exhibit S-3; and *CAFR, 1995*, exhibit S-1.

Proposal for a Fair Federal Payment

It is in the national interest to have a capital city that functions well. A
fair federal payment would recognize the District's role as the nation's
capital, compensate the District for its role, and ensure that it remains
viable and its tax costs competitive with surrounding jurisdictions and
other cities. Congress must now meet these responsibilities in order to
make America's capital city world renowned again.

Congress has never adopted a federal payment formula that reflected
its own interpretation of the federal government's fiscal responsibility to
the capital. In fact, the only time it ever enacted a formula-based payment
was the "percentage of own source revenue" formula that existed from
1878 to 1925 and briefly resurfaced in 1993. That formula is flawed,
however, because a decline in own-source revenues, indicating the District is in need of additional funds, perversely triggers a reduction in the

federal payment. In addition, the formula provides an incentive for the District to inflate its budget. In the case of the 50-50 formula, for every dollar of expenditure increase in the budget, the District would only have to raise fifty cents in taxes or fees. Such a formula is also unfair because it does not link the federal payment to the fiscal impact of the federal government on the District of Columbia.

We propose a *new fiscal relationship with the federal government*. This relationship would have three elements. Each addresses a particular part of the District's revenue shortage that results from its unique nature of the nation's capital.

—The federal government should make a payment in lieu of taxes (PILOT) to cover fully the services received by the 41 percent of the District's property tax base that is, by federal determination, exempt from taxation. This would allow property taxes to be reduced for all owners.

—The federal government should provide state-type aid of an amount comparable to that received from their state governments by cities of similar size. This would simply provide parity for the District compared with other American cities.

—There should be a 50-50 sharing of state-type spending, including the state share of medicaid and welfare. This categorical aid would partially compensate the District for the fact that it has no state to provide a range of state services while providing an incentive for efficient service delivery. The compensation would not be necessary, of course, if the federal government chose to provide these services directly to District residents.

The following sections set out the logic of each of these elements and derive values for them.

The PILOT

The District's tax base is severely constrained because it is the nation's capital. Forty-one percent of the property is exempt from property taxes. Sixty-five percent of the people who work in the District live elsewhere and do not contribute to the income tax base. Congress does not allow the District to impose a nonresident tax to help pay for public services provided to commuters during their workday. The District cannot collect taxes on the purchases or income of the large number of military personnel and foreign diplomats living and doing business there. Finally, the federal government does not pay sales tax on purchases or personal property taxes on its equipment.

From the perspective of a city, property tax exemptions are the most significant lost source of revenue, and our PILOT focuses exclusively on that.[8] First, the exemption is a subsidy to certain public and private organizations that is proportional to their use of real property. Thus the existence of tax-exempt property bears an opportunity cost equal to the alternative taxable use of property owned by tax-exempt entities.[9] Second, taxable property owners may face higher tax burdens to finance services provided to tax-exempt properties.[10] In cities with high tax burdens and increasing service demands, large amounts of tax-exempt property may also result in fiscal stress because there is a limited tax base to fund services.[11] Third, tax-exempt entities tend to concentrate in areas where there is already a large portion of tax-exempt property. The District has such a concentration because many nonprofit organizations have established headquarters in the city, a development that has often been attributed to their desire to be located near the federal government. Thus, economic analysis would indicate that the District suffers from inefficient land use, high tax burdens, potential fiscal stress, and the further erosion of the tax base because of its role as the seat of the national government.

The economic inefficiency and burden of imposing so much tax-exempt property on the District suggest to some that the efficacy of property tax exemptions should be reexamined. However, the exemption of government property and the property of universities, cultural institutions, nonprofits, and churches is a common practice. As a result, there are strong arguments for payments that represent full tax equivalency from higher levels of government to local jurisdictions.[12]

The most frequent counterargument to full-tax-equivalency PILOTs is that such an approach does not consider the benefits that accrue to a

8. Property tax exemptions and payments in lieu of taxes are discussed more fully in appendix C.

9. Henry J. Raimondo, "Compensation Policy for Tax-Exempt Property in Theory and Practice," *Land Economics*, vol. 56 (February 1980), pp. 34–42; and John M. Quigley and Roger W. Schmenner, "Property Tax Exemption and Public Policy," *Public Policy*, vol. 23 (Summer 1975), pp. 259–97.

10. Quigley and Schmenner, "Property Tax Exemption," p. 260.

11. John K. Mullen, "Property Tax Exemptions and Local Fiscal Stress," *National Tax Journal*, vol. 43 (December 1990), p. 474.

12. Some scholars argue for a two-part formula with a payment-for-services portion and a PILOT or direct taxation to address the tax base burden. Christina Fong and Jeff Kuenzi, *Reimbursing Municipalities for the Presence of State-Owned Properties* (University of Massachusetts, Office of Institutional Research and Planning, 1994), pp. 10–11.

jurisdiction as a result of the tax-exempt property located there. This argument is not persuasive. First, the benefits of tax exemptions are enjoyed by a much larger constituency than the local taxpayers who bear the resulting higher tax burden. Second, the consideration of the benefits of government property as a criterion for the amount of taxes paid is profoundly unfair. As many economists have noted, no other property pays taxes that net-out their contribution to the jurisdiction.[13] "All businesses (and probably other organizations as well) will create some favorable economic effects in providing jobs and income. A city could not remove all such property from the tax rolls if these economic effects or benefits exceeded the lost revenue from property tax exemption. To exempt *some* property on this basis and not *all* of it violates the rules of equity in tax administration."[14]

Overall, the determination by the federal government of property tax exemptions reflects an unfunded mandate placed on the District, a mandate much like those states place on their cities. The federal government should compensate the District for the cost of the tax exemptions through a full-tax-equivalency PILOT.

Playing the State Parent

This study accepts the present congressional governance of the District and focuses on revenue solutions within it.[15] There has been continuing federal concern, expressed directly in legislation, that the District's tax burden be comparable to the burden in surrounding jurisdictions and other cities. Currently, the District's taxes are among the highest in the nation.[16] As the sovereign government responsible for the District of

13. For example, see Michael E. Bell, "Alternative Treatments of Governmentally Owned Tax-Exempt Properties in Urban Economies," in *1977 Proceedings of the Seventieth Annual Conference on Taxation* (Columbus, Ohio, 1978), p. 180; and Advisory Commission on Intergovernmental Relations, *Payments in Lieu of Taxes on Federal Real Property*, A-90 (Washington, 1981), p. 81.

14. Richard L. Pfister, "A Reevaluation of the Justifications for Property Tax Exemption," *Public Finance Quarterly*, vol. 4 (October 1976), pp. 431–52.

15. The analysis of the revenue components presented here might be helpful in analyzing different governance options, such as statehood and retrocession.

16. The District has the second highest level of taxes per capita among the fifty states and the highest level of taxes per capita compared with major U.S. cities. Thomas N. Edmonds and Raymond J. Keating, *D.C. by the Numbers* (University Press of America, 1995), pp. 20, 21. See this study's table 1-1 for comparisons with Boston, Baltimore, and Memphis and chapter 2 for comparisons with surrounding jurisdictions.

Columbia, the federal government must also act as the "state," the intermediating level of government in American federalism. This involves providing general "state aid" as well as specific aid for certain types of services, or even providing direct services.

There is a general order to American federalism and the resulting revenue and spending responsibilities of the various levels of government. The states, having constitutional sovereignty, have delegated considerable power to the national government. Since the Employment Act of 1946, the national government has taken responsibility for using monetary and fiscal policy to keep the economy at high levels of employment and growth with reasonable price stability. In addition, it has taken the lead as redistributor of income and wealth, modifying the market-determined distribution in line with goals of social equity, especially providing assistance to the poor. As Edwin Cannon noted in 1896, "Measures adopted to produce greater equality are . . . exceedingly unsuitable for local authorities. The smaller the locality the more capricious and ineffectual are likely to be any efforts it may make to carry out such a policy. It seems clearly desirable that all such measures should be applied to the largest possible area."[17]

Although the national government provides some public goods, like national defense, most such goods and services are provided through state and local governments. The states have the constitutional responsibility for ensuring freedom, quality of life, and a measure of justice for their residents. These days, states limit their direct provision of services to large, basic infrastructure systems—the courts, prisons, licensing and regulation, universities, and highways—but they provide the funding and the rules for the provision of local-level services such as elementary and secondary education, child care, and foster care. Through municipal home rule legislation, states delegate varying degrees of responsibilities to local governments. Most American cities share those responsibilities with overlapping or contiguous counties. Typically, under home rule arrangements the state controls city taxes, setting the rates and defining the base. Often the state administers the tax or allows the city to piggyback on a state tax; sometimes it charges for administration.[18]

17. Carol O'Cleireacain, "Cities' Role in the Metropolitan Economy and the Federal Structure," in Henry G. Cisneros, ed., *Interwoven Destinies: Cities and the Nation* (Norton, 1993), p. 171.

18. For example, only fourteen states allow cities or counties to levy local income taxes. See Advisory Commission on Intergovernmental Relations, *Significant Features of Fiscal Federalism*, vol. 1: *Budget Processes and Tax Systems* (Washington, 1995), tables 20, 21.

No two American cities are alike in their revenue or spending respon-sibilities, but they share the common characteristic that when trouble hits, there is a state government to which they can turn and that has the authority to take charge. The fiscal crises of New York City, Philadelphia, Orange County, Bridgeport, and, most recently, Miami represent a va-riety of fiscal problems and state-generated solutions, including control boards, state-appointed auditors, state backing in credit markets and help in restructuring debt. States have also taken over provision of certain services. During the New York City fiscal crisis of the mid-1970s, the state permanently shifted the funding and administration of the senior colleges of the city university system and the city court system to the state government. State takeovers of problem school districts in New Jersey and Illinois demonstrate that, even with home rule, ultimate responsibil-ity for local services in the American federal structure rests with the state government.

Without a state government, the nation's capital is orphaned. Al-though the District does not receive the state aid that other cities get, it has to provide a range of public services that states typically provide. In the current fiscal crisis the federal government has stepped in, establishing a control board with emergency powers and providing emergency ser-vices. In doing so, it has followed the state model of governance and home rule. This report expands the model to include a restructuring of the revenue relationship between the District and its higher governmental authority.

As table 1-1 showed, Massachusetts provides Boston with about $429 million and Maryland provides Baltimore with more than $650 million in state aid. These revenues substitute for city taxes that might be levied. State aid represents a form of revenue sharing within the state, which is a larger and more diverse economy than any locality. "Through its grants the state can redistribute resources to aid localities with low fiscal capac-ities and can help in the provision of goods of local merit or those that have positive spillovers. . . . [Often] the aid . . . serves as an alternative to state assumption of full responsibility for . . . functions such as edu-cation, highways, and welfare, leaving administration and performance . . . primarily in local hands."[19]

In the case of central cities, state aid especially represents a way to ease the burdens of higher service needs and weaker fiscal health: "A

---

19. J. Richard Aronson and John L. Hilley, *Financing State and Local Government,* 4th ed. (Brookings, 1986), pp. 78, 81.

city's fiscal health depends on . . . economic and social factors . . . and on its state-determined fiscal institutions, including its access to broad-based taxes, the taxes collected by overlying jurisdictions, its service responsibilities, and the intergovernmental grants it receives from its state."[20] The District is not only lacking in these forms of state support, it is providing the support itself.

Of course, in the case of other cities it is *a portion* of state taxes paid by residents that flows back in the form of state aid. The remainder of the financing comes from the rest of the state, with higher burdens borne by richer areas. In the case of the District, if the federal government were to act as the state, the "state aid" would be financed from national revenue, with only a very small amount coming out of the District's economy. This does not invalidate the parity argument. First, because all states seek to export as much of their tax burden as possible, levying taxes in ways in which the costs are passed on to national and even international shareholders, customers, or workers, it is simply not possible to locate where the ultimate tax burden rests.[21] Second, state aid flows to all localities and to counties. Certainly, the District contributes to federal tax revenues; the contribution is simply a small part of total federal collections. In this way, the District is to the federal "state" no different than any number of small counties to their states. They pay taxes, however small a part of the total, and they receive state aid.

In addition, Massachusetts and Maryland share with the federal government in providing medicaid and welfare for Boston and Baltimore's poor.[22] State taxes cover the state share. The District's "state" share, at 50 percent, amounts to $440.7 million, currently raised from District taxes. If the federal government were to pick up the entire "state" share for the District, the city might be able to function more like Boston and Baltimore. Of course, the federal government would either have to run the programs or exercise extraordinary oversight with strict penalties, since local administration with no resources at stake provides no incentive for cost efficiency. Further, with the federal government fully exercising state responsibilities for medicaid in the District, the nation's tax-

20. Helen F. Ladd and John Yinger, *America's Ailing Cities: Fiscal Health and the Design of Urban Policy* (John Hopkins University Press, 1989), p. 14.

21. Severance taxes on oil and minerals, sales and special taxes on tourism, and Michigan's business activity tax are a few examples.

22. Medicaid spending is considerably larger than welfare, and given the lack of experience with the recent move to a federal block grant to states for welfare, this discussion will use the term *medicaid* to cover the income redistribution programs.

payers would bear all of the cost of the poor residents of the nation's capital, a federal role exercised nowhere else.[23]

Thus less than 100 percent federal funding for medicaid would, at the moment, appear to be required on grounds of efficiency and political expediency. That leaves the city-type model of medicaid spending. About one-quarter of the states require a portion of medicaid be paid by localities, but those are usually counties. New York City, though, pays 25 percent of the cost of medicaid (New York State pays 25 percent and the federal government pays half).[24] New York City is subject to the eligibility requirements, reporting rules, auditing strictures, and other oversight required by New York State and the federal government. The District would face only federal rules and oversight. In that way, it would resemble Mississippi, West Virginia, and Arkansas, which provide 25 percent or less of their own resources toward medicaid and run their own programs.[25]

Of course, the District provides other state-type services that are funded only by its residents. The federal government can play the role of the state by providing these state-type services directly, or it can compensate the District, or it might combine both approaches. To do so requires agreement between the federal government and the District as to which services can legitimately be classified as state-type and which are clearly not. There are perhaps as many definitions of state services as there are states. A recent study by Philip Dearborn and Carol Meyers for the District's Control Board categorized the District's expenditures as state-type or local-type or as typically shared between states and localities. As table 7-1, which reproduces their study's distributions, shows, the largest categories of state-type spending by the District are medicaid, welfare, mental health, foster care, and higher education. The amount of spending commonly shared by state and local governments, which is dominated

---

23. Although many have argued that this approach would be the best national model of income redistribution, unless it were applied to the fifty states, it is doubtful Congress would bestow it on the District. In particular, Alice M. Rivlin makes a strong case that the federal government should take responsibility for health coverage and health care containment, including medicaid, which would remove the fastest rising unfunded mandate from states and place the national government in the principal role in income distribution policy. See *Reviving the American Dream: The Economy, the States and the Federal Government* (Brookings, 1992),

24. Carol O'Cleireacain, "A Case Study in Fiscal Federalism: New York City and New York State," *Fordham Urban Law Journal*, vol. 19, no. 3 (1992), pp. 727–45.

25. Advisory Commission on Intergovernmental Relations, *Significant Features of Fiscal Federalism*, vol. 2: *Revenues and Expenditures* (Washington, 1994), table 95.

Table 7-1. *District of Columbia State-Type and City-Type Services, Appropriated Expenditures, 1995*

Millions of dollars

Service	State-type	City-type	Both
AFDC	62.8		
SSI supplements	5.2		
General relief	7.5		
Need determination	23.3		
Foster care	59.5		
Development disabilities	27.0		
Child day care			23.8
Elderly services		20.2	
Homeless		12.7	
Rehabilitation	6.8		
Child support	2.9		
Disease prevention			5.7
Medical examiner		1.9	
School health		4.6	
Health labs	1.4		
Medicaid	377.9		
D.C. General Hospital			56.7
Health clinics		20.2	
Long-term care	4.0		
HIV/AIDS			6.1
Alcohol and drugs		23.0	
Mental health	113.7		
Public schools			613.7
Higher education	53.9		
Training			14.1

by public education, debt service, and adult corrections, is more than twice the amount of state-type spending. State aid should cover much of this typically shared spending. With respect to state-type spending, the federal government could provide the service directly or by contracting with a neighboring state to provide it. In some cases, economies of scale might lead to lower costs. We have not determined either the feasibility or the cost of such an option. Rather, since this is a revenue study, we have focused on estimating the compensation to the District if there were to be no direct federal provision of state-type services.

Of course, the federal government could decide that rather than assume the responsibilities of a state by itself, it would spread the burden to the surrounding region. If so, the logic of an earnings tax on nonresidents employed in the District is inescapable. The small city-type com-

Table 7-1. *(Continued)*

Service	State-type	City-type	Both
Police		366.8	
Adult corrections			238.8
Juvenile corrections			35.3
Parole	5.4		
Mass transit		123.1	
Streets			37.0
Parking enforcement		9.2	
Vehicle registration and related	5.7		
Fire and emergency medical services		150.4	
Courts			87.3
Pretrial services		3.2	
Indigent representation		37.9	
Parks and recreation			25.2
Public library		19.8	
Arts and humanities			1.7
Regulations		34.9	
Housing and community development		15.4	
Economic development			7.8
Settlements and judgments			14.5
Solid waste		21.0	
City planning		3.2	
Legislative			7.7
Elections		2.5	
Financial management			36.5
Debt service		366.4	
Totals	757.0	870.0	1,578.3

Source: Philip W. Dearborn and Carol S. Meyers, "The Necessity and Costs of District of Columbia Services," Greater Washington Research Center, August 1966, table 7.

muter tax estimated in chapter 4 could provide an alternative source of funding for state aid.[26]

An Alternative: Federal Tax Expenditure

There are, of course, other approaches that the federal government might take to compensate the District. For example, Eleanor Holmes Norton, the District's nonvoting delegate to Congress, has proposed a 15 percent federal flat income tax for District residents.[27]

26. A flat 2 percent tax on nonresident income would raise $361 million.
27. This is based on the legislation introduced in the 104th Congress, HR 3244, April 15, 1996.

The Norton proposal would reduce the federal income tax on District residents by changing the current five-rate, progressive federal income tax to one rate (the current minimum of 15 percent) on wages earned in the greater metropolitan area and on District-source nonwage income. Capital gains would be exempt if their source is in the District. The proposal would also increase exemptions for bona fide residents from the current IRS standard deduction plus one exemption of $6,400, to $15,000 for single filers, $25,000 for heads of households, and $30,000 for joint filers, thus effectively eliminating the federal income tax on a family of four at $30,000.

The 15 percent flat tax would only benefit District residents currently paying federal income tax. About 45 percent of residents do not pay any federal income tax, with many receiving the earned income tax credit. Among the 55 percent with a federal tax liability, the greatest benefits of the cut would go to those with the highest incomes because of the progressivity of the federal personal income tax. Taxpayers with annual incomes in excess of $200,000 would receive 28.5 percent of the total benefit—on average a 6.4 percent tax reduction worth $34,680 (tables 7-2 and 7-3). Middle-income taxpayers, earning from $40,000 to $75,000 annually, would receive a tax cut in the range of $2,210 to $2,700 a year.[28]

The immediate cost to the federal government would be an estimated $675 million to $750 million in income tax revenues, based on current residents and current incomes. If policy were to succeed in attracting residents to the District, the annual cost to the federal Treasury would be greater. The Joint Committee on Taxation estimates that by 2006 the annual cost could grow to $1.8 billion.[29]

Unfortunately, the Norton proposal does not provide direct budget relief to the District as it struggles to reach fiscal balance under its four-year plan. The assumption of the proposal is that the lowered federal taxes will lure families who have left for the neighboring suburbs back to the District. But there are no empirical studies as to whether tax cuts of this magnitude will indeed generate relocation.[30] In assessing the like-

28. Citizens for Tax Justice and Institute on Taxation and Economic Policy, "Microsimulation Tax Model," April 1996.

29. "Microsimulation Tax Model"; and Kenneth Kies, "Written Testimony of the Staff of the Joint Committee on Taxation regarding H.R. 3244, the District of Columbia Economic Recovery Act," Subcommittee on the District of Columbia of the House Committee on Government Reform and Oversight, 104 Cong., July 31, 1996, p. 15.

30. A thorough study of the possible effect of supply-side tax cuts was done by Joseph Cordes and others, "Analysis of Jack Kemp's Proposals for the District of Columbia," *State Tax Notes*, vol. 9 (October 30, 1995), pp. 1271–83.

Table 7-2. *District of Columbia Household Average Earnings and Income Taxes, 1995*

Dollars unless otherwise specified

Income	Percent of families[a]	Average income	Average income taxes		
			Federal	District	Total
Less than 10,000	26.2	4,100	− 180	− 210	− 390
10,000–20,000	19.7	15,200	− 40	− 80	− 120
20,000–30,000	16.9	24,900	1,630	1,050	2,680
30,000–40,000	10.8	34,500	3,370	1,840	5,210
40,000–50,000	7.9	44,500	5,170	2,730	7,900
50,000–75,000	8.6	59,800	7,610	3,580	11,190
75,000–100,000	3.8	86,400	12,650	5,550	18,200
100,000–200,000	4.3	130,000	20,470	8,210	28,680
More than 200,000	1.8	546,000	107,740	32,970	140,710
Total	100.0	39,600	5,000	2,000	7,000

Source: Citizens for Tax Justice and Institute on Taxation and Economic Policy, "Microsimulation Tax Model," April 1996.

a. Taxpayers and nonfilers.

lihood, one needs to measure whether families left because of tax costs or for other reasons. The standard public finance theory argues that households base their location decisions on the locality's package of taxes and services.[31] Indeed, the debate within the District continues to be whether residents will return, regardless of the tax burden, before the local government has turned around its failure to provide adequate schools, public safety, passable streets, and drinkable water. For example, for middle-income families earning $40,000 to $75,000 a year, about 17 percent of present District taxpayers, the Norton tax cut would be $2,100 to $2,700 a year. For those earning $100,000 a year, the cut would be $6,500 to $7,000, roughly the cost to send one child to private school.

As this study has shown, for the nation's capital city to have a sustainable and competitive revenue structure, one on a par with cities of similar size, it will require additional help from a higher level of government. Given current District service levels, such parity would require $450 million to $500 million. Might Delegate Norton's proposal eventually generate such a level of revenues? Raising that amount in tax revenue by attracting new residents would require 100,000 middle-income families of four to move into the District.[32]

31. Charles M. Tiebout, "A Pure Theory of Local Expenditures," *Journal of Political Economy* (October 1956).

32. This is derived by dividing $475 million (midpoint) by $4,557 (average tax burden for a resident family of four at the $50,000 income level). District of Columbia Department of Finance and Revenue, *A Comparison of Tax Rates and Burdens in the Washington Metropolitan Area* (1995), p. 11.

Table 7-3. *Effect of the Norton Proposal for a 15 Percent Federal Flat Tax for District of Columbia Residents, 1995*
Dollars unless otherwise specified

Income	Percent of families[a]	Average Income	Flat tax of 15 percent					
			Federal	District	Total	Change[b]	Chg/Inc. (percent)	Percent of total
0–10,000	26.2	4,100	–180	–210	–390	…	…	…
10–20,000	19.7	15,200	630	–80	550	–590	–3.9	5.2
20–30,000	16.9	24,900	490	1,050	1,540	–1,140	–4.6	8.6
30–40,000	10.8	34,500	1,870	1,840	3,710	–1,500	–4.4	7.2
40–50,000	7.9	44,500	2,960	2,730	5,690	–2,210	–5.0	7.8
50–75,000	8.6	59,800	4,910	3,580	8,490	–2,700	–4.5	10.3
75–100,000	3.8	86,400	7,930	5,550	13,480	–4,720	–5.5	8.0
100–200,000	4.3	130,000	12,780	8,210	20,990	–7,690	–5.9	14.7
200,000+	1.8	546,000	73,060	32,970	106,030	–34,680	–6.4	28.5
Totals	100.0	39,600	2,750	2,000	4,750	–2,350	–5.7	100.0

Source: "Microsimulation Tax Model," April 1996.
a. Taxpayers and nonfilers.
b. Compared to table 7-2, column 5.

Whether such an influx is possible, how long it might take, and what the implications are for public services are open to debate. Should such a relocation take place, it would ultimately add $221 million to the federal cost of the flat tax program, bringing the total to $991 million. The federal government would be spending almost $1 billion to provide potentially about $0.5 billion of budget relief to the nation's capital.

It is not hard to understand the appeal of Delegate Norton's proposal for District residents since it represents for most of them a windfall benefit without obvious cost and does not obviously harm the rest.

Using this study's yardsticks for evaluation, the most favorable element of the flat tax is that it is simple. However, simplicity for the taxpayer will not be matched by simplicity of administration. As localities have discovered, when financial advantages are linked to geographic location, the incentives for fraud are enormous, and enforcement is not only difficult, it is expensive and time consuming. The 15 percent flat tax rate is to be restricted to "bona fide residents" of the District. The ability to enforce that definition, even at a very high cost, is certainly in doubt. And attempting to enforce it will require greater intrusion into taxpayers' privacy, so as not to create a flood of federal revenue losses, than any of the commentary on the Norton plan has yet recognized.

In terms of fairness, any flat tax represents an erosion of vertical equity and a moving away from the principle of ability to pay. Although this proposal makes no one in the District worse off, it does not directly benefit 45 percent of the households. It also distributes the greatest benefits to those in the remaining 55 percent with the largest incomes. In the context of the District's governance, many argue that there should be no taxation without representation, an appeal that residents hope has historical resonance around the country. So in the sense of political equity, it would be an improvement from the present situation. Combined with the fact that the remaining tax burden is more unevenly distributed, that does not represent an improvement.

From the nation's point of view this is an inefficient policy for providing revenue stability for the District. Transferring tax revenues to private individuals could ultimately cost the federal government twice what the District would receive in public revenues. In addition, the plan would place an open-ended future liability on the federal government, putting at political risk the existing federal payment of $660 million.

Finally, this proposal ultimately reinforces rather than assuages the unique status of the District. The federal government has already refused to allow the District to tax incomes of nonresidents, failed to provide

Table 7-4. *Proposed Restructured Relationship between the Federal Government and the District of Columbia, Fiscal Year 1995*
Millions of dollars

Category		Estimated revenue
PILOT[a]		382.5
Federal government property	280.9	
Traditional local exemptions required by Congress	69.5	
Foreign property	14.0	
Special act of Congress and executive order exemptions	18.1	
Direct state aid		434.2
Shared costs for state redistributive services (medicaid and welfare)		220.4
Shared costs for other state services[b]		158.2
TOTAL		1,195.3

Sources: Author's calculations based on District of Columbia Department of Finance and Revenue, *Study of Property, Income and Sales Tax Exemptions in the District of Columbia* (April 1995); District of Columbia Department of Finance and Revenue, *Schedule of Organizations in the District of Columbia Exempted from Real Property Taxation by Acts of Congress, 1996 Assessment*; Philip Dearborn and Carol Meyers, "The Necessity and Cost of District of Columbia Services," August 1996: and *FY 1995 Boston Comprehensive Annual Financial Report*.

a. Not included in PILOT are other tax exemptions that reduce the District's tax base and the estimated revenue forgone: sales tax on military purchases, $10.9 million; sales tax on diplomatic purchases, $11.2 million; income tax on military personnel, $21.1 million; income tax on diplomatic personnel, $25.6 million; federal and special act of Congress personal property, $52.6 million; and federal sales tax (not available).

b. State services provided by the District include the following: SSI supplements, general relief, need determination, foster care, development disabilities, rehabilitation, child support, health labs, long-term care, mental health, higher education, parole, and vehicle registration.

state-type aid, and imposed a range of state-type functions. Long-term fiscal stability will require shaping a competitive revenue structure for the District that is not unique, but more like that of a typical American city.

The Restructured Fiscal Relationship

Table 7-4 outlines the elements of the proposed federal payment. These numbers should be treated as approximate because changes in events will generate changes here. For example, the estimates are based on current District spending. If spending became more efficient, necessary revenues would decrease. The PILOT is based on Department of Finance and Revenue assessed values for exempt property. Because the assessments are required by law but are not used for any revenue purpose, they are probably outdated and inexact. They might change significantly with improvements in the assessment techniques and greater oversight. In addition, included in the medicaid amount is aid for families with dependent children (AFDC), a program recently ended and replaced by a block grant, which will generate a change in the District's spending. Finally, the amount of state aid mimics another jurisdiction. If that behavior changed, so would this amount.

The real property PILOT is based on full tax equivalency using the District's estimates for the value of tax-exempt property. The value of the PILOT will depend on the tax rate used. At the current commercial property tax rate, the PILOT would total $609 million. However, we propose reducing the commercial property tax rate to $1.35 per $100 of assessed valuation. The value of the PILOT would then be $382 million.[33]

The PILOT would compensate the District for federal government property, foreign government property (which is a direct result of the federal presence), traditional local exemptions required by Congress, and property exempted by special acts of Congress and executive order of the president. The District government property has been omitted from the federal PILOT. The traditional local exemptions date to a federal law passed December 24, 1942, and include libraries, hospitals, educational institutions, and religious properties.[34] Congress has also specifically exempted by statute such institutions as the American Association of University Women, the National Education Association, the National Society of Colonial Dames, and the Brookings Institution.[35] Finally, international institutions such as the Organization of American States and the International Monetary Fund have been exempted by executive order of the president. There is nothing, of course, to prevent the federal government from eliminating some of these exemptions, tying them to certain community services or charitable actions, or even pressuring nondiplomatic entities to pay PILOTs of their own (see appendix C).

The federal PILOT would be part of the section of the federal budget that includes other PILOTs, and it would be determined by the assessed value of the exempt property and the commercial property tax rate (which this study has lowered and constrained not to exceed 150 percent of the residential rate). At least at the beginning of this new PILOT, there would be an advantage for the federal and District governments to form a part-

33. It would be $303 million at the median suburban rate of $1.07 and $272 at the current residential rate of $0.96.

34. See 56 Stat. 1089, chap. 826. In other cities exemptions of this type are required by state law or state constitution.

35. In 1995 the Brookings Institution's property tax exemption was worth $250,000. Under the new lower commercial property tax rate proposed in this study ($1.35 per $100 assessed value) and assuming the same assessed value, the exemption would be about $157,000.

nership with the International Association of Assessing Officers (IAAO) to ensure state-of-the-art valuation for some of the unique properties in the nation's capital. There are valuation techniques available; for example, New York City values Central Park and receives PILOTs from the state of New York for the World Trade Center and Battery Park City.

The amount of state aid shown in table 7-4 is derived from the amount of aid that Boston receives per capita from Massachusetts multiplied by the current District population.[36] This would be a discretionary revenue for the District to spend as it determines or to substitute for existing tax revenue.

We have divided the compensation for state-type services into medicaid and welfare and all others. We propose that the federal government pick up an additional 25 percent share, thus paying 75 percent of the cost of medicaid. This would put the District's share at 25 percent, like New York City, the only city paying for this burden. The cost would be about $220.4 million.

For the other state-type services that the District provides, it spends about $316 million (table 7-1). We are proposing 50-50 sharing of the actual cost, amounting to $158.2 million.

The total federal resources committed in this new relationship amount to about $1.2 billion, based on present spending patterns. These resources would pass to the District in three ways: as a PILOT, which would be a substitute for property tax revenue for the District; as state aid, a formula-based discretionary revenue for the District; and as a 50-50 split for state-type services, including medicaid, which would be categorical revenue that the District would be able to spend only on these services and subject to oversight.

In sum, as the calculations in this book show, the federal payment currently falls $535 million (45 percent) short of fully compensating the District for being the nation's capital. Increasing the resources, basing them on the logic of the burdens borne by the nation's capital, and making them predictable would help provide ongoing budget balance for the District. It would also allow the District to simplify and lower taxes on residents and businesses. The new fiscal relationship would cost the average American annually about $4.50. This is the price for a capital city that is, as the nation's founders intended, separate from any state government and that reflects the nation's purpose well.

36. Boston's state aid amount comes roughly to half of the cost of the two largest services—education and adult corrections—that Dearborn and Meyers categorize as being commonly shared between state and local governments around the country (table 7-1). It is reassuring when two distinct logics lead to roughly the same conclusions.

Epilogue

THIS BOOK comes at a crucial time and in a special context. From the beginning of the 1990s the federal government has become more closely involved with the financial problems of the nation's capital. It has increased the federal payment four times. In 1995 Congress took control of the District's finances by declaring a fiscal emergency, empowering a presidentially appointed Control Board to achieve a balanced budget by 1999, and ensuring an independent chief financial officer for the District. In 1996 the board took control of both the District's lottery operation and the public schools.[1] With the federal government's attention and interest in the District's problems of long-run solvency, the public's attention has refocused from daily administrative and budget problems to the fundamental matters of structure and survival.

This study accepted the urgency of reorienting the District toward achieving long-term structural budget balance. My researchers and I began with recent studies of the District's financial problems (see appendix D for a selected list). Assuming that after the 1996 national elections, a new administration and Congress would turn again to the District's fiscal situation, we set January 1997 as our reporting deadline. A shortened version of the findings and recommendations of this study was released as Brookings Institution Policy Brief #11 on January 14, 1997.

On that same day President Clinton outlined his initiative for the nation's capital city. That action opened a historic opportunity to restructure the relationship between the federal government and the nation's capital. It guaranteed that the future of the District would be on the policy agenda for the 105th Congress and into the twenty-first century.

---

1. The board placed the chief financial officer in charge of the lottery and appointed a new superintendent and oversight board for the schools.

The President's Proposal

The President's National Capital Revitalization and Self-Government Improvement Plan is a work in progress. The January outline contained a mixture of proposals for federal relief to the District. It included the federal government's taking back responsibility for the unfunded pension system it passed to the District with home rule in the mid-1970s; spending on some state-type services; federal aid for capital and infrastructure spending; economic development incentives; and administrative help. In exchange the president proposed to eliminate the federal payment and insisted, in support of the Control Board, that the District move to a budget balanced in accordance with generally accepted accounting principles (GAAP) in fiscal year 1998, one year earlier than required under existing law.

In January 1997 the President's Office of Management and Budget costed the entire plan, including the economic development component and the elimination of the federal payment, at $339 million over five years. However, because the proposal combined operating budget relief with capital budget spending, it was not easy for the District, Congress, or outside analysts to estimate the value that this proposal would provide annually for the District's operating budget and four-year financial plan.

The White House said that the president's proposal was budget neutral to the District for fiscal 1998.[2] Any analysis of the proposal at the time this volume is going to press is very tentative because of the lack of details. Also, it would not be terribly useful, since the details are subject to change during negotiations with the District and Congress.

Accrued Pension Liability

The Clinton administration proposed that the federal government assume the payment for retired and vested District employees, which would reduce the District's pension spending by half and eliminate the present unfunded liability. As Andrew Brimmer, chair of the Control Board, noted, "the unfunded pension liability has always been the responsibility

---

2. Preliminary analyses by a number of sources confirm this. For example, see Philip M. Dearborn, "Assessing the Fiscal Effects of President Clinton's Proposal on the District," statement of the executive director of the D.C. Tax Revision Commission before the Council of the District of Columbia's Committee on Finance and Revenue, February 13, 1997.

of the Federal government."[3] To many, this action represented the federal government's publicly admitting what officials previously would say only privately and what District residents and political leaders talked about openly for a long time: that the fiscal relationship agreed upon at the time of the Home Rule Act was not a good deal for the District. Congress did not provide funding of the pension rights that had accrued for the employees—police, firefighters, teachers, judges—who left federal service and became District employees. At the time home rule became a reality, the retirement obligations had not been actuarially funded; the liability then was $2 billion; it is now about $5 billion, even with the District's contributions over the intervening years.

Under the administration's initial proposal, new and not-yet-vested employees would be covered by a new pension plan to be set up and funded entirely by the District. The savings to the District from this proposal would depend entirely on the plan. Immediately, the federal government, which would take control of the old plan, would gain about $3.5 billion from the transfer of the District's pension assets.[4] At a time when both the administration and Congress are struggling to balance the federal budget by 2002, the transfer of the District's assets to the federal government helps in the short term by generating considerable federal deficit relief as a result of the federal budget scoring rules.[5]

Capital and Operating Relief from State-Type Services, Including Infrastructure

The president's proposal focused on funding four state-type services: courts, prisons, medicaid, and transportation infrastructure. For the first two, the administration proposed that the federal government provide the service directly, relieving the District of both current and capital spending.[6] With medicaid, the president, like this study, proposed that

3. Andrew F. Brimmer, "Testimony before the Subcommittee on the District of Columbia Committee on Government Reform and Oversight, United States House of Representatives," March 13, 1997, p. 7.

4. The White House puts the asset size at $3.4 billion; the Control Board, at $3.6 billion. The exact number will be determined only at time of transfer.

5. Assets are not expected to be depleted until 2007.

6. However, negotiations over these issues already have revealed that the amount of spending relief to the District will depend on the extent to which "court operations" include social services, probation, indigent representation, and the ongoing maintenance of the physical facilities and whether the assumption of responsibility for sentenced prisoners includes the young adults at the Lorton prison complex.

the federal government pick up a part of the "state" share. The OMB chose an additional 20 percent; this study chose 25 percent on the argument of parity with New York City. The Control Board argued that the federal government should treat the District as states treat their cities.[7] With respect to transportation, the Clinton plan provided $125 million for capital spending in 1998, which could be used to pay the District's Metrorail commitment and save future debt service. It also proposed an Infrastructure Trust Fund into which private contributions might be made.

Economic Development

The president proposed a new Economic Development Corporation (EDC) for the District, where seven of the nine members of the governing board would be appointed by him. The EDC would be capitalized by the federal government at $50 million, $20 million of which would be earmarked for nonprofit institutions. This was presented as a ten-year commitment by the federal government to the District to create an institution acting as both facilitator and coordinator of big projects to spur private investment in the nation's capital. The EDC would be able to offer tax incentives ($250 million) similar to those in empowerment zones, which were discussed in chapter 2. There would be employment tax credits for hiring low- or moderate-income residents, investment tax credits and additional expensing for certain small businesses on their federal corporate income tax, the ability to issue some tax-exempt bonds for private development, and the ability to use such powers as eminent domain, expedited planning review, and site acquisition and disposal to speed development projects.[8]

IRS Administration

The president proposed that the Internal Revenue Service collect the District's personal income tax and payroll taxes beginning in 1999 and estimated it would cost the agency $25 million annually. However, one cannot expect equal budgetary savings for the District from this part of

7. Brimmer, "Testimony," pp. 4–5.
8. The president also directed federal agencies to assemble a list of federal land that can be amassed and private sector actions that can be joined with this effort by mid-May 1997.

the proposal. As this study makes clear, the state of the District's Department of Finance and Revenue will not allow staff reductions or staff transfers as a result of the move to IRS collection. But improved enforcement might be expected to yield increased revenues.

Borrowing and Debt

The proposal also allowed for loans from the U.S. Treasury to bond out the District's accumulated deficit, an offer providing a cost advantage only if the District's access to the public credit markets is restricted, since Treasury borrowing is taxable and the District's borrowing is tax exempt. It substituted a Treasury bond financing role for the present Treasury duty of providing short-term (cash-flow) financing, which has been backed by the federal payment. In addition, the District's debt limit, 14 percent of discretionary revenue, would decrease with the elimination of the federal payment, beginning in fiscal 1998.

The Issues

This volume has presented the case that, for long-run fiscal survival, the nation's orphaned capital needs a state. Therefore, it has been extremely reassuring to see the president, the Control Board, and some members of Congress embrace the concept of the federal government's taking on the role of the missing state. In stepping up to help the District, the president said that one of the major problems of the nation's capital is that it is a " 'not quite' place. It's not quite a state, but it's not quite a city. So it has been loaded up with responsibilities that normally are only borne by states. I think that is wrong."[9]

The president's initial proposal was, as Control Board Chair Andrew Brimmer stated, "a very good start."[10] But it omitted consideration of important issues. First, it did not go all the way toward having the federal government act as the state to the nation's capital city. In the case of state-type spending, for example, the Control Board recommended that "the President consider . . . support to the District for mental health

9. Remarks by the president in "District of Columbia College Reading Tutor Announcement" at Garrison Elementary School, Washington, February 21, 1997.
10. Brimmer, "Testimony," p. 10.

services."[11] Further, there are smaller state-type services that the president's initial proposal ignored. To the argument that the federal government does not believe itself equipped to provide these, as has been outlined in chapter 7, it should compensate the District for providing them.

In the case of revenues, the District government and the Control Board expressed strong opposition to the proposed end of the federal payment. Chairman Brimmer argued that "the federal payment is not a gift. Nor is it a payment . . . for the provision of statelike functions."[12] The case presented in this book for a federal payment in lieu of taxes and state aid would "compensate for the National Government's presence in the District," as Brimmer argued.

Neither did the plan address fiscal stability and budget balance for the District. This study argues that the long-run solvency of the nation's capital is in the national interest. Clearly, the president and Congress accepted this view when they established the Control Board. The Control Board demonstrated convincingly that grafting the president's initial proposal onto the board's four-year financial plan meant that the District would "start to experience an operating deficit that increases to approximately $112 million by FY 2000 . . . principally due to the structural imbalance exacerbated by the absent Federal Payment."[13] In addition, the fiscal pressure on the District's budget over the coming years cannot offer the opportunity to address the pressing issue of tax overload on the dwindling District tax base, which this study has convincingly demonstrated.

Finally, District residents and members of Congress have raised a number of governance issues that the president's initial proposal did not address. In particular, considerable focus on the shortcomings of the District government's management and provision of services has led to an effort to place a professional city manager at the top of the District government. A number of arguments for this were put forward, from the institutionalization of strong professional management throughout the government, to depoliticizing the workings of local government, to making the District's governance resemble more closely that of cities in the surrounding area and of similar or smaller size, to a desire to look beyond

11. The board also recommended that the District and the federal government revisit the issue of ownership and operation of St. Elizabeth's Hospital, which the federal government has insisted the District take over and which has never operated in the black. See Brimmer, "Testimony," p. 9.

12. Brimmer, "Testimony," p. 15.

13. Brimmer, "Testimony," p. 12.

the fiscal and economic issues for structural changes. Whatever the reason, the governance structure, efficiency in service delivery, and management accountability are on the agenda of many, including members of Congress, who have a role in determining the final package for the District for fiscal 1998 and beyond.

The Process

Throughout the spring and summer of 1997 there will be two processes proceeding simultaneously regarding the District and its fiscal 1998 budget. One will involve the District's budget proposals; the other, the president's plan. Under existing law the District's proposed budget must go to Congress by June 15, 1997. It is a given that the proposed 1998 budget going to Congress on June 15, 1997, will be balanced according to GAAP.

With respect to the president's proposal for the District, there have been lengthy and ongoing negotiations between the administration and the District government (both the executive and council) over myriad details, agency by agency, as to how this plan would work. The president proposed bringing an agreement between the District and the administration to Congress in the form of a memorandum of understanding, which would in effect represent a long-term blueprint for the restructured relationship. As the drafting of the memorandum proceeded, the details of the president's proposal changed in an effort to reach agreement. When the memorandum is finally signed by the administration and the District government, it will be an enhanced package compared to the outline released in January 1997. And there will be detail involving District and federal responsibilities that the initial outline lacked. Also, it will stand separately from the president's budget proposal and move through both the Control Board and Congress on a separate track from the District's fiscal 1998 budget.[14]

Once the memorandum arrives at Congress, the legislative process will begin. And until it is completed, the District's proposed fiscal 1998 budget must reflect existing law. The timetable for the budget is extremely tight, so that the longer it takes to reach agreement on the memorandum

14. The Control Board, a fourth party to this process, will not be a signatory to the memorandum. It is likely to issue a side letter regarding any roles, such as overseer, monitor, and enforcer, that the administration and District are expecting it to fill.

and adjusting that agreement into one with Congress (and the Control Board), the greater the probability that the District will begin fiscal 1998 on October 1, 1997, without Congress having acted on the president's plan and with the District's budget balanced according to GAAP and reflecting current law.[15] The administration does not expect to present the memorandum as legislation. Rather, there is an agreement with Congress to proceed in a manner similar to that used to establish the Control Board, where the legislation was formed in consultation. Thus the public cannot expect to see the legislation embodying the president's plan until there is agreement on it between Congress and the administration. It is not clear how independent and how visible will be the roles of both the executive and legislative branches of the District government, as a signatory to the memorandum, and the Control Board in the process.

President Clinton's proposal in January 1997 represented a giant step forward by recognizing the problem of the missing state for the orphaned capital. As this study demonstrates, the forces pushing for change are compelling. The District of Columbia remains a small open economy, with its revenues stagnating. Its residents and businesses are overburdened by high tax rates necessitated by a limited local tax base. Increasingly, its tax policies are constrained by the policies of jurisdictions in the surrounding region. Its economic and fiscal survival as well as its physical security are in the national interest. Restructuring the relationship by having the federal government take on the role of the missing state cannot be accomplished in one year or with one budget. And it will take place as both the District of Columbia and the federal government proceed toward sustainable budget balance. There certainly is much to do.

---

15. If that were to happen, congressional adoption of part or all of the president's plan will require amending the District's budget.

Revenue Definitions, Data, and Sources: Supplement to Figure 1-3 and Tables 1-2 and 1-4

T HE DISTRICT budget consists of a general fund and a number of enterprise funds that together total $5.1 billion. Discretionary revenues may be spent on the entire range of services that the District government provides. They are determined by subtracting federal categorical aid, special funds, and nonallocated other revenues. In fiscal year 1995 the District collected $3.3 billion in discretionary revenues (table A-1). Almost three-quarters ($2.36 billion) of the discretionary revenues come from taxes, one-fifth ($660 million) from the federal payment, and about 8 percent ($274 million) from nontaxes—fees, fines, charges, and the lottery.

Definition of Taxes

Nineteen taxes feed the discretionary revenues. Unfortunately, the District does not present the exact number of taxes or other revenue sources in a form that is easy to follow. The fiscal year 1995 *Comprehensive Annual Financial Report (CAFR)* lists twenty taxes (p. 52), while the latest Department of Finance and Revenue *Tax Facts* lists twenty-one (p. 1). Starting from the *CAFR*, this study takes what the report lists as "transfer taxes" and separates them into two component taxes, the deeds transfer tax and the tax on the transfer of special interests. It also adds the professional license fee, which is collected as a tax (subject to penalty and interest) and which would raise the count to twenty-two taxes. Proceeding from fiscal year 1995, however, one needs to subtract from discretionary taxes the public safety fee, which from 1995 onward is dedicated to funding the new sports arena; the motor vehicle fuel tax,

Table A-1. *District of Columbia Discretionary Revenue,*
Fiscal Year 1995

Thousands of dollars

Source	Subtotals	Totals
Taxes		2,363,823
Real property		654,284
Personal income		643,676
General sales and use		485,651
General business taxes		221,984
Corporation	121,407	
Unincorporated business	39,272	
Personal property	61,305	
Selective gross receipts		210,269
Public utility	131,012	
Toll telecommunication	44,554	
Insurance companies	34,703	
Selective sales and excise taxes		63,839
Alcoholic beverage	4,930	
Cigarette	20,117	
Hotel occupancy	8,352	
Motor vehicles	30,440	
Other		84,120
Inheritance and estate	16,807	
Recordation, Transfer	22,691	
Economic interest transfer	21,826	
Public space rental	14,754	
Professional license[a]	8,042	
Federal payment		660,000
Nontax revenue		273,609
Licences and permits		39,541
Business licenses	21,901	
Nonbusiness licenses	17,640	
Fines and forfeits		42,447
Charges for services		52,687
Court fees	5,991	
Other	46,696	
Miscellaneous revenues		53,834
Interest	17,994	
Other	35,840	
Other financing sources–Lottery		85,100
Total revenues		3,297,432

Source: *District of Columbia Comprehensive Annual Financial Report, September 30, 1995* (hereafter *CAFR, 1995*).

a. Not provided in *CAFR, 1995*. This amount provided by the Department of Finance and Revenue collections files as of June 30, 1996 (copy July 17, 1996).

which, as of October 1, 1995, is dedicated to the Highway Trust Fund; and the tax on health care providers, which ends with fiscal year 1996.[1] This brings to nineteen the total number of taxes that constitute general fund discretionary revenues.

This number does not treat the corporate surcharge as a separate tax; it treats five sales tax rates applied to different sales tax bases as one general sales tax; and it ignores the parking space tax ("Clean Air Act compliance fee") of $20 a month (approximately $1 a working day), which the District has not enforced since putting it on the books in 1994.[2]

Definition of Nontax Revenues

There is no official published comprehensive list of nontax revenues. Charges, licenses, permits, fees, and fines are collected and recorded in the agencies administering them, resulting in a fragmentation of revenue reporting, verification, and tracking. By our count there are 115 different nontax revenues. Table A-2 presents a summary of the District agencies by the size and number of nontax revenues they collect. Table A-3 presents the full range of nontax revenues by type and by agency. Both of these tables are derived from the working list supplied by the comptroller's office as the backup to the *CAFR*. They are presented here to record as complete a picture as possible of the user fees and charges imposed by the District.[3] They should not be considered reliable financial statements, because the individual collections are not monitored or comprehensively matched to receipts.

Data Sources

Precision on the number of revenue sources and the amounts raised by each is not a hallmark of the District's financial management. The *CAFR*, recording the actual events of the fiscal year, provides a complete list of revenues from individual taxes, with the auditors' qualified opinion with

1. District of Columbia Department of Finance and Revenue, *Tax Facts, Fiscal Years 1993 and 1994*, p. 31.
2. D.C. Law 10-242; District Code 47-2731.
3. It took months of searching to find this list, the location of which was news to the tax policy staff of the Department of Finance and Revenues and the economic development staff of the city council.

Table A-2. *District of Columbia Nontax Revenues by Department, Fiscal Year 1995*

Department	Number of nontax revenues	Amount of nontax revenue collected (dollars)
Public Works	22	79,644,687.10
Financial Management	4	40,792,821.87
Consumer and Regulatory Affairs	32	25,121,472.73
Finance and Revenue	5	20,232,022.98
Public Service Commission	4	6,812,944.14
Corrections	3	6,463,118.69
Superior Court	5	5,990,006.91
Administrative Services	6	4,869,151.54
Fire Department	3	4,236,686.56
Office of People's Council	1	2,651,000.00
Office of Cable Television	1	2,156,589.88
Taxicab Commission	8	1,430,440.47
Court of Appeals	3	1,260,983.27
Metropolitan Police Department	8	542,570.85
Secretary of the District of Columbia	2	151,924.10
Corporation Council	1	22,369.99
Office of Economic Development	1	14,050.00
Office of Campaign Finance	1	5,207.40
Board of Elections and Ethics	2	881.40
Human Services	3	(5,848,468.28)
Total	115	196,550,461.60

Source: District of Columbia Controller's Office, "Appropriated Revenue Excluding Taxes and Intergovernmental, FY 1995," August 8, 1996.

respect to the business tax revenues, but it aggregates nontax revenues.[4] The executive budget for fiscal year 1995 does not provide a full list of the revenues, including taxes, or a tax-by-tax forecast of revenues expected in the coming year. Rather, future tax revenues and recent past tax performance are treated at an aggregated level, with only the real property tax and the personal income tax distinctly discernible.[5] Indeed, the fiscal year 1995 budget's 30 pages on revenues stands in slim contrast to its 570 or so pages of spending.

4. The qualified opinion related to the auditors' "inability to obtain sufficient evidence supporting general fund business taxes receivables and Water and Sewer Enterprise Fund customer receivables." KPMG Peat Marwick, "Independent Auditors' Report on the Internal Control Structure," Washington, January 23, 1995, p. 1. Noted in *CAFR, 1995*, p. 18.

5. For a full list and description of all the taxes, one must go to the District's Department of Finance and Revenue's *Tax Facts*, published irregularly and considerably after the fiscal year.

Much of the tax revenue, tax exemption, assessment, taxpayer, and other data used in this study comes from unpublished files of the District's Department of Finance and Revenue, including special computer runs that they produced for their own use or at our request. The economists and analysts there are the first to admit to the limitations of their data. We have no independent means to verify the accuracy of either the published or the unpublished data relied on in this study. Where we have encountered obvious issues involving the quality of the data, we have noted it directly in the individual chapters.

Table A-3. *District of Columbia Nontax Revenues by Source, Fiscal Year 1995*

Revenue source	Amount (dollars)	Department
Licenses and permits		
Business licenses		
Consumer goods and repair license	14,386.00	Consumer and Regulatory Affairs
Business mileage fee	3,969.14	Public Service Commission
Self-unloading permit	710,678.50	Consumer and Regulatory Affairs
Notary public	37,540.00	Secretary of the District of Columbia
Security broker fees	1,692,085.00	Public Service Commission
Public space excavation permit	195,765.00	Consumer and Regulatory Affairs
Refrigerator and plumbing permit	845,341.00	Consumer and Regulatory Affairs
Other business licenses	3,444,987.15	Consumer and Regulatory Affairs
Occupational and professional license	2,680,440.18	Consumer and Regulatory Affairs
Electric permit	1,052,900.70	Consumer and Regulatory Affairs
Boxing and wrestling	20,926.76	Consumer and Regulatory Affairs
Certificate of occupancy permit	278,312.68	Consumer and Regulatory Affairs
Professional license	8,041,201.01	Finance and Revenue
Healing arts license	1,109,048.02	Consumer and Regulatory Affairs
Insurance license	701,238.75	Consumer and Regulatory Affairs
Alcoholic beverage license	2,420,435.77	Consumer and Regulatory Affairs
Building and equipment permit	5,922,244.99	Consumer and Regulatory Affairs
Other business license	48,937.00	Public Works
Taxicab license	409,446.35	Taxicab Commission
Other business license	45,210.00	Taxicab Commission
Hacker's license	268,512.12	Taxicab Commission
Subtotal	29,943,606.12	

Nonbusiness permits

Reciprocity permit	312,545.00	Public Works
Bicycle registration	1,269.00	Metropolitan Police Department
Motor vehicle registration	583,659.00	Taxicab Commission
Other nonbusiness license	85,415.60	Consumer and Regulatory Affairs
Motor vehicle registration	14,776,649.87	Public Works
Motor vehicle operators permit	45,100.00	Taxicab Commission
Boat registration	107,063.10	Metropolitan Police Department
Motor vehicle operators permit	1,727,872.27	Public Works
Subtotal	17,639,573.84	
Total licenses and permits	47,583,179.96	

Fines and forfeits

Fines and forfeits—courts	534,197.60	Superior Court
Traffic fines	640,427.50	Superior Court
Booting fees	392,955.00	Public Works
Impoundment fee	236,571.00	Public Works
Hacker's fines	76,705.00	Taxicab Commission
Sale of abandoned property	512,415.99	Administrative Services
Towing fees	861,075.00	Public Works
Traffic fines	39,192,619.20	Public Works
Total fines and forfeits	42,446,966.29	

Charges for services
Court fees

Court fees and charges	4,730,306.67	Superior Court
Court reports and copies	109,028.27	Court of Appeals
Court registration fees	1,127,400.00	Court of Appeals
Court fees and charges	24,555.00	Court of Appeals
Subtotal	5,991,289.94	

Table A-3. *District of Columbia Nontax Revenues by Source, Fiscal Year 1995 (Continued)*

Revenue source	Amount	Department
Other		
Pharmaceutical, medical device fee	231,863.21	Consumer and Regulatory Affairs
Street and gutter	4,531.67	Public Works
Surveyor fees	211,760.00	Public Works
Water and sewer	514.80	Public Works
Solid waste disposa! fee	1,147,800.99	Public Works
Third party payments	(4,222,801.87)	Human Services
Health facility fee	20,976.00	Consumer and Regulatory Affairs
Pay patients	(1,709,280.98)	Human Services
Reproduction of reports	994,287.50	Public Works
Condo certification fee	1,875.00	Consumer and Regulatory Affairs
Boiler inspection	51,900.00	Consumer and Regulatory Affairs
Smoke regulation permit	1,080.00	Taxicab Commission
Charges—other services	6,605.00	Consumer and Regulatory Affairs
Reproduction of reports	728.00	Taxicab Commission
Condo registration	8,385.00	Consumer and Regulatory Affairs
Elevator inspection license	169,249.00	Consumer and Regulatory Affairs
Recordation fee—corporation	3,698,387.09	Consumer and Regulatory Affairs
Parking fees and permits	773,931.08	Public Works
Rental accommodations fee	715,672.58	Consumer and Regulatory Affairs
Fingerprints and photographs	9,253.50	Metropolitan Police Department
Charges—other services	199,766.69	Corrections
Firearm user fee	4,523.00	Metropolitan Police Department
Reproduction of reports	24,601.50	Metropolitan Police Department
Police hauling and storage	68,018.00	Metropolitan Police Department
Transcript of records	781.40	Board of Elections and Ethics
Transcript of records	139,261.81	Finance and Revenue
Emergency ambulance service	4,232,639.07	Fire Department

	Amount	Department
Quarters and subsistence	6,251.00	Corrections
Utility assessment	2,651,000.00	Office of People's Council
Charges—other services	100.00	Board of Elections and Ethics
Reproduction of reports	54,593.88	Consumer and Regulatory Affairs
Social service facility fee	38,269.19	Consumer and Regulatory Affairs
Reproduction of reports	1,776.49	Fire Department
Smoke regulation permit	7,573.00	Consumer and Regulatory Affairs
Wharves and markets	32,555.00	Consumer and Regulatory Affairs
Utilities assessment	4,825,000.00	Public Service Commission
Motor vehicle titles	1,653,244.50	Public Works
Motor vehicle inspection	2,233,278.00	Public Works
Transcript of records	141,689.00	Metropolitan Police Department
Cable TV franchise fee	2,156,589.88	Office of Cable Television
Parking fees and permits	158,380.76	Administrative Services
Sale of procurement digest	11,579.98	Administrative Services
Wharves and markets	20,249.42	Administrative Services
Charges—other services	114,384.10	Secretary of the District of Columbia
Transcript of records	113.50	Consumer and Regulatory Affairs
Recordation fee	2,716,060.47	Finance and Revenue
Investment advisors act	291,890.00	Public Service Commission
Rental of land	4,147.71	Public Works
Parking meters	12,977,212.26	Public Works
Arena fee	9,118,469.42	Finance and Revenue
Subtotal	46,695,653.57	
Total charges for services	52,686,943.51	

Miscellaneous

Interest

	Amount	Department
Interest income	28,846.44	Superior Court
Interest income	17,964,656.53	Financial Management
Subtotal	17,993,502.97	

Table A-3. *District of Columbia Nontax Revenues by Source, Fiscal Year 1995 (Continued)*

Revenue source	Amount	Department
Other		
Disposition of unclaimed property	16,666,188.42	Financial Management
Reimbursement from other government	30.00	Public Works
Reimbursement from other government	6,257,101.00	Corrections
Other revenue	83,614.57	Human Services
Other revenue	738,846.41	Public Works
Other revenue	(608,705.28)	Financial Management
Other revenue	56,228.70	Superior Court
Bus shelter advertisement	660,940.87	Public Works
Other revenue	2,271.00	Fire Department
Other revenue	186,153.75	Metropolitan Police Department
Other revenue	217,030.27	Finance and Revenue
Pesticide registration	89,400.00	Consumer and Regulatory Affairs
Other revenue	5,207.40	Office of Campaign Finance
Other revenue	8,918.09	Consumer and Regulatory Affairs
Holding account	14,050.00	Office of Economic Development
KEG registration fund	9,860.00	Consumer and Regulatory Affairs
Other revenue	6,770,682.20	Financial Management
Other revenue	22,369.99	Corporation Council
Sale of realty	3,136,941.88	Administrative Services
Concession income	1,029,583.51	Administrative Services
Civil infractons	493,156.09	Consumer and Regulatory Affairs
Subtotal	35,839,868.87	
Total miscellaneous	53,833,371.84	
Total nontax revenues	196,550,461.60	

Source: District of Columbia Controller's Office, "Appropriated Revenue Excluding Taxes and Intergovernmental, FY 1995," August 8, 1996.

APPENDIX B

Results of the Econometric Study

THIS APPENDIX presents the results of empirical testing relating the District's tax policy and the fortunes of its private economy. As chapter 2 shows, the tax burden borne by District businesses is considerably greater than that borne by their suburban counterparts and competitors. Because the District is a small, open economy, businesses can be expected to be sensitive to the District's high taxes.

Among the factors affecting the likelihood that a new business will form in the District of Columbia or an established business will expand are the costs of doing business, the preferences of the labor force, the demands of potential clients, including the federal government, and the prosperity of the metropolitan area. The District has some control over the costs of doing business through the tax rates it sets and the bases it elects to tax. One factor it has little control over is the growth of the metropolitan area, but the District economy can benefit from its location at the heart of a growing area.[1] The focus of the model, then, is the effects of District tax policy on the share of private sector metropolitan area jobs locating in the District.

The Model

The model estimates the factors causing changes in the District's share of regional employment from 1976 through 1994.

1. The increase in the number of jobs in the Washington metropolitan area between 1985 and 1989 was second in the United States only to the increase in greater Los Angeles. Bureau of Census, *State and Metropolitan Area Data Book 1991*, 4th ed., p. xliii (Department of Commerce).

*Factors Affecting the District's Share of the Region's
Private Employment*

There are four factors affecting the District's share of metropolitan
area private employment. First is the overall size, measured in total employment, of the area. The District has fixed boundaries and is thoroughly
developed. Growth in the metropolitan area will tend to expand the
boundaries, build on less developed land, and shrink the District's share
of the economy. As the area expands, the District's share of employment
should shrink.

The second factor is the effect of taxes. Because taxes are part of the
cost of doing business, the District's tax rates, especially in comparison
with Maryland's and Virginia's, may be instrumental in determining the
relative profitability of District enterprises. The expansion of existing
businesses and the launching of new enterprises will hinge on the relative
profitability of potential sites. Insofar as a company is indifferent between
conducting its business in the District or the suburbs, a tax rate increase
in one of the locations could upset the balance: expansion would take
place in another location. Of course, if the tax increase were spent on
public services as valuable to the company as the amount of the tax
increase, no harmful effect would be observed.

Taxes also increase the prices of intermediate goods. A business need
not be the direct payer of a tax to be affected by it. Rent on commercial
property, for example, must reimburse a developer for property tax payments in addition to other costs. A high tax raises the rent. Again, an
employer indifferent to locating in the District or in the suburbs might
be swayed by a rent increase downtown. Insofar as the property tax
cannot be added to the rent, the developer's earnings will decrease. A
higher tax would then have a dampening effect on commercial development. In either case a decrease in jobs will be associated with a higher
tax. One therefore expects the District's commercial property tax, currently 40 percent higher than the region's next highest rate, to affect
employment.

The other tax imposed uniformly on a wide range of businesses is the
sales and use tax. The District's general rate is 5.75 percent; Virginia's is
4.5 percent and Maryland's 5 percent. The sales and use tax is in effect
due when both buyer and seller reside in the taxed jurisdiction. The rate
difference provides an incentive for one or both to locate outside the
District. The economic effect of a sales tax over time can be difficult to
measure because sales taxes change infrequently. The difference between

the District's and Virginia's rates, however, as it reflects rate changes in both jurisdictions, has taken on six different values between 1975 and 1993, the period covered in this study. The variability of this difference should be sufficient to show an effect on employment if the sales tax rates are a significant factor.

Also included among the tax variables are the District, Maryland, and Virginia corporate income tax rates and average unemployment insurance costs, both of which are relatively high in the District. The corporate income tax and the unincorporated business income tax, however, do not apply to many of the District's businesses. Unincorporated professional businesses are not subject to the latter tax. In the survey cited in chapter 2, businesses did cite the unemployment insurance tax rates as a reason to locate outside the District. This is also an attractive variable in an employment regression because it is a cost associated with each worker.

In light of the rationale articulated above and the results of Timothy Bartik's survey of studies relating economic activity to tax rates, one would expect the commercial property tax to show the most significant depressing effect on the District's share of metropolitan area employment.[2]

The third factor possibly affecting the location of businesses is the customer base. The model considers the effect of both population and federal employment on the number of private jobs. Both represent a market for business and should work to increase employment. To some extent, however, population and federal employment also compete with business, driving up rents and consuming other sorts of services, which may mute their beneficial effect.

The fourth factor is time. Relating a shrinking job base to the passage of time does not constitute an explanation. Rather, it concedes that there are other factors correlated with time that are contributing to the changing economic landscape.

If the four factors do have some bearing on the location decisions of business, it should be possible to associate an expected share of the metropolitan employment base locating in the District with a fixed combination of relevant factors. Observing the District's share of metropolitan private employment, one notices continual change, mostly shrinkage.

2. Timothy J. Bartik, "The Effects of Property Taxes and Other Local Public Policies on the Intrametropolitan Pattern of Business Location," in Henry W. Herzog Jr. and Alan M. Schlottman, *Industry Location and Public Policy* (University of Tennessee Press, 1991), pp. 57–82.

This movement can be characterized as District employment approaching this expected share, which depends on the factors already discussed. Let us refer to this hypothetical fraction as the steady-state share, not because it stays constant but because it represents the center toward which the observed share is continually moving. Were the relevant factors to remain constant, the District's share of private metropolitan employment would achieve this share and remain. Changing the factors that determine the steady-state share will immediately change this target. The actual District share will then begin to move in the direction of the new steady state.

The empirical study examines a number of observed shares and likely factors and tests whether the changes in the shares can be characterized as an approach toward a steady state and how that state is related to the factors.

Results

Equation 1 represents our best estimate of the District's steady-state share of metropolitan area private employment. Each of the variables— the difference between District and suburban property taxes, the difference between District and Virginia sales taxes, the growth in jobs in the metropolitan area, and time in years—had a significant effect on the District's share of employment, the first three in the direction expected.[3] Each year the level of employment will move about one-fourth of the way toward the current steady-state level. The formula derived is as follows.[4]

$$(1) \quad SSE = 0.44 - 5.52 \times CPTD - 1.61 \times DCVASD$$
$$- 0.12 \times GRJM - 1.55 \times 10^{-3} \times YR,$$

where SSE represents the District's steady state employment share, $CPTD$ the difference between the District commercial property tax rate and suburban rates (lagged three years), $DCVASD$ the difference between the general sales tax in the District and in Virginia (lagged one year), $GRJM$

3. The difference between District sales taxes and a weighted average of suburban sales tax rates posed a technical problem. As the Maryland sales tax rate did not change at all, the weighted average reflected the changing weight given Virginia taxes (Virginia employment) as much as it reflected the tax rates themselves. The difference between sales tax rates in the District and Virginia proved to be a better predictor of growth than the difference between the rates in the District and Maryland.

4. The applicable differences in the property tax rates are those from three years before and for the sales tax rates those from one year before.

the percentage increase of jobs in the metropolitan area, and *YR* the year minus 1985. The coefficients in equation 1 above are derived from those shown in table B-1, which estimates the changes in *DCShare*. In order to convert the finding into an equation for the steady state level, the lagged level, *DCShare* (-1), is dropped, and the coefficients of the other variables are divided by its coefficient, 0.24. The model is shown explicitly in the methodology section below.

Currently the commercial property tax is $1.11 per $100 assessed value higher than the average suburban rate, and the general sales tax rate in the District is 1.25 percentage points higher than Virginia's. If the property tax rate differential were reduced by $0.10 as the District rate decreased from $2.15 per $100 to $2.05, the District's predicted steady-state share of metropolitan employment would increase from the 1994 level of 22.97 percent to 23.52 percent, an additional 11,300 jobs. This increase would be achieved gradually, with about 7,000 jobs gained within five years of the reduction.[5] Changes in taxes work over time. The lags used in this model reflect the years required for the tax rate differentials to show their greatest effect. The three-year lag in the property tax rate is not surprising, given the length of leases in the commercial rental market and the required response time involved in commercial development.

Based on the 1994 commercial levy, a reduction of $0.10 per $100 of assessed value would cost the District $22.5 million annually.[6] The annual cost per new job after the steady-state increase of 11,300 is achieved comes to $2,000.

If the general sales tax rate were reduced by 0.1 percentage point, from 5.75 percent to 5.65 percent, the analysis predicts a gain in employment share of 0.16 percentage points eventually 3,300 jobs, more than half of them achieved within three years.[7] The District's general sales tax generated about $486,000,000 in fiscal 1995, with about half coming from the basic rate of 5.75 percent.[8] If the 5.75 percent were reduced to 5.65

5. Three years after the property tax decrease, employment begins its increase, moving each year one-fourth of the way toward the 11,300 increase in jobs. The total increase will be 3,000 jobs after three years, 5,100 after four, and 6,700 after five.

6. The total commercial assessment was $20.274 billion and the total levy $436 million, according to District of Columbia Department of Finance and Revenue, *District of Columbia Tax Facts, Fiscal Years 1993 and 1994* (1995).

7. The process begins after one year. Then 800 new jobs are produced in the first year, 1,400 after two, and 1,800 after three.

8. Most of the remainder comes from the hotel and restaurant sales taxes, imposed at 10 percent and 13 percent, respectively. DFR, *Tax Facts, Fiscal Years 1993 and 1994*, p. 28.

percent, the tax revenue would drop from the present $242 million to $238 million. If this were to produce 3,300 jobs, as the steady-state estimate predicts, the annual cost per job would be $1,200.

Growth in metropolitan area employment was also found to be a significant factor in explaining the District's share. The District will not grow as fast as the metropolitan area. In 1994 area private employment stood at 2.047 million jobs, 470,000 of them in the District. An increase of 100,000 area jobs would bring total metropolitan employment to 2.147 million, and would represent 4.88 percent growth. If this increase came after a year of no growth in the region, the District's share would be expected to decline by 0.57 percent (0.12 × 4.88 percent), or from the current 22.97 percent to 22.40 percent, or 480,000 jobs. Metropolitan area growth, that is, disproportionately favors the suburbs. Independent of tax differences, just 10 percent of the growth would occur in the District. *According to these results, a small decrease in the commercial property tax would produce more jobs in the District than an excellent year of growth for the metropolitan area.* The District's economy is somewhat buoyed by growth in the metropolitan area, but changes in its own policies would seem to produce a greater impact.

A time trend is included in the regression to account for omitted variables correlated with time that might affect the District's equilibrium employment share. These apparently do exist. The quantities involved are somewhat smaller than the changes associated with the 0.1 percent decrease in taxes, so that increases in the District's share of employment would be predicted to more than offset the annual unexplained decline. The coefficient above shows that each year, independent of tax differences or metropolitan area growth, the steady-state share of private employment will decline by 0.15 percent, at present about 3,000 jobs. The omitted factors could include a gradual decline in the quality of District services delivered to businesses, an improvement in the services provided by some of the suburban locales, or technological changes that have gradually altered the private sector's locational needs.

This study used specific tax rates rather than some measure of overall burden so as to assist in the refinement of District tax policy. Employment changes seem to have the expected negative relationship with lagged values of the tax rates specified earlier. This does not mean, however, that the other taxes do not matter. The sales and commercial property taxes are broad-based ones that all businesses pay, directly increasing their expenditures on space and materials. The rates are an excellent indicator of the burden these taxes impose. In the case of the corporate and unincorporated business franchise taxes, however, the rates are a weaker reflection of the burden.[9] This does not mean the business income taxes do not have an adverse effect on employment levels, but only that the rates do not have the explanatory power of the simpler, broader based taxes. Unemployment compensation tax and workers' compensation insurance also will vary widely among employers. The average value used in the model may not be a good indication of the costs that different businesses face.

The conclusion here is that high tax rates appear to be a factor in the District's decreasing employment share. For the commercial property tax and the general sales tax, this effect is statistically significant (at a 99 percent level of confidence), and the measured effects are reported. The effect of the other taxes on employment will be more selective and distributed unevenly, as are the burdens of the other taxes.

Calculation of Elasticity

The District's 1994 share of metropolitan area employment was 22.97 percent. The current commercial property tax rate is 2.15 percent. An increase of 0.552 percent in the employment share resulting from a reduction of ten basis points in the commercial rate reflects an elasticity of

$$(0.552/22.97) / (-0.1/2.15) = -0.52.$$

For the general sales tax rate a change of ten basis points would reveal an elasticity of

$$(0.161/22.97) / (-0.1/5.75) = -0.40.$$

These elasticities are considerably lower than the average of -2.0 that Timothy Bartik finds in a number of studies on the impact of the property tax on location.[10] Still, this work corroborates the significant negative

9. According to the Department of Finance and Revenue, the corporate franchise tax and the unincorporated business franchise taxes had about 20,000 and 8,000 payers, respectively, in 1994.

In the process of determining a District taxable net income, firms will produce amounts that are possibly out of step with the size (in space, employees, and dollars) of their District activities. Losses generated in other states and in past years can offset current District earnings and warp the relation between activity and taxable income. Also, since the decision in *Bishop v. District of Columbia* in 1979, many partnerships and unincorporated businesses do not face a business income tax. Thousands of other businesses do.

10. Bartik, "Effects of Property Taxes," p. 75.

Table B-1. *Best-Fit Equation Explaining Changes in the District of Columbia Share of Metropolitan Area Private Employment, 1976–94*

Independent variable	Coefficient (t-statistics)
Constant	0.105
	(13.834)
DCShare (−1)[a]	−0.240
	(−19.630)
CPTD (−3)[b]	−1.327
	(−9.662)
DCVASD (−1)[c]	−0.387
	(−12.540)
GRJM[d]	−0.028
	(−4.687)
YR[e]	$−0.37*10^{-3}$
	(−3.435)
R^2	0.987
Auto correlation coefficient	−0.676
	(−3.734)

a. Level of the District's share of metropolitan area private employment.
b. The difference between the District commercial property tax rate and suburban rates.
c. The difference between the general sales tax in the District and that in Virginia.
d. The growth in jobs in the metropolitan area.
e. Year minus 1985.

effect, which other studies have also found, of local taxes on economic activity. The lower elasticity is perhaps not surprising because the two choices the firms in this study face are between locating in the District or the Washington suburbs, and these options are qualitatively distinct. Two suburbs, for example, are closer substitutes than a suburban and a District location.

Test of Predictive Power

As a test of the predictive power of the derived relation shown in table B-1, we perform the same regression from 1976 through 1990 and attempt to predict the movement in the *DCShare* from 1992 to 1993 and from 1993 to 1994. Table B-2 shows those results. The new equation for the steady-state employment share becomes

$$(2) \quad SSE = 0.397 - 6.816 \times CPTD - 1.737 \times DCVASD$$
$$- 0.070 \times GRJM - 0.477 \times 10^{-3} \times YR.$$

The coefficients in equation 2 are derived from those shown in table B-2, which estimates changes in *DCShare*. As was necessary for equation

Table B-2. *Best-Fit Equation through 1990*

Independent variable	Coefficient (t-statistics)
Constant	0.085
	(2.809)
DCShare (-1)[a]	−0.214
	(−3.546)
CPTD (-3)[b]	−1.461
	(−7.983)
DCVASD (-1)[c]	−0.372
	(−11.136)
GRJM[d]	−0.0015
	(−0.986)
YR[e]	−0.012
	(−0.185)
R^2	0.984
Auto correlation coefficient	−0.756
	(−4.095)

a. Level of the District's share of metropolitan area private employment.
b. The difference between the District commercial property tax rate and suburban rates.
c. The difference between the general sales tax in the District and that in Virginia.
d. The growth in jobs in the metropolitan area.
e. Year minus 1985.

1, the steady state equation requires dropping the lagged level, *DCShare* (-1), and dividing the coefficients of the other independent variables by its coefficient, 0.21 in this case.

Equation 2 predicts a steady state share of 23.19 percent of regional employment for the District in 1992, 22.00 percent in 1993, and 21.86 percent in 1994. The decrease is almost entirely attributable to the increase in the commercial property tax rate differential, which reflects the increase in 1990 of the District's commercial property tax rate from 2.03 percent to 2.15 percent. Based on the 1992 level of *DCShare* equal to 23.80 percent and an *M* equal to 0.214, the coefficient of the lagged value of *DCShare*, the share should be expected to move about a fifth of the way to the new 1993 equilibrium level of 22.00 percent (see equations 3 through 6). The estimation predicts a 1993 share of 23.41 percent. In fact, the 1993 *DCShare* was 23.38 percent. Starting from 23.38 percent in 1993 and moving toward the new steady-state share of 21.86 percent, the estimation predicts a share of 23.05 percent in 1994, when *DCShare* in fact decreased to 22.97 percent. Like any other economic variable, *DCShare* will be subject to many more forces and factors than one can build into a predictive model. It does appear, however, from these estimates and from inspection of table B-3 that the magnitude of the decreases bears some relation to movements in the estimated steady-state

Table B-3. *Actual Values of Key Factors Affecting District of Columbia Steady-State Share of Metropolitan Private Employment*
Percent unless otherwise noted

Variable	1988	1989	1990	1991	1992	1993	1994
DCShare	24.291	23.977	23.949	23.976	23.797	23.375	22.972
CPTD	0.910	0.959	1.104	1.111	1.089	1.081	1.080
DCVASD	1.5	1.75	1.5	1.5	1.5	1.5	2.1875
GRJM	1.049	1.023	1.007	0.969	0.997	1.018	1.025
(Year– 1985) = YR	(1988– 1985) = 3	(1989– 1985) = 4	(1990– 1985) = 5	(1991– 1985) = 6	(1992– 1985) = 7	(1993– 1985) = 8	(1994– 1985) = 9

share, which reflects past increases in the commercial property tax rate. And given that 1994's estimated equilibrium share of 21.86 percent is well below the current share of 22.97 percent, further sharp decreases would be predicted.

Methodology

Using a time series analysis with the District's share of metropolitan area private employment as the dependent variable focuses the analysis on the District and produces results that cannot be applied to another part of the area or another city altogether, because all other relevant factors would be different. The luxury afforded by a time-series analysis is the relative stability of other factors as, year after year, the same places are being compared. This study was also made possible by an unusual data source. Since 1975 the District has been required to publish its tax rates each year and, for comparative purposes, the tax rates of cities around the country as well as rates around the metropolitan area.[11] This comparison provides a time series of area tax rates during the past twenty years. Such a data set may not be so readily available for another metropolitan area.

Two tax differentials, metropolitan area growth, time, and the specification of a process converging to a steady state explained a great deal of the District's share of the region's employment. A bias from omitted variables will affect the coefficients insofar as the variables left out are positively or negatively correlated with the independent variables. In the

11. District of Columbia Department of Revenue and Finance *Tax Rates and Burdens in the in the District of Columbia: A Nationwide Comparison* (1995). Congress required publication of such a document as part of the home rule agreement.

case of the District, however, although the commercial property tax rate increased from 2.03 percent to 2.15 percent between 1986 and 1995, real expenditures on activities that businesses might benefit from have changed very little.[12] There is no reason to expect that such other omitted variables as crime, traffic congestion, or efficiency of service delivery would be correlated with the differences between city and suburban property or sales taxes rates.

The process modeled is a partial-adjustment model.[13] Each year the District's share of private employment will move part way from the previous year's level toward the steady state, reflecting the private sector's ultimate response to the District's economic advantages and disadvantages, including the parameters outlined earlier. If *DCShare* represents the District's share of employment, the process supposed is

(3) $DCShare = DCShare(-1) + M[DCShare^* - DCShare(-1)].$

In the brackets is the difference between last year's employment fraction, *DCShare(−1)*, and the steady state the tax rates and other factors produce, *DCShare**. The fraction of that difference that the District will make up in one year is represented by *M*. The regressions performed were based on the growth in the District's fraction of metropolitan employment. The analysis attempts to quantify the relationship between the change in *DCShare*, the lagged value *DCShare(−1)*, and the parameters that determine *DCShare**. That is,

(4) $DCShare = DCShare^* - DCShare(-1)$
$$= MDCShare^* - MDCShare(-1).$$

So that if a regression finds that

(5) $DCShare = MDCShare(-1) + \beta X,$

---

12. According to the *District of Columbia Comprehensive Annual Financial Report, September 30, 1995,* and some simple calculations, the real growth in a group of taxes paid mostly by business—real property, general sales, business franchise, personal property, and gross receipts—was 3.77 percent. The real growth in expenditures that directly affect business—economic development, public safety, and public works—was −4.89 percent. The expenditure items with the greatest growth were debt service and human services.

13. L. Jay Helms, "The Effect of State and Local Taxes on Economic Growth: A Time Series–Cross Section Approach," *Review of Economics and Statistics,* vol. 67 (November 1985), pp. 574–84; and Robert Carroll and Michael Wasylenko, "Do State Business Climates Still Matter? Evidence of a Structural Change," *National Tax Association Journal,* vol. 47 (March 1994), pp. 19–33.

where X represents the factors purporting to influence the steady state, the estimate for the equilibrium level will be

$$(6) \qquad SSE = DCShare^* = \beta/M(X).$$

The regression results can be found in table B-4.[14] The first three columns test the impact of the three groups of explanatory variables. The first column tests three tax rates and the difference between the average weekly cost of unemployment insurance tax in the District and in the suburbs. The most likely candidate, the property tax rate differential, proves to be highly significant and negative. Like the property tax, the sales tax rate is a good indicator of the burden it imposes on businesses, and shows a negative and significant effect on steady-state employment. The amounts by which the corporate tax rate and the unemployment insurance tax exceed their suburban counterparts add very little to this regression.

The second column shows the predictive power of the District's shares of metropolitan area federal government employment and population. The share of government employment has the expected positive sign. The coefficient on population indicates that the shrinkage in population and employment share in the District are distinct phenomena. The loss in employment share is not a result of the decline in population. The steady-state share of private employment, however, does appear to be connected to the District's share of federal government employment.

Column three tests the extent to which the growth of the metropolitan area and the passage of time account for the District's reduced share of metropolitan employment. Both are significant, particularly the growth in the total metropolitan employment. District employment will represent a diminishing fraction of growing metropolitan area employment.

Among the first three columns the tax rates in column one provide the most explanatory power. In the fourth column, all the independent variables are combined in one regression. Although this overloads the nineteen observations with nine explanatory variables, it is instructive to see

14. Because the process this analysis supposes has differences in the employment share negatively correlated with past levels, they may also be correlated with past differences. The regression on these differences may show some autocorrelation. The results presented are based on a first-degree autoregressive process. An ordinary least squares regression was also performed. The same variables are significant. Neither the coefficients nor the t-statistics are meaningfully different. The R^2 for the ordinary least squares regressions are less than their autoregressive counterparts by 0.02 or 0.03.

Table B-4. Testing Groups of Factors and All Factors Combined in Explaining Changes in the District of Columbia Share of Metropolitan Private Employment, 1976–94

Independent variable	Taxes	Markets	Growth, Time	All independent variables	Underlying structure
Constant	0.084 (12.229)	-0.122 (-3.837)	0.121 (2.742)	0.0835 (2.464)	0.014 (1.805)
DCShare (-1)[a]	-0.244 (-14.824)	-0.201 (-3.200)	-0.182 (-2.055)	-0.294 (-13.310)	-0.073 (-2.658)
CPTD (-3)[b]	-1.888	...	...	-1.026	...
DCVASD (-1)[c]	-0.361	...	...	-0.386 (-9.728)	...
CORPE (-1)[d]	-0.086 (-1.591)	...	...	-0.105 (-2.120)	...
UNEMPD(-1)[c]	$0.31*10^{-6}$	...	...	$-0.38*10^{-5}$ (1.410)	...
POP	...	0.045 (4.339)	...	$-0.27*10^{-3}$ (-0.002)	...
DCFMSH	...	0.308 (4.339)	...	0.078 (1.733)	...
GRJM[f]	...	...	-0.074 (-2.793)	-0.031 (-3.915)	...
YR	...	...	$-0.84*10^{-3}$ (-1.366)	$-0.67*10^{-3}$ (-1.101)	...
R^2	0.972	0.812	0.767	0.990	0.659
Auto	-0.509	0.138	0.637	-0.877	0.413
Correlation Coefficient	(-2.161)	(0.253)	(1.977)	(-7.034)	(1.895)

a. The District's share of metropolitan area private employment.
b. The difference between the District's commercial property tax rate and suburban rates.
c. The difference between the general sales tax in the District and that in Virginia.
d. The difference between the corporate income tax rates in the District and the suburb[s]
e. The difference between the average per employee cost of unemployment compensation
f. The growth in jobs in the metropolitan area.

that the significance of the sales and property tax differentials survives the inclusion of all the variables considered.

The regression shown in table B-1 combines the significant variables from the foregoing analysis to produce a regression that explains the most variation in the District's share of metropolitan employment with the fewest number of variables. Each included variable adds significant explanatory power to the regression. None of the excluded variables add information to the regression shown. The coefficients in this regression result produce the estimation shown in equation 1. The positive effect of the share of federal employment does not persist in combination with the tax differentials. Although it does move with the steady-state private employment share, it does not add information to the "best fit" regression.

Payments in Lieu of Taxes
for Exempt Property

THIS STUDY proposes that the federal government make a full-tax-equivalency payment in lieu of taxes (PILOT) to the District of Columbia in compensation for the 41 percent of the value of property in the nation's capital which, detailed in chapter 3, is exempt from property taxation. A short review of the property tax exemption and PILOTs is presented here.

The Property Tax Exemption and Its Economic Implications

Property tax law is governed by states. State constitutional provisions either directly provide the exemption for specific types of property or grant the legislature power to accord tax-exempt status. In the case of the District of Columbia (lacking a state and a state constitution), Congress and, to a limited degree, the president have determined the property tax exemptions.

The exemption for higher levels of government is an expression of sovereign immunity. Although this principle was not articulated in the U.S. Constitution, it was set forth by the Supreme Court in *McCulloch v. Maryland,* which accepted the argument that state and local governments could erode the power of the federal government through taxation.[1] In addition, the exemption for nongovernment property is perva-

---

1. Alfred Balk, *The Free List: Property without Taxes* (Russell Sage Foundation, 1971), p. 23; and Richard L. Pfister, "A Reevaluation of the Justification for Property Tax Exemption," *Public Finance Quarterly*, vol. 4 (October 1976), p. 435.

sive around the United States.[2] It is based on one of two arguments: that property that does not earn an income from trade or commerce is, effectively, in public use, or that the organization that is granted the exemption provides services that would otherwise be provided by the state.[3]

The economic effect of a property tax exemption is identical to a subsidy. In this case the subsidy is based on the use of real property, which effectively lowers its cost to the user. Thus there is an incentive for tax-exempt organizations to operate in a "more real estate intensive [manner] than would otherwise be desirable."[4] Further, such an "overuse" of real property directly reduces the amount of taxable property available, which is already limited within any jurisdiction, so the opportunity cost of the exemption is the alternative taxable use to which such property could be put.[5]

Second, owners of taxable property may face higher tax burdens to finance services provided to tax-exempt properties.[6] In cities with high tax burdens and increasing service demands, large amounts of tax-exempt property may result in fiscal stress because there is a limited tax base to fund services. Empirical evidence suggests that property tax exemptions are a significant source of fiscal stress for local jurisdictions in New York State, so that both complete and partial exemptions are "generally detrimental to fiscal health in a manner roughly comparable to a direct reduction in capacity."[7]

Third, tax-exempt entities will tend to concentrate in areas where there is already a large portion of tax-exempt property. The District of Columbia illustrates this concentration. Many nonprofit organizations have established headquarters in the city. Although this has often been attrib-

2. Thirty-six state constitutions provide the property tax exemption themselves to nonprofits, or allow state legislatures to add statutes granting immunity. In the remaining states, constitutional provisions are more broad and permit the legislature to grant a tax exemption to any institution, including charitable entities. See Cynthia F. Burns, "Higher Education Institutions and Property Taxation: The Hidden Costs of Community Financial Stress," College of William and Mary, October 1995, for examples and for a bibliography.

3. John M. Quigley and Roger W. Schmenner, "Property Tax Exemption and Public Policy," *Public Policy*, vol. 23 (Summer 1975), pp. 259–97.

4. Henry J. Aaron, *Who Pays the Property Tax: A New View* (Brookings, 1975), p. 85.

5. Henry J. Raimondo, "Compensation Policy for Tax-Exempt Property in Theory and Practice," *Land Economics*, vol. 56 (February 1980), p. 35; and Quigley and Schmenner, "Property Tax Exemption," p. 261.

6. Quigley and Schmenner, "Property Tax Exemption," p. 260.

7. John K. Mullin, "Property Tax Exemptions and Local Fiscal Stress," *National Tax Journal*, vol. 43, no. 4 (1990), p. 474.

uted to the organizations' desire to be located near the federal government, there is an economic rationale as well.

> Because these institutions do not pay property taxes, they are sensitive only to the sale price of property, not the tax load. In a world where fiscal differences across tax jurisdictions are capitalized, the lowest selling price for otherwise identical properties will be found in the jurisdictions with the highest property tax rate. Hence, other things equal, tax-exempt institutions will be drawn to the jurisdictions with the highest tax rates. If tax-exempt institutions erode the tax base and cause property taxes to increase further, then tax-exempt institutions will find it even more attractive based on the selling price to locate or to expand in these high-tax jurisdictions. Hence the influx of tax-exempt institutions may feed on itself.[8]

The District, as has been noted, has the highest commercial property tax rate in the region.

Finally, there is often a mismatch between the recipients of the subsidy and the population that is supposed to benefit from the services of the exempt organization.[9] This is particularly true in the District, where the benefits of the tax exemption on federal property are enjoyed by citizens of the entire nation, in the form of an independent capital city, and citizens of the region in terms of federal jobs in the District, but the costs are borne by the resident taxpayers.

The economic implications of real property tax exemptions pose difficult challenges for jurisdictions with large amounts of tax-exempt property. They suffer from inefficient land use, high tax burdens, potential fiscal stress, and the further erosion of the tax base resulting from the further concentration of tax-exempt entities. And those benefiting from the tax exemption may be very different from those receiving the services for the exempt organizations.

The PILOT Agreement for Government Property

In regard to exempt government property, there is a range of policy options to redress the economic effects described above. One is that

8. William A. McEachern, "Tax-Exempt Property, Tax Capitalization, and the Cumulative Urban Decay Hypothesis," *National Tax Journal,* vol. 34, no. 2 (1981), p. 191.

9. Quigley and Schmenner, "Property Tax Exemption," p. 261.

federal and state property should simply be subject to local property taxes, which "would eliminate many of the inequities that exist for local taxing jurisdictions in which such property is concentrated."[10] Another is to recognize that exempt property imposes two distinct burdens on municipalities: the "impact burden" of the service demands of the property, and the "tax base burden" of the property tax revenue forgone.[11] A policy response would include a "payment for services" as reimbursement for the impact burden, especially in areas where user fees are the norm, and a PILOT or direct taxation to address the tax-base burden.[12]

This study has focused on a third policy option. We find strong arguments for full-tax-equivalency payments from higher levels of government to local jurisdictions. The federal and state governments should make payments to local governments according to the tax liability of the property.[13] Support for full-tax-equivalency PILOTs can also be found within the federal government in *Payments in Lieu of Taxes on Federal Real Property* by the Advisory Commission on Intergovernmental Relations (ACIR), a bipartisan body created by Congress in 1959 to monitor and recommend improvements in the operation of the American federal system.[14] "*By acquiring real property, the government has assumed a responsibility borne by private taxable property owners.* Thus, it should make payments in lieu of taxes on much the same basis as owners of private property pay real estate taxes. Failure to treat the federal government in this manner violates the horizontal equity canon of public finance, that 'equals be treated equally,' with the index of equality here being the value of real property that is owned."[15]

The most frequent counterargument to full-tax-equivalency PILOTs is that they ignore the benefits that accrue to a jurisdiction as a result of tax-exempt government property. Direct benefits of tax-exempt property include the services provided to local residents by tax-exempt institutions.[16] Indirect benefits are possible improvement in property values stemming from greater private demand for sites bordering the exempt

---

10. Pfister, "Reevaluation," p. 450.

11. Christina Fong and Jeff Kuenzi, *Reimbursing Municipalities for the Presence of State-Owned Properties* (University of Massachusetts, Office of Institutional Research and Planning, 1994), p. 4.

12. Fong and Kuenzi, *Reimbursing Municipalities*, pp. 10–11.

13. Quigley and Schmenner, "Property Tax–Exemption," p. 281.

14. Advisory Commission on Intergovernmental Relations, *Payments in Lieu of Taxes on Federal Real Property*, report no. A-90 (1981), front cover.

15. ACIR, *Payments in Lieu of Taxes*, p. 81.

16. Raimondo, "Compensation Policy," 35.

property.[17] However, such arguments fail to address adequately the equity implications of tax exemptions. First, the benefits of tax exemptions are enjoyed by a much larger constituency than those people who most pay for them. Second, consideration of the benefits conferred by government property as a criterion for the amount of taxes paid is profoundly unfair. Including the benefits in a PILOT calculation results in special treatment of government property because no other property taxes are based on the enhancements they confer on the jurisdiction.[18] "All businesses (and probably other organizations as well) will create favorable economic effects in providing jobs and income. A city could not remove all such property from the tax rolls if these economic effects or benefits exceeded the lost revenue from property tax exemption. To exempt *some such* property on this basis and not *all* of it violates the rules of equity in tax administration."[19] Overall, an equitable compensation policy for tax-exempt government property demands some form of full tax equivalency.

In fact, the federal government has several PILOT programs to reimburse local governments. The most wide-ranging program was created by the Payments in Lieu of Taxes Act of 1976 and paid $102 million in fiscal year 1995 to various states with federal lands.[20] In addition, thirty-four states have policies designed to reimburse municipalities for tax-exempt property.[21]

The Case of Nongovernmental Tax Exemptions

The implications of nongovernmental tax exemptions for religious, educational, and other nongovernmental institutions are different from those for governmental institutions. Many nonprofit organizations provide local constituencies with direct benefits that do not spill over into neighboring jurisdictions. In addition, the economic viability of some of

17. Dick Netzer, "Property Tax Exemptions and Their Effects: A Dissenting View," in National Tax Association, *1972 Proceedings of the Sixty-Fifth Annual Conference on Taxation* (1973), p. 272.

18. Michael E. Bell, "Alternative Treatments of Governmentally Owned Tax-Exempt Properties in Urban Economies," in National Tax Association, *1977 Proceedings of the Seventieth Annual Conference on Taxation* (1978), p. 180.

19. Pfister, "Reevaluation," pp. 438–39.

20. *Appendix: Budget of the United States Government Fiscal Year 1997*, p. 551.

21. Fong and Kuenzi, *Reimbursing Municipalities*, p. 1.

these organizations may be threatened if they fully lost the subsidy provided by the property tax exemption.

In the District the broad categories of exemption, including libraries, hospitals, educational institutions, and religious properties, were established by federal law on December 24, 1942.[22] In addition, Congress evaluates the status of institutions that are not automatically exempt and passes specific legislation to exempt those that it finds worthy of exemption.[23]

Congressional authority over property tax exemption policy in the District of Columbia is a direct parallel to state legislative and constitutional authority over exemption policy around the country. In recent years local governments in a number of states, reacting to fiscal pressures and to long-standing town-gown tensions, have become increasingly aggressive in asserting their objection toward states' property tax exemption for nonprofits. Universities in particular have come under challenges to their tax-exempt status, although not successfully so long as the property is used for educational purposes. The most common approaches are challenges to the property that may be used for noneducational purposes, such as residence halls, sports stadiums, parking lots, day care centers, faculty housing, and vacant land; challenges to leased property; challenges to the institution's purpose; and demands for payments in lieu of taxes. Often the first three approaches end up in court; sometimes they result in voluntary payments. The fourth approach is yielding payments directly from schools to localities.[24]

22. 56 Stat. 1089, chap. 826.

23. The National Society of Colonial Dames currently occupies 53,738 square feet of property with a total assessed value of $2,771,735 that, if taxable, would yield $67,458. In regard to the society, Alfred Balk has remembered, "During one of my visits the District I learned of introduction of a bill to exempt a half-acre of property bought by the National Society of Colonial Dames. Its assessed valuation was $150,000, producing some $4,500 in taxes annually. When I asked a member of the District government if he had any idea what might happen to the bill, he replied, 'We know what will happen, the property will be added to that exempt list, unless there is a miracle.' There was none." Balk, "Free List," p. 50. See also District of Columbia Department of Finance and Revenue, *Schedule of Organizations in the District of Columbia Exempted from Real Property Taxation by Acts of Congress. 1996 Assessments.*

24. These challenges have been going on for years. New Haven challenged Yale in 1899, and Cambridge sought taxes from Harvard in 1900, both unsuccessfully at the time. However, as universities have expanded their activities and contracted out a number of activities, the areas exposed to challenge have expanded. See Cynthia Burns, "Rendering unto Caesar: The Movement to Tax Colleges," *Planning for Higher Education*, vol. 25 (Fall 1996).

The popularity of the PILOT approach for nonprofits is growing. It begins with a public request for a voluntary payment. And a fair proportion of colleges, in states that restrict as well as states that allow challenges to tax exemptions, have finally agreed. For example, in 1990 Yale agreed to pay $4.2 million to New Haven, Connecticut, and to place the university's golf course on the tax rolls. Other university PILOTs are Dartmouth, $1 million; Harvard, $970,000; MIT, $900,000; UC Berkeley, $200,000; and Princeton, $35,000.[25] The mayor of Providence, Rhode Island, has recently appointed a commission to look into the possibility of obtaining revenue, by fee for service or by PILOT, from nonprofit hospitals and universities. Further, in 1994 the mayor of Philadelphia issued an executive order requesting that all tax-exempt organizations, except churches and synagogues, make payments equal to 40 percent of their property tax liability or face litigation. All of the Philadelphia colleges and universities have entered into PILOTs rather than risk litigation, and Philadelphia has linked the tax exemption for hospitals to services for the indigent community.[26]

In determining the scope of tax exemptions for nongovernmental property in the District, one cannot ignore the role of the national capital.[27] The religious, educational, and nonprofit exemptions in the District of Columbia mirror those of traditionally exempt property around the country but bring into direct focus the conflicts between what residents of the city may see as their interests and the federal government sees as

---

25. Burns, "Rendering unto Caesar," p. 30.

26. This is largely the result of the unsettled legal terrain in Pennsylvania, which has a state constitutional provision that permits the exemption of organizations "of purely public charity." In 1985 the Pennsylvania Supreme Court listed five criteria meriting a charitable exemption: advance a charitable purpose; donate or render gratuitously a substantial portion of its services; benefit a substantial and indefinite class of persons who are legitimate subjects of charity; relieve the government of some of its burden; and operate entirely free from the private profit motive. See *Hospital Utilization Project* v. *Commonwealth*, 507 Pa.1,487 A2d 1306 (1985). In addition, there is a statutory provision that limits exemptions to organizations "founded, endowed, and maintained by public or private charity" and a court of commons pleas decision holding that Washington and Jefferson College was not purely charitable and eligible for exemption. This case is on appeal to the Supreme Court, but the uncertainty has opened the door to PILOT negotiations. So far the state legislature has not acted to clear up the ambiguities.

27. The property of embassies and multilateral institutions, while not U.S. government property, clearly is public or governmental property covered by reciprocal or international agreements.

the national interest. For that reason, this study has included those traditionally exempt properties in the suggested federal PILOT. Whether the federal government is acting in the national interest or acting the role of the state to the capital city, the exemptions, their economic effects, and their revenue consequences, are its responsibility.

Selected Previous Studies of the District's Financial Condition

Technical Aspects of the District's Tax System. Studies and papers prepared for the District of Columbia Tax Revision Commission Committee on the District of Columbia. House of Representatives, 95 Cong. 2 sess., December 1978.

Commission on Budget and Financial Priorities of the District of Columbia (Rivlin Commission). *Financing the Nation's Capital.* Washington, November 1990.

Dearborn, Philip. "Avoiding a District of Columbia Financial Emergency." Greater Washington Research Center, December 1992.

Dearborn, Philip. "Balancing the District's Budgets." Greater Washington Research Center, March 1993.

Moore, Stephen, and Dean Stansel. "The Myth of America's Underfunded Cities." Cato Institute, February 1993.

General Accounting Office. "Financial Status: District of Columbia Finances." Briefing report, June 1994.

McKinsey and Company and the Urban Institute. "Assessing the District of Columbia's Financial Future." Report to the Federal City Council, October 1994.

KPMG Peat Marwick LLP. "Four Years Later—The Rivlin Report Revisited: An Assessment of Progress in the District of Columbia." Washington, December 1994.

General Accounting Office. "District of Columbia: Information on the District of Columbia and Other Cities." Briefing report, June 1995.

General Accounting Office. "District of Columbia: Information on the District's Financial Crisis." Briefing report, July 1995.

DC Appleseed Center for Law and Justice. "The Case for a More Fair and Predictable Federal Payment for the District." Washington, November 1995.

General Accounting Office. "District Government: Information on Its Fiscal Condition and the Authority's First Year of Operations." July 1996.

Brookings D.C. Revenue Project Business-Civic Advisory Group

CALVIN CAFRITZ
Cafritz Company

PEGGY COOPER CAFRITZ
*Lincoln Theatre/U Street Theatre
    Foundation*

OLIVER T. CARR
Carr Realty Corporation

TIM COUGHLIN
Riggs National Bank

SHIREEN DODSON
*Center for African American
    History & Culture
Smithsonian Institution*

JULIAN FORE
Arthur Andersen & Co.

JANE FORTSON
Progress & Freedom Foundation

WILLIAM M. FREEMAN
Bell Atlantic

JAMES O. GIBSON
D.C. Agenda

ROBERT M. GLADSTONE
Quadrangle Corporation

TERRENCE D. GOLDEN
Host Marriott

DONALD E. GRAHAM
The Washington Post

MICHELE V. HAGANS
*University of the District of
    Columbia*

KWASI HOLMAN
*District of Columbia Chamber of
    Commerce*

JOSEPH HORNING
Horning Bros.

HARRIET IVEY
Fannie Mae Foundation

LARRY KANAREK
McKinsey & Company, Inc.